1973

FOUR PLAYS BY
Lillian Hellman

THE CHILDREN'S HOUR

DAYS TO COME

THE LITTLE FOXES

WATCH ON THE RHINE

WITH AN INTRODUCTION BY
THE AUTHOR

THE
MODERN LIBRARY
NEW YORK

Random House IS THE PUBLISHER OF

THE MODERN LIBRARY

BENNETT A. CERF · DONALD S. KLOPFER · ROBERT K. HAAS

Manufactured in the United States of America

By H. Wolff

CONTENTS

INTRODUCTION

by LILLIAN HELLMAN

LAST night I finished reading the proofs of these four plays. I had never read them before, nor, beyond the rehearsal period, have I ever seen them played through. I had, of course, read parts of the plays—always the parts I liked, and I have seen parts of the plays once they had opened—always the parts I liked. There is a blessed door that leads from the orchestra out to the lobby. With practice you close it without a creak and what you don't like is behind you. Reading the proofs last night, carefully, slowly, thinking I was reading for the errors of the printer, I soon forgot the printer and was reading for myself.

Long ago I made a rule not to return to finished work: communion with what was ended seemed to me unhealthy. If you returned too often to what you had already done, I thought, you would come to like it and yourself too well, or dislike it and yourself too much. The work of the years before, or last year, or last month, was as far away as childhood, and your chance was ahead and not behind. Stirring the pole of memory in depths long buried, Henry James said it could be. My extreme dislike of that pole ended in a kind of pseudo-forgetfulness. I cannot remember: I cannot forget: I have always to be reminded that I had problems in writing the plays. I have to be told the first three drafts of *The Children's Hour* had a third set and three or four more people; *Days to Come* once had a scene in the town's main street; in *The Little Foxes* Addie had a daughter and Horace another disease; *Watch on the Rhine* started out in

Ohio. I have always to be told writing was hard work, and will be again.

Last night, finishing the proofs, I began to examine this state of forgetfulness with less amusement. There must be many reasons for it, but one came clear and simple: I have never before *really* wished to see, to examine, to evaluate myself. It is true that I, more than many writers, pay polite lip-service to criticism, to my own and to that of the few people for whose judgment I would give a penny. I have thought I was a cold audience for myself only because I was somewhat less warm than some other writers were about themselves. But comparative coldness is not necessarily cold at all. Last night, however, I think I saw most of what was wrong in the plays and—although I do not like these words, I will not apologize for them—most of what was right.

I started reading the proofs, as I started writing these plays, with *The Children's Hour*. It took a year and a half of stumbling stubbornness to do the play. I remembered, in the hodge-podge that came back last night, how many times I tore it up, how many characters I took out and put back and took out again; how I reached back into my own childhood and found the day *I* finished *Mlle. de Maupin;* the day *I* faked a heart attack; the day *I* saw an arm get twisted. And I thought again of the world of the half-remembered, the half-observed, the half-understood which you need so much as you begin to write. It is always there for you. God help you to use it right. Right? Right for what? Right to have something to say and to say it well.

There are, of course, many things wrong with *The Children's Hour*. (Even with my new clarity I have not seen them all, which is just as well, and better for my health.) The play probably should have ended with Martha's suicide: the last scene is tense and over-burdened. I knew this at the time, but I could not help myself. I am a moral writer, often too moral a writer, and I cannot avoid, it seems, that last summing-up. I think that is only a mistake when it fails to achieve its purpose, and I would rather make the attempt, and fail, than fail to make the attempt.

The theme of *The Children's Hour* was good and evil. The theme of *Days to Come* is good and evil: evil, this time, in the hands of people who don't understand it. *Days to Come* was a failure. It got bad reviews in the press, played six performances, and closed. Reading it now, I have no apologies for it. I spoiled a good play. I returned to the amateur's mistake: everything you think and feel must be written *this* time, because you may never have another chance to write it. I knew a woman like Cora and I hated her, and *that* hate had to go in the play; I knew a woman like Julie, I pitied her, and *that* pity had to go in the play; I had been raised with the Ellicotts of the world, and what I felt about them had to go in the play, too; I knew Leo Whalen and I wanted to say how much I respected men who work for other men. I wanted to say too much. And I began thinking of new ways to say it. People in life, I told myself, don't always make the direct answer, or follow the immediately preceding thought. (That is why, in the play, people answer, or understand, much later than the question or answer is offered them.) If you had lived in another place, or been richer or been poorer, or worked harder or worked less, or read a different book, perhaps you might have been. . . . And so I gave the leading characters their counterparts: Leo Whalen is the good Wilkie; Firth the simple Andrew Rodman; Cora the sick Hannah. I played this theme all alone: a solitary composer with a not very interesting quarter note. The subtleties of failures are seldom discovered, and that is just as well.

But with all that is wrong, all the confusion, the jumble, the attempt to do too much, I stand on the side of *Days to Come*. I am only sorry that the confusion in the script confused the best director in the theatre, who, in turn, managed to confuse one of its most inadequate casts.

(There were exceptions, of course.) On the opening night actors moved as figures in the dream of a frightened child. The death-dance of collapse was slow and unreal. It was my fault, I suppose, that it happened. I do not believe actors break plays, or make them, either. And nothing would have affected the play if I had done what the writer must do: kick and fight his way through until the whole is good, and the audience will not stop to worry about the parts. If he cannot do that, he has failed. In that sense, *Days to Come* failed, and only in that sense does its failure matter to me now.

It was with *Days to Come,* or perhaps it was with *The Little Foxes*—this forgetting has its cheery side—that I began to examine the two descriptions that some critics have found so handy for me: the plays are too well-made, the plays are melodramas. By the well-made play, I think is meant the play whose effects are contrived, whose threads are knit tighter than the threads in life and so do not convince.

Obviously, I can have no argument with those whom my plays do not convince. Something does not convince you. Very well, and that is all. But if they convince you, or partly convince you, then the dislike of their being well-made makes little sense. The theatre has limitations: it is a tight, unbending, unfluid, meager form in which to write. And for these reasons, compared to the novel, it is a second-rate form. (I speak of the form, not the content.) Let us admit that. Having admitted it—a step forward, since most of us are anxious to claim the medium by which we earn a living is a fine and fancy thing—we can stop the pretentious lie that the stage is unhampered. What the author has to say is unhampered: his means of saying it are not. He may do without scenery, he may use actors not as people but as animals or clouds, and he still must *pretend* the empty stage is a garden or an arena, and he still must *pretend* that living people are animals. He has three walls of a theatre and he has begun his pretense with the always rather comic notion that the audience is the fourth wall. He must pretend and he must represent. And if there is something vaguely awry, for me, about the pretense of representation—since by the nature of the stage it can never be done away with—it is not that I wish to deny to other writers their variations of the form, but that, for me, the realistic form has interested me most.

Within this form there must be tricks—the theatre is a trick—and they are, I think, only bad when they are used trickily and stop you short. But if they are there, simple, and come to hand, they are justified. In the last act of *Watch on the Rhine*, Kurt Müller is about to leave. He wants to say good-bye to his children who are upstairs. He asks his wife to bring them down. Now it is most probable that in real life a man would go upstairs, find the children in their room, say good-bye there. But it seemed to me, when this problem came up, that kind of un-well-madeness was not worth the candle. It seemed messy to ring in another set, to bring down the curtain, to interfere with a mood and a temper. The playwright, unlike the novelist, must—and here is where I think the charge of well-madeness should be made—trick up the scene. This is how he has to work. It is too bad, but it is not his fault. If he is good, and drives ahead, it will not matter much. If he is not good, the situation will worry him, and he will begin to pretend it doesn't exist and, by so pretending, fret and lengthen it.

I think the word melodrama, in our time, has come to be used in an almost illiterate manner. By definition it is a violent dramatic piece, with a happy ending. But I think we can add that it uses its violence for no purpose, to point no moral, to say nothing, in say-nothing's worse sense. (This, of course, does not mean, even by inference, that violence plus the *desire* to say something will raise the level of the work. A great many bad writers want to say something: their intention may make them fine men, but it does not make them fine writers. Winning the girl, getting the job, vanquishing the slight foe, are not enough.) But when violence is actually the needed stuff of the work and comes toward a large enough end, it has been and always will be in the good writer's field. George Moore said there was so much in *War and Peace* that Tolstoi must surely have awakened in the night frightened that he had left out a yacht race or a High Mass. There is a needed return to the correct use of the word melodrama. It is only then the critic will be able to find out whether a writer justifies his use of violence, and to scale him against those who have used it.

I do not want to talk here of *Watch on the Rhine*. Only eleven months have gone by since it was finished, and that is not time enough for me to see it clearly. Even now, of course, I know many ideas should have come clearer, many speeches cleaner, many things should have been said with more depth and understanding. I have not wanted to write here any final word on the plays. Some day, perhaps. Some day when I have greater faith that I will be the writer I now, on January 14, 1942, want to be. In any case, while there is much in all the plays that is wrong—and it did not hurt me to see it last night, as it once would have hurt me to half-see it— this much has been right: I tried. I did the best I could do at the time each play was written. Within the limitations of my own mind and nature, my own understanding, my own knowledge, it was the best I could do with what I had. If I did not hope to grow, I would not hope to live.

There have been two people—there have been others, good friends—who have been closely connected with these plays. I shall not, because I should not, thank them. One thanks for candy or a kindness, but not for what I owe them both. Herman Shumlin has directed and produced all four of the plays. On all four he has worked with the high seriousness which is the first requirement of a good artist.

He has done more than interpret these plays: he has wrung from them more than was in them, and hidden things in them which should not be seen. Mr. Shumlin's patient work on the plays has only been exceeded by his patient work with their author, and that is patience and sympathy of a high degree. It is one of the mysteries of the theatre—a mystery which irritates those who really *work* in the theatre —that very little is known, by the critics and the public, of the director's function. When a director is as good as Mr. Shumlin, his work is very important indeed. Important to the play and important to the actors who must interpret the play. Mr. Shumlin has made many an actor into a star, and many a star into a decent actor. The theatre, for him, is not a place to show off; not for himself, not for the actor. He is one of the few directors who believes in the *play:* he is one of the very few who has the sharp clarity, the sensitivity, the understanding, which should be the director's gift to the play.

By 1930 I had decided not to be a writer. I had tried, all my life, not too hard, I suppose, and certainly not too well. That year I thought I wouldn't ever be a good writer and if I couldn't be a good writer I didn't want to write at all. I had accepted that, but it made me sad. That I tried again is entirely due to Dashiell Hammett. Patiently and persistently, he hammered away. He began by attacking most of what I had written, teaching me along the way that writers must go to school at writing, and learn and read and think and study. He had made me believe that I should try once more. When I tried to write a play, he spared me nothing. Over and over again he would tell me how bad was the first draft, the second, the fifth, the sixth; over and over again I would bring the next drafts, giving them to him with what I thought was the truthful notice that if this wasn't any good I would never write again and might kill myself. It was meant to intimidate him, and it never did. If I never wrote again, he said, what difference did it make? If I wasn't going to be any good, I should stop writing anyway. Go back now and try again.

All that was more than friendship. It was the care and sacrifice of a scholarly and warm-hearted man who knows about writing, who wants it to be good, who is generous enough to give help. If he had never said much more to me— but that with pride—than that he thought I would be all right some day, it would still be the nicest compliment I have ever had.

January, 1942

THE CHILDREN'S HOUR

FOR

D. HAMMETT

WITH THANKS

The Children's Hour was first produced at Maxine Elliot's Theatre, New York City, on November 20, 1934, with the following cast:

(In the order of their appearance)

PEGGY ROGERS	EUGENIA RAWLS
MRS. LILY MORTAR	ALINE MCDERMOTT
EVELYN MUNN	ELIZABETH SECKEL
HELEN BURTON	LYNNE FISHER
LOIS FISHER	JACQUELINE RUSLING
CATHERINE	BARBARA LEEDS
ROSALIE WELLS	BARBARA BEALS
MARY TILFORD	FLORENCE MCGEE
KAREN WRIGHT	KATHERINE EMERY
MARTHA DOBIE	ANNE REVERE
DOCTOR JOSEPH CARDIN	ROBERT KEITH
AGATHA	EDMONIA NOLLEY
MRS. AMELIA TILFORD	KATHERINE EMMET
A GROCERY BOY	JACK TYLER

Produced and directed by HERMAN SHUMLIN
Settings designed by ALINE BERNSTEIN

SCENE

ACT ONE

Living room of the Wright-Dobie School.
Late afternoon in April.

ACT TWO

Scene I. Living room at Mrs. Tilford's. A few hours later.
Scene II. The same. Later that evening.

ACT THREE

The same as Act One. November.

THE CHILDREN'S HOUR

ACT ONE

SCENE: *A room in the Wright-Dobie School for girls, a converted farm-house eighteen miles from the town of Lancet. It is a comfortable, unpretentious room used as an afternoon study-room and at all other times as the living room.*

A large door Left Center faces the audience. There is a single door Right. Against both back walls are bookcases. A large desk is at Right; a table, two sofas, and eight or ten chairs.

It is early in an afternoon in April.

AT RISE: MRS. LILLY MORTAR *is sitting in a large chair Right Center, with her head back and her eyes closed. She is a plump, florid woman of forty-five with obviously touched-up hair. Her clothes are too fancy for a class-room.*

Seven girls, from twelve to fourteen years old, are informally grouped on chairs and sofa. Six of them are sewing with no great amount of industry on pieces of white material. One of the others, EVELYN MUNN, *is using her scissors to trim the hair of* ROSALIE, *who sits, nervously, in front of her. She has* ROSALIE's *head bent back at an awkward angle and is enjoying herself.*

The eighth girl, PEGGY ROGERS, *is sitting in a higher chair than the others. She is reading aloud from a book. She is bored and she reads in a singsong, tired voice.*

PEGGY (*reading*). "It is twice blest; it blesseth him that gives and him that takes: 'tis mightiest in the mightiest; it becomes the throned monarch better than his crown; his sceptre shows the force of temporal power, the attribute to awe and majesty, wherein . . ." (MRS. MOR-TAR *suddenly opens her eyes and stares at the hair-cutting. The children make efforts to warn* EVELYN. PEGGY *raises her voice until she is shouting*) "doth sit the dread and fear of kings; but mercy is above . . ."

MRS. MORTAR. Evelyn! What are you doing?

EVELYN (*inanely. She lisps*). Uh—nothing, Mrs. Mortar.

MRS. MORTAR. You are certainly doing something. You are ruining the scissors, for one thing.

PEGGY (*loudly*). "But mercy is above. It . . ."

MRS. MORTAR. Just a moment, Peggy. It is very unfortunate that you girls cannot sit quietly with your sewing and drink in the immortal words of the immortal bard. (*She sighs*) Evelyn, go back to your sewing.

EVELYN. I can't get the hem thtraight. Honeth, I've been trying for three weekth, but I jutht can't do it.

MRS. MORTAR. Helen, please help Evelyn with the hem.

HELEN (*rises, holding up the garment* EVELYN *has been working on. It is soiled and shapeless, and so much has been cut off that it is now hardly large enough for a child of five. Giggling*). She can't ever wear *that*, Mrs. Mortar.

MRS. MORTAR (*vaguely*). Well, try to do something with it. Make some handkerchiefs or something. Be clever about it. Women must learn these tricks. (*To* PEGGY) Continue. "Mightiest in the mightiest."

PEGGY. " 'Tis mightiest in the mightiest; it becomes the throned monarch better than his crown; his sceptre— his sceptre shows the force of temporal power, the attribute to awe and majesty, wherein—"

LOIS (*from the back of the room chants softly and mo-*

notonously through the previous speech). Ferebam, ferebas, ferebat, ferebamus, ferebatis, fere, fere—

CATHERINE (*two seats away, the book propped in front of her*). Fere*bant*.

LOIS. Ferebamus, ferebatis, fere*bant*.

MRS. MORTAR. Who's doing that?

PEGGY (*the noise ceases. She hurries on*). "Wherein doth sit the dread and fear of kings; but mercy is above this sceptred sway, it is enthroned in the hearts of kings, it is an attribute to God himself—"

MRS. MORTAR (*sadly, reproachfully*). Peggy, can't you imagine yourself as Portia? Can't you read the lines with some feeling, some pity? (*Dreamily*) Pity. Ah! As Sir Henry said to me many's the time, pity makes the actress. Now, why can't *you* feel pity?

PEGGY. I guess I feel pity.

LOIS. Ferebamus, ferebatis, fere—fere—fere—

CATHERINE. Fere*bant*, stupid.

MRS. MORTAR. How many people in this room are talking? Peggy, read the line again. I'll give you the cue.

PEGGY. What's a cue?

MRS. MORTAR. A cue is a line or word given the actor or actress to remind them of their next speech.

HELEN (*softly*). To remind *him* or *her*.

ROSALIE (*a fattish girl with glasses*). Weren't you ever in the movies, Mrs. Mortar?

MRS. MORTAR. I had many offers, my dear. But the cinema is a shallow art. It has no—no— (*Vaguely*) no fourth dimension. Now, Peggy, if you would only try to submerge yourself in this problem. You are pleading for the life of a man. (*She rises and there are faint sighs from the girls, who stare at her with blank, bored faces. She recites hammily, with gestures*) "But mercy is above this sceptred sway; it is enthroned in the hearts of kings, it is an attribute to God himself; and earthly power doth then show likest God's when mercy seasons justice."

LOIS (*almost singing it*). Utor, fruor, fungor, potior, and vescor take the dative.

CATHERINE. Take the *ablative*.

LOIS. Oh, dear. Utor, fruor, fung—

MRS. MORTAR (*to LOIS, with sarcasm*). You have something to tell the class?

LOIS (*apologetically*). We've got a Latin exam this afternoon.

MRS. MORTAR. And you intend to occupy the sewing and elocution hour learning what should have been learnt yesterday?

CATHERINE (*wearily*). It takes her more than yesterday to learn it.

MRS. MORTAR. Well, I cannot allow you to interrupt us like this.

CATHERINE. But we're finished sewing.

LOIS (*admiringly*). I bet you were good at Latin, Mrs. Mortar.

MRS. MORTAR (*conciliated*). Long ago, my dear, long ago. Now, take your book over by the window and don't disturb our enjoyment of Shakespeare. (CATHERINE and LOIS *rise, go to window, stand mumbling and gesturing*) Let us go back again. "It is an attribute of—" (*At this point the door opens far enough to let* MARY TILFORD, *clutching a slightly faded bunch of wild flowers, squeeze cautiously in. She is fourteen, neither pretty nor ugly. She is an undistinguished-looking girl, except for the sullenly dissatisfied expression on her face*) "And earthly power doth then show likest God's when mercy seasons justice. We do pray for mercy, and that same prayer doth teach—"

PEGGY (*happily*). You've skipped three lines.

MRS. MORTAR. In my entire career I've never missed a line.

PEGGY. But you did skip three lines. (*Goes to* MRS. MORTAR *with book*) See?

MRS. MORTAR (*seeing* MARY *sidling along wall toward other end of the room, turns to her to avoid* PEGGY *and the book*). Mary!

HELEN (*in whisper to* MARY). You're going to catch it now.

MRS. MORTAR. Mary!

MARY. Yes, Mrs. Mortar?

MRS. MORTAR. This is a pretty time to be coming to your sewing class, I must say. Even if you have no interest in your work you might at least remember that you owe me a little courtesy. Courtesy is breeding. Breeding is an excellent thing. (*Turns to class*) Always remember that.

ROSALIE. Please, Mrs. Mortar, can I write that down?

MRS. MORTAR. Certainly. Suppose you all write it down

PEGGY. But we wrote it down last week.

(MARY *giggles.*)

MRS. MORTAR. Mary, I am still awaiting your explanation. Where have you been?

MARY. I took a walk.

MRS. MORTAR. So you took a walk. And may I ask, young lady, are we in the habit of taking walks when we should be at our classes?

MARY. I am sorry, Mrs. Mortar, I went to get you these flowers. I thought you would like them and I didn't know it would take so long to pick them.

MRS. MORTAR (*flattered*). Well, well.

MARY (*almost in tears*). You were telling us last week how much you liked flowers, and I thought that I would bring you some and—

MRS. MORTAR. That was very sweet of you, Mary; I always like thoughtfulness. But you must not allow anything to interfere with your classes. Now run along, dear, and get a vase and some water to put my flowers in. (MARY *turns, sticks out her tongue at* HELEN, *says:* "A-a-a," *and exits Left*) You may put that book away, Peggy. I am sure your family need never worry about your going on the stage.

PEGGY. I don't want to go on the stage. I want to be a lighthouse-keeper's wife.

MRS. MORTAR. Well, I certainly hope you won't read to him.

(*The laughter of the class pleases her.* PEGGY *sits down among the other girls, who are making a great show of doing nothing.* MRS. MORTAR *returns to her chair, puts her head back, closes her eyes.*)

CATHERINE. How much longer, O Cataline, are you going to abuse our patience? (*To* LOIS) Now translate it, and for goodness' sakes try to get it right this time.

MRS. MORTAR (*for no reason*). "One master passion in the breast, like Aaron's serpent, swallows all the rest."

(*She and* LOIS *are murmuring during* KAREN WRIGHT'S *entrance.* KAREN *is an attractive woman of twenty-eight, casually pleasant in manner, without sacrifice of warmth or dignity. She smiles at the girls, goes to the desk. With her entrance there is an immediate change in the manner of the girls: they are fond of her and they respect her. She gives* MORTAR, *whose quotation has reached her, an annoyed look.*)

LOIS. "Quo usque tandem a*butere.* . . ."

KAREN (*automatically*). "Abutere." (*Opens drawer in desk*) What's happened to your hair, Rosalie?

ROSALIE. It got cut, Miss Wright.

KAREN (*smiling*). I can see that. A new style? Looks as though it has holes in it.

EVELYN (*giggling*). I didn't mean to do it that bad, Mith Wright, but Rothalie'th got funny hair. I thaw a picture in the paper, and I wath trying to do it that way.

ROSALIE (*feels her hair, looks pathetically at* KAREN). Oh, what shall I do, Miss Wright? (*Gesturing*) It's long here, and it's short here and—

KAREN. Never mind. Come up to my room later and I'll see if I can fix it for you.

MRS. MORTAR. And hereafter we'll have no more hair-cutting.

KAREN. Helen, have you found your bracelet?

HELEN. No, I haven't, and I've looked everywhere.

KAREN. Have another look. It must be in your room somewhere.

(MARY *comes in Right, with her flowers in a vase. When she sees* KAREN, *she loses some of her assurance.* KAREN *looks at the flowers in surprise.*)

MARY. Good afternoon, Miss Wright. (*Sits down, looks at* KAREN, *who is staring hard at the flowers.*)

KAREN. Hello, Mary.

MRS. MORTAR (*fluttering around*). Peggy has been reading Portia for us.

(PEGGY *sighs.*)

KAREN (*smiling*). Peggy doesn't like Portia?

MRS. MORTAR. I don't think she quite appreciates it, but—

KAREN (*patting* PEGGY *on the head*). Well, I didn't either. I don't think I do yet. Where'd you get those flowers, Mary?

MRS. MORTAR. She picked them for me. (*Hurriedly*) It made her a little late to class, but she heard me say I loved flowers, and she went to get them for me. (*With a sigh*) The first wild flowers of the season.

KAREN. But not the very first, are they, Mary?

MARY. I don't know.

KAREN. Where did you get them?

MARY. Near Conway's cornfield, I think.

KAREN. It wasn't necessary to go so far. There was a bunch exactly like this in the garbage can this morning.

MRS. MORTAR (*after a second*). Oh, I can't believe it!

What a nasty thing to do! (*To* MARY) And I suppose you have just as fine an excuse for being an hour late to breakfast this morning, and last week— (*To* KAREN) I haven't wanted to tell you these things before, but—

KAREN (*hurriedly, as a bell rings off stage*). There's the bell.

LOIS (*walking toward door*). Ad, ab, ante, in, de, inter, con, post, præ— (*Looks up at* KAREN) I *can't* seem to remember the rest.

KAREN. Præ, pro, sub, super. Don't worry, Lois. You'll come out all right. (LOIS *smiles, exits.* MARY *attempts to make a quick exit*) Wait a minute, Mary. (*Reluctantly* MARY *turns back as the girls file out.* KAREN *moves the small chairs, clearing the room as she talks*) Mary, I've had the feeling—and I don't think I'm wrong— that the girls here were happy; that they liked Miss Dobie and me, that they liked the school. Do you think that's true?

MARY. Miss Wright, I have to get my Latin book.

KAREN. I thought it was true until you came here a year ago. I don't think you're very happy here, and I'd like to find out why. (*Looks at* MARY, *waits for an answer, gets none, shakes her head*) Why, for example, do you find it necessary to lie to us so often?

MARY (*without looking up*). I'm not lying. I went out walking and I saw the flowers and they looked pretty and I didn't know it was so late.

KAREN (*impatiently*). Stop it, Mary! I'm not interested in hearing that foolish story again. I *know* you got the flowers out of the garbage can. What I do want to know is why you feel you have to lie out of it.

MARY (*beginning to whimper*). I *did* pick the flowers near Conway's. You never believe me. You believe everybody but me. It's always like that. Everything I say you fuss at me about. Everything I do is wrong.

KAREN. You know that isn't true. (*Goes to* MARY, *puts her*

arm around her, waits until the sobbing has stopped)
Look, Mary, look at me. (*Raises* MARY'S *face with her
hand*) Let's try to understand each other. If you feel
that you *have* to take a walk, or that you just *can't* come
to class, or that you'd like to go into the village by
yourself, come and tell me—I'll try and understand.
(*Smiles*) I don't say that I'll always agree that you
should do exactly what you want to do, but I've had
feelings like that, too—everybody has—and I won't be
unreasonable about yours. But this way, this kind of
lying you do, makes everything wrong.

MARY (*looking steadily at* KAREN). I got the flowers near
Conway's cornfield.

KAREN (*looks at* MARY, *sighs, moves back toward desk
and stands there for a moment*). Well, there doesn't
seem to be any other way with you; you'll have to be
punished. Take your recreation periods alone for the
next two weeks. No horseback-riding and no hockey.
Don't leave the school grounds for any reason what-
soever. Is that clear?

MARY (*carefully*). Saturday, too?

KAREN. Yes.

MARY. But you said I could go to the boat-races.

KAREN. I'm sorry, but you can't go.

MARY. I'll tell my grandmother. I'll tell her how everybody treats me here and the way I get punished for
every little thing I do. I'll tell her, I'll—

MRS. MORTAR. Why, I'd slap her hands!

KAREN (*turning back from door, ignoring* MRS. MORTAR'S
speech. To MARY). Go upstairs, Mary.

MARY. I don't feel well.

KAREN (*wearily*). Go upstairs now.

MARY. I've got a pain. I've had it all morning. It hurts
right here (*pointing vaguely in the direction of her
heart*). Really it does.

KAREN. Ask Miss Dobie to give you some hot water and bicarbonate of soda.

MARY. It's a bad pain. I've never had it before.

KAREN. I don't think it can be very serious.

MARY. My heart! It's my heart! It's stopping or something. I can't breathe. (*She takes a long breath and falls awkwardly to the floor.*)

KAREN (*sighs, shakes her head, kneels beside* MARY. *To* MRS. MORTAR). Ask Martha to phone Joe.

MRS. MORTAR (*going out*). Do you think—? Heart trouble is very serious in a child.

(KAREN *picks* MARY *up from the floor and carries her off Right. After a moment* MARTHA DOBIE *enters Center. She is about the same age as* KAREN. *She is a nervous, high-strung woman.*)

KAREN (*enters Right*). Did you get Joe?

MARTHA (*nodding*). What happened to her? She was perfectly well a few hours ago.

KAREN. She probably still is. I told her she couldn't go to the boat-races and she had a heart attack.

MARTHA. Where is she?

KAREN. In there. Mortar's with her.

MARTHA. Anything really wrong with her?

KAREN. I doubt it. (*Sits down at desk and begins to mark papers*) She's a problem, that kid. Her latest trick was kidding your aunt out of a sewing lesson with those faded flowers we threw out. Then she threatened to go to her grandmother with some tale about being mistreated.

MARTHA. And, please God, Grandma would believe her and take her away.

KAREN. Which would give the school a swell black eye. But we ought to do something.

MARTHA. How about having a talk with Mrs. Tilford?

KAREN (*smiling*). You want to do it? (MARTHA *shakes her*

head) I hate to do it. She's been so nice to us. (*Shrugging her shoulders*) Anyway, it wouldn't do any good. She's too crazy about Mary to see her faults very clearly —and the kid knows it.

MARTHA. How about asking Joe to say something to her? She'd listen to him.

KAREN. That would be admitting that we can't do the job ourselves.

MARTHA. Well, we can't, and we might as well admit it. We've tried everything we can think of. She's had more attention than any other three kids put together. And we still haven't the faintest idea what goes on inside her head.

KAREN. She's a strange girl.

MARTHA. That's putting it mildly.

KAREN (*laughs*). It's funny. We always talk about the child as if she were a grown woman.

MARTHA. It's not so funny. There's something the matter with the kid. That's been true ever since the first day she came. She causes trouble here; she's bad for the other girls. I don't know what it is—it's a feeling I've got that it's wrong somewhere—

KAREN. All right, all right, we'll talk it over with Joe. Now what about our other pet nuisance?

MARTHA (*laughs*). My aunt the actress? What's she been up to now?

KAREN. Nothing unusual. Last night at dinner she was telling the girls about the time she lost her trunks in Butte, Montana, and how she gave her best performance of Rosalind during a hurricane. Today in the kitchen you could hear her on what Sir Henry said to her.

MARTHA. Wait until she does Hedda Gabler standing on a chair. Sir Henry taught her to do it that way. He said it was a test of great acting.

KAREN. You must have had a gay childhood.

MARTHA (*bitterly*). Oh, I did. I did, indeed. God, how I used to hate all that—

KAREN. Couldn't we get rid of her soon, Martha? I hate to make it hard on you, but she really ought not to be here.

MARTHA (*after a moment*). I know.

KAREN. We can scrape up enough money to send her away. Let's do it.

MARTHA (*goes to her, affectionately pats her head*). You've been very patient about it. I'm sorry and I'll talk to her today. It'll probably be a week or two before she can be ready to leave. Is that all right?

KAREN. Of course. (*Looks at her watch*) Did you get Joe himself on the phone?

MARTHA. He was already on his way. Isn't he always on his way over here?

KAREN (*laughs*). Well, I'm going to marry him some day, you know.

MARTHA (*looking at her*). You haven't talked of marriage for a long time.

KAREN. I've talked of it with Joe.

MARTHA. Then you *are* thinking about it—soon?

KAREN. Perhaps when the term is over. By that time we ought to be out of debt, and the school should be paying for itself.

MARTHA (*nervously playing with a book on the table*). Then we won't be taking our vacation together?

KAREN. Of course we will. The three of us.

MARTHA. I had been looking forward to some place by the lake—just you and me—the way we used to at college.

KAREN (*cheerfully*). Well, now there will be three of us. That'll be fun, too.

MARTHA (*after a pause*). Why haven't you told me this before?

KAREN. I'm not telling you anything we haven't talked about often.

MARTHA. But you're talking about it as *soon* now.

KAREN. I'm glad to be able to. I've been in love with Joe a long time. (MARTHA *crosses to window and stands looking out, her back to* KAREN. KAREN *finishes marking papers and rises*) It's a big day for the school. Rosalie's finally put an "l" in could.

MARTHA (*in a dull, bitter tone, not turning from window*). You really *are* going to leave, aren't you?

KAREN. I'm not going to leave, and you know it. Why do you say things like that? We agreed a long time ago that my marriage wasn't going to make any difference to the school.

MARTHA. But it will. You know it will. It can't help it.

KAREN. That's nonsense. Joe doesn't want me to give up here.

MARTHA (*turning from window*). I don't understand you. It's been so damned hard building this thing up, slaving and going without things to make ends meet—think of having a winter coat without holes in the lining again! —and now when we're getting on our feet, you're all ready to let it go to hell.

KAREN. This is a silly argument, Martha. Let's quit it. You haven't listened to a word I've said. I'm not getting married tomorrow, and when I do, it's not going to interfere with my work here. You're making something out of nothing.

MARTHA. It's going to be hard going on alone afterward.

KAREN. For God's sake, do you expect me to give up my marriage?

MARTHA. I don't mean that, but it's so—

(*Door Center opens and* DOCTOR JOSEPH CARDIN *comes in. He is a large, pleasant-looking, carelessly dressed man of about thirty-five.*)

CARDIN. Hello, darling. Hi, Martha. What's the best news?

MARTHA. Hello, Joe.

KAREN. We tried to get you on the phone. Come in and look at your little cousin.

CARDIN. Sure. What's the matter with her now? I stopped at Vernie's on the way over to look at that little black bull he bought. He's a baby! There's going to be plenty of good breeding done in these hills.

KAREN. You'd better come and see her. She says she has a pain in her heart. (*Goes out Right.*)

CARDIN (*stopping to light a cigarette*). Our little Mary pops up in every day's dispatches.

MARTHA (*impatiently*). Go and see her. Heart attacks are nothing to play with.

CARDIN (*looks at her*). Never played with one in my life. (*Exits Right.*)

(MARTHA *walks around room and finally goes to stare out window.*)

(MRS. MORTAR *enters Right.*)

MRS. MORTAR. *I* was asked to leave the room. (MARTHA *pays no attention*) It seems that I'm not wanted in the room during the examination.

MARTHA (*over her shoulder*). What difference does it make?

MRS. MORTAR. What difference does it make? Why, it was a deliberate snub.

MARTHA. There's very little pleasure in watching a man use a stethoscope.

MRS. MORTAR. Isn't it natural that the child should have me with her? Isn't it natural that an older woman should be present? (*No answer*) Very well, if you are so thick-skinned that you don't resent these things—

MARTHA. What are you talking about? Why, in the name of heaven, should *you* be with her?

MRS. MORTAR. It—it's customary for an older woman to be present during an examination.

MARTHA (*laughs*). Tell that to Joe. Maybe he'll give you a job as duenna for his office.

MRS. MORTAR (*reminiscently*). It was I who saved Delia Lampert's life the time she had that heart attack in Buffalo. We almost lost her that time. Poor Delia! We went over to London together. She married Robert Laffonne. Not seven months later he left her and ran away with Eve Cloun, who was playing the Infant Phenomenon in Birmingham—

MARTHA. Console yourself. If you've seen one heart attack, you've seen them all.

MRS. MORTAR. So you don't resent your aunt being snubbed and humiliated?

MARTHA. Oh, Aunt Lily!

MRS. MORTAR. Karen is consistently rude to me, and you know it.

MARTHA. I know that she is very polite to you, and— what's more important—very patient.

MRS. MORTAR. Patient with me? *I*, who have worked my fingers to the bone!

MARTHA. Don't tell yourself that too often, Aunt Lily; you'll come to believe it.

MRS. MORTAR. I *know* it's true. Where could you have gotten a woman of my reputation to give these children voice lessons, elocution lessons? Patient with me! Here I've donated my services—

MARTHA. I was under the impression you were being paid.

MRS. MORTAR. That small thing! I used to earn twice that for one performance.

MARTHA. The gilded days. It was very extravagant of them to pay you so much. (*Suddenly tired of the whole thing*) You're not very happy here, are you, Aunt Lily?

MRS. MORTAR. Satisfied enough, I guess, for a poor relation.

MARTHA (*makes a motion of distaste*). But you don't like the school or the farm or—

MRS. MORTAR. I told you at the beginning you shouldn't have bought a place like this. Burying yourself on a farm! You'll regret it.

MARTHA. We like it here. (*After a moment*) Aunt Lily, you've talked about London for a long time. Would you like to go over?

MRS. MORTAR (*with a sigh*). It's been twenty years, and I shall never live to see it again.

MARTHA. Well, you can go any time you like. We can spare the money now, and it will do you a lot of good. You pick out the boat you want and I'll get the passage. (*She has been talking rapidly, anxious to end the whole thing*) Now that's all fixed. You'll have a grand time seeing all your old friends, and if you live sensibly I ought to be able to let you have enough to get along on. (*She begins to gather books, notebooks, and pencils.*)

MRS. MORTAR (*slowly*). So you want me to leave?

MARTHA. That's not the way to put it. You've wanted to go ever since I can remember.

MRS. MORTAR. You're trying to get rid of me.

MARTHA. That's it. We don't want you around when we dig up the buried treasure.

MRS. MORTAR. So? You're turning me out? At my age! Nice, grateful girl you are.

MARTHA. Oh, my God, how can anybody deal with you? You're going where you want to go, and we'll be better off alone. That suits everybody. You complain about the farm, you complain about the school, you complain about Karen, and now you have what you want and you're still looking for something to complain about.

MRS. MORTAR (*with dignity*). Please do not raise your voice.

MARTHA. You ought to be glad I don't do worse.

MRS. MORTAR. I absolutely refuse to be shipped off three thousand miles away. I'm not going to England. I shall go back to the stage. I'll write to my agents tomorrow, and as soon as they have something good for me—

MARTHA. The truth is I'd like you to leave soon. The three

of us can't live together, and it doesn't make any difference whose fault it is.

MRS. MORTAR. You wish me to go tonight?

MARTHA. Don't act, Aunt Lily. Go as soon as you've found a place you like. I'll put the money in the bank for you tomorrow.

MRS. MORTAR. You think I'd take your money? I'd rather scrub floors first.

MARTHA. I imagine you'll change your mind.

MRS. MORTAR. I should have known by this time that the wise thing is to stay out of your way when *he's* in the house.

MARTHA. What are you talking about now?

MRS. MORTAR. Never mind. I should have known better. You always take your spite out on me.

MARTHA. Spite? (*Impatiently*) Oh, don't let's have any more of this today. I'm tired. I've been working since six o'clock this morning.

MRS. MORTAR. Any day that he's in the house is a bad day.

MARTHA. When *who* is in the house?

MRS. MORTAR. Don't think you're fooling me, young lady. I wasn't born yesterday.

MARTHA. Aunt Lily, the amount of disconnected unpleasantness that goes on in your head could keep a psychologist busy for years. Now go take your nap.

MRS. MORTAR. I know what I know. Every time that man comes into this house, you have a fit. It seems like you just can't stand the idea of them being together. God knows what you'll do when they get married. You're jealous of him, that's what it is.

MARTHA (*her voice is tense and the previous attitude of good-natured irritation is gone*). I'm very fond of Joe, and you know it.

MRS. MORTAR. You're fonder of Karen, and I know that. And it's unnatural, just as unnatural as it can be. You

don't like their being together. You were always like
that even as a child. If you had a little girl friend, you
always got mad when she liked anybody else. Well,
you'd better get a beau of your own now—a woman of
your age.

MARTHA. The sooner you get out of here, the better. Your
vulgarities are making me sick and I won't stand for
them any longer. I want you to leave—

(*At this point there is a sound outside the large doors
Center.* MARTHA *breaks off, angry and ashamed. After
a moment she crosses to the door and opens it.* EVELYN
and PEGGY *are to be seen on the staircase. For a second
she stands still as they stop and look at her. Then,
afraid that her anger with her aunt will color anything
she might say to the children, she crosses the room
again and stands with her back to them.*)

MARTHA. What were you doing outside the door?

EVELYN (*hurriedly*). We were going upthtairth, Mith
Dobie.

PEGGY. We came down to see how Mary was.

MARTHA. And you stopped long enough to see how we
were. Did you deliberately listen?

PEGGY. We didn't mean to. We heard voices and we
couldn't help—

MRS. MORTAR (*fake social tone*). Eavesdropping is something nice young ladies just don't do.

MARTHA (*turning to face the children*). Go upstairs now.
We'll talk about this later. (*Slowly shuts door as they
begin to climb the stairs.*)

MRS. MORTAR. You mean to say you're not going to do
anything about that? (*No answer. She laughs nastily*)
That's the trouble with these new-fangled notions of
discipline and—

MARTHA (*thoughtfully*). You know, it's really bad having
you around children.

MRS. MORTAR. What exactly does that mean?

MARTHA. It means that I don't like them hearing the things you say. Oh, I'll "do something about it," but the truth is that this is their home, and things shouldn't be said in it that they can't hear. When you're at your best, you're not for tender ears.

MRS. MORTAR. So now it's my fault, is it? Just as I said, whenever he's in the house you think you can take it out on me. You've got to have some way to let out steam and—

(*Door opens Right and* CARDIN *comes in.*)

MARTHA. How is Mary?

(MRS. MORTAR, *head in air, gives* MARTHA *a malicious half-smile and makes what she thinks is majestic exit Center.*)

MRS. MORTAR. Good day, Joseph.

CARDIN. What's the matter with the Duchess? (*Nods at door Center.*)

MARTHA. Just keeping her hand in, in case Sir Henry's watching her from above. What about Mary?

CARDIN. Nothing. Absolutely nothing.

MARTHA (*sighs*). I thought so.

CARDIN. I could have managed a better faint than that when I was six years old.

MARTHA. Nothing the matter with her at all, then?

CARDIN (*laughs*). No, ma'am, not a thing. Just a little something she thought up.

MARTHA. But it's such a silly thing to do. She knew we'd have you in. (*Sighs*) Maybe she's not so bright. Any idiots in your family, Joe? Any inbreeding?

CARDIN. Don't blame her on me. It's another side of the family. (*Laughs*) You can look at Aunt Amelia and tell: old New England stock; never married out of Boston; still thinks honor is honor and dinner's at eight thirty. Yes, ma'am, we're a proud old breed.

MARTHA. The Jukes were an old family, too. Look, Joe, have you any idea what is the matter with Mary? I mean, has she always been like this?

CARDIN. She's always been a honey. Aunt Amelia's spoiling hasn't helped any, either.

MARTHA. We're reaching the end of our rope with her. This kind of thing—

CARDIN (*looking at her*). Aren't you taking this too seriously?

MARTHA (*after a second*). I guess I am. But you stay around kids long enough and you won't know what to take seriously, either. But I do think somebody ought to talk to Mrs. Tilford about her.

CARDIN. You wouldn't be meaning me now, would you, Miss Dobie?

MARTHA. Well, Karen and I were talking about it this afternoon and—

CARDIN. Listen, friend, I'm marrying Karen, but I'm not writing Mary Tilford in the contract. (MARTHA *moves slightly.* CARDIN *takes her by the shoulders and turns her around to face him again. His face is grave, his voice gentle*) Forget Mary for a minute. You and I have got something to fight about. Every time anything's said about marrying—about Karen marrying me—you—(*She winces*) There it is. I'm fond of you. I always thought you liked me. What is it? I know how fond you are of Karen, but our marriage oughtn't to make a great deal of difference—

MARTHA (*pushing his hands from her shoulders*). God damn you. I wish— (*She puts her face in her hands.* CARDIN *watches her in silence, mechanically lighting a cigarette. When she takes her hands from her face, she holds them out to him. Contritely*) Joe, please, I'm sorry. I'm a fool, a nasty, bitter—

CARDIN (*takes her hands in one of his, patting them with his other hand*). Aw, shut up. (*He puts an arm around*

her, and she leans her head against his lapel. They are
standing like that when KAREN *comes in Right.*)

MARTHA (*to* KAREN, *as she wipes her eyes*). Your friend's
got a nice shoulder to weep on.

KAREN. He's an admirable man in every way. Well, the
angel child is now putting her clothes back on.

MARTHA. The angel child's influence is abroad even while
she's unconscious. Her room-mates were busy listening
at the door while Aunt Lily and I were yelling at each
other.

KAREN. We'll have to move those girls away from one
another.

(*A bell rings from the rear of the house.*)

MARTHA. That's my class. I'll send Peggy and Evelyn
down. You talk to them.

KAREN. All right. (*As* MARTHA *exits Center,* KAREN *goes
toward door Right. As she passes* CARDIN *she kisses
him*) Mary!

(MARY *opens door, comes in, stands buttoning the neck
of her dress.*)

CARDIN (*to* MARY). How's it feel to be back from the
grave?

MARY. My heart hurts.

CARDIN (*laughing. To* KAREN). Science has failed. Try a
hairbrush.

MARY. It's *my* heart, and it hurts.

KAREN. Sit down.

MARY. I want to see my grandmother. I want to—

(EVELYN *and* PEGGY *timidly enter Center.*)

KAREN. Sit down, girls, I want to talk to you.

PEGGY. We're awfully sorry, really. We just didn't think
and—

KAREN. I'm sorry too, Peggy. (*Thoughtfully*) You and
Evelyn never used to do things like this. We'll have to
separate you three.

EVELYN. Ah, Mith Wright, we've been together almotht a year.

KAREN. It was evidently too long. Now don't let's talk about it. Peggy, you will move into Lois's room, and Lois will move in with Evelyn. Mary will go in with Rosalie.

MARY. Rosalie hates me.

KAREN. That's a very stupid thing to say. I can't imagine Rosalie hating anyone.

MARY (*starting to cry*). And it's all because I had a pain. If anybody else was sick they'd be put to bed and petted. You're always mean to me. I get blamed and punished for everything. (*To* CARDIN) I do, Cousin Joe. All the time for everything.

(MARY *by now is crying violently and as* KAREN *half moves toward her,* CARDIN, *who has been frowning, picks* MARY *up and puts her down on the couch.*)

CARDIN. You've been unpleasant enough to Miss Wright. Lie here until you've stopped working yourself into a fit. (*Picks up his hat and bag, smiles at* KAREN) I've got to go now. She's not going to hurt herself crying. The next time she faints, I'd wait until she got tired lying on the floor. (*Passing* MARY, *he pats her head. She jerks away from him.*)

KAREN. Wait a minute. I'll walk to the car with you. (*To girls*) Go up now and move your things. Tell Lois to get her stuff ready.

(*She and* CARDIN *exit Center. A second after the door is closed,* MARY *springs up and throws a cushion at the door.*)

EVELYN. Don't do that. She'll hear you.

MARY. Who cares if she does? (*Kicks table*) And she can hear that, too.

(*Small ornament falls off table and breaks on floor.* EVELYN *and* PEGGY *gasp, and* MARY'S *bravado disappears for a moment.*)

EVELYN (*frightened*). Now what are you going to do?

PEGGY (*stooping down in a vain effort to pick up the pieces*). You'll get the devil now. Dr. Cardin gave it to Miss Wright. I guess it was kind of a lover's gift. People get awfully angry about a lover's gift.

MARY. Oh, leave it alone. She'll never know we did it.

PEGGY. *We* didn't do it. You did it yourself.

MARY. And what will you do if I say *we* did do it? (*Laughs*) Never mind, I'll think of something else. The wind could've knocked it over.

EVELYN. Yeh. She'th going to believe that one.

MARY. Oh, stop worrying about it. I'll get out of it.

EVELYN. Did you really have a pain?

MARY. I fainted, didn't I?

PEGGY. I wish I could faint sometimes. I've never even worn glasses, like Rosalie.

MARY. A lot it'll get you to faint.

EVELYN. What did Mith Wright do to you when the clath left?

MARY. Told me I couldn't go to the boat-races.

EVELYN. Whew!

PEGGY. But we'll remember everything that happens and we'll give you all the souvenirs and things.

MARY. I won't let you go if I can't go. But I'll find some way to go. What were *you* doing?

PEGGY. I guess we shouldn't have done it, really. We came down to see what was happening to you, but the doors were closed and we could hear Miss Dobie and Mortar having an awful row. Then Miss Dobie opens the door and there we were.

MARY. And a lot of crawling and crying you both did too, I bet.

EVELYN. We were thort of thorry about lithening. I gueth it wathn't—

MARY. Ah, you're always sorry about everything. What were they saying?

PEGGY. What was who saying?

MARY. Dobie and Mortar, silly.

PEGGY (*evasively*). Just talking, I guess.

EVELYN. Fighting, you mean.

MARY. About what?

EVELYN. Well, they were talking about Mortar going away to England and—

PEGGY. You know, it really wasn't very nice to've listened, and I think it's worse to tell.

MARY. You do, do you? You just don't tell me and see what happens.

(PEGGY *sighs*.)

EVELYN. Mortar got awful thore at that and thaid they juth wanted to get rid of her, and then they thtarted talking about Dr. Cardin.

MARY. What about him?

PEGGY. We'd better get started moving; Miss Wright will be back first thing we know.

MARY (*fiercely*). Shut up! Go on, Evelyn.

EVELYN. They're going to be married.

MARY. Everybody knows that.

PEGGY. But everybody doesn't know that Miss Dobie doesn't want them to get married. How do you like that?

(*The door opens and* ROSALIE WELLS *sticks her head in.*)

ROSALIE. I have a class soon. If you're going to move your things—

MARY. Close that door, you idiot. (ROSALIE *closes door, stands near it*) What do you want?

ROSALIE. I'm trying to tell you. If you're going to move your things—not that I want you in with me—you'd better start right now. Miss Wright's coming in a minute.

MARY. Who cares if she is?

ROSALIE (*starts for door*). I'm just telling you for your own good.

PEGGY (*getting up*). We're coming.

MARY. No. Let Rosalie move our things.

ROSALIE. You crazy?

PEGGY (*nervously*). It's all right. Evelyn and I'll get your things. Come on, Evelyn.

MARY. Trying to get out of telling me, huh? Well, you won't get out of it that way. Sit down and stop being such a sissy. Rosalie, you go on up and move my things and don't say a word about our being down here.

ROSALIE. And who was your French maid yesterday, Mary Tilford?

MARY (*laughing*). You'll do for today. Now go on, Rosalie, and fix our things.

ROSALIE. You crazy?

MARY. And the next time we go into town, I'll let you wear my gold locket and buckle. You'll like that, won't you, Rosalie?

ROSALIE (*draws back, moves her hands nervously*). I don't know what you're talking about.

MARY. Oh, I'm not talking about anything in particular. You just run along now and remind me the next time to get my buckle and locket for you.

ROSALIE (*stares at her a moment*). All right, I'll do it this time, but just 'cause I got a good disposition. But don't think you're going to boss me around, Mary Tilford.

MARY (*smiling*). No, indeed. (ROSALIE *starts for door*) And get the things done neatly, Rosalie. Don't muss my white linen bloomers—

(*The door slams as* MARY *laughs.*)

EVELYN. Now what do you think of that? What made her tho agreeable?

MARY. Oh, a little secret we got. Go on, now, what else did they say?

PEGGY. Well, Mortar said that Dobie was jealous of them, and that she was like that when she was a little girl, and that she'd better get herself a beau of her own because it was unnatural, and that she never wanted anybody to like Miss Wright, and that was unnatural. Boy! Did Miss Dobie get sore at that!

EVELYN. Then we didn't hear any more. Peggy dropped a book.

MARY. What'd she mean Dobie was jealous?

PEGGY. What's unnatural?

EVELYN. Un for not. Not natural.

PEGGY. It's funny, because everybody gets married.

MARY. A lot of people don't—they're too ugly.

PEGGY (*jumps up, claps her hand to her mouth*). Oh, my God! Rosalie'll find that copy of *Mademoiselle de Maupin*. She'll blab like the dickens.

MARY. Ah, she won't say a word.

EVELYN. Who getth the book when we move?

MARY. You can have it. That's what I was doing this morning—finishing it. There's one part in it—

PEGGY. What part?

(MARY *laughs.*)

EVELYN. Well, what wath it?

MARY. Wait until you read it.

EVELYN. Don't forget to give it to me.

PEGGY. It's a shame about being moved. I've got to go in with Helen, and she blows her nose all night. Lois told me.

MARY. It was a dirty trick making us move. She just wants to see how much fun she can take away from me. She hates me.

PEGGY. No, she doesn't, Mary. She treats you just like the rest of us—almost better.

MARY. That's right, stick up for your crush. Take her side against mine.

PEGGY. I didn't mean it that way.

EVELYN (*looks at her watch*). We'd better get upthtairth.

MARY. I'm not going.

PEGGY. Rosalie isn't so bad.

EVELYN. What you going to do about the vathe?

MARY. I don't care about Rosalie and I don't care about the vase. I'm not going to be here.

EVELYN *and* PEGGY (*together*). Not going to be here! What do you mean?

MARY (*calmly*). I'm going home.

PEGGY. Oh, Mary—

EVELYN. You can't do that.

MARY. Can't I? You just watch. (*Begins to walk around the room*) I'm not staying here. I'm going home and tell Grandma I'm not staying any more. (*Smiles to herself*) I'll tell her I'm not happy. They're scared of Grandma—she helped 'em when they first started, you know—and when she tells 'em something, believe me, they'll sit up and listen. They can't get away with treating me like this, and they don't have to think they can.

PEGGY (*appalled*). You just going to walk out like that?

EVELYN. What you going to tell your grandmother?

MARY. Oh, who cares? I'll think of something to tell her. I can always do it better on the spur of the moment.

PEGGY. She'll send you right back.

MARY. You let me worry about that. Grandma's very fond of me, on account my father was her favorite son. I can manage *her* all right.

PEGGY. I don't think you ought to go, really, Mary. It's just going to make an awful lot of trouble.

EVELYN. What'th going to happen about the vathe?

MARY. Say I did it—it doesn't make a bit of difference any more to me. Now listen, you two got to help. They won't miss me before dinner if you make Rosalie shut the door and keep it shut. Now, I'll go through the field to French's, and then I can get the bus to Homestead.

EVELYN. How you going to get to the thtreet-car?

MARY. Taxi, idiot.

PEGGY. How are you going to get out of here in the first place?

MARY. I'm going to walk out. You know where the front door is, or are you too dumb even for that? Well, I'm going right out that front door.

EVELYN. Gee, I wouldn't have the nerve.

MARY. Of course you wouldn't. You'd let 'em do anything to you they want. Well, they can't do it to me. Who's got any money?

EVELYN. Not me. Not a thent.

MARY. I've got to have at least a dollar for the taxi and a dime for the bus.

EVELYN. And where you going to find it?

PEGGY. See? Why don't you just wait until your allowance comes Monday, and then you can go any place you want. Maybe by that time—

MARY. I'm going today. *Now.*

EVELYN. You can't *walk* to Lanthet.

MARY (*goes to* PEGGY). You've got money. You've got two dollars and twenty-five cents.

PEGGY. I—I—

MARY. Go get it for me.

PEGGY. No! No! I won't get it for you.

EVELYN. You can't have *that* money, Mary—

MARY. Get it for me.

PEGGY (*cringes, her voice is scared*). I won't. I won't. Mamma doesn't send me much allowance—not half as much as the rest of you get—I saved this so long—you took it from me last time—

EVELYN. Ah, she wantth that bithycle tho bad.

PEGGY. I haven't gone to the movies, I haven't had any candy, I haven't had anything the rest of you get all the time. It took me so long to save that and I—

MARY. Go upstairs and get me the money.

PEGGY (*hysterically, backing away from her*). I won't. I won't. I won't.

(MARY *makes a sudden move for her, grabs her left arm, and jerks it back, hard and expertly.* PEGGY *screams softly.* EVELYN *tries to take* MARY'S *arm away. Without releasing her hold on* PEGGY, MARY *slaps* EVELYN'S *face.* EVELYN *begins to cry.*)

MARY. Just say when you've had enough.

PEGGY (*softly, stiflingly*). All—all right—I'll get it.

(MARY *smiles, nods her head as the Curtain falls.*)

ACT TWO

SCENE I

SCENE: *Living room at* MRS. TILFORD'S. *It is a formal room, without being cold or elegant. The furniture is old, but excellent. The exit to the hall is Left; glass doors Right lead to a dining room that cannot be seen.*

AT RISE: *Stage is empty. Voices are heard in the hall.*

AGATHA (*off-stage*). What are *you* doing here? Well, come on in—don't stand there gaping at me. Have they given you a holiday or did you just decide you'd get a better dinner here? (AGATHA *enters Left, followed by* MARY. AGATHA *is a sharp-faced maid, not young, with a querulous voice*) Can't you even say hello?

MARY. Hello, Agatha. You didn't give me a chance. Where's Grandma?

AGATHA. Why aren't you in school? Look at your face and clothes. Where have you been?

MARY. I got a little dirty coming home. I walked part of the way through the woods.

AGATHA. Why didn't you put on your middy blouse and your old brown coat?

MARY. Oh, stop asking me questions. Where's Grandma?

AGATHA. Where ought any clean person be at this time of day? She's taking a bath.

MARY. Is anybody coming for dinner?

AGATHA. She didn't say anything about you coming.

MARY. How could she, stupid? She didn't know.

AGATHA. Then what are you doing here?

34

MARY. Leave me alone. I don't feel well.

AGATHA. Why don't you feel well? Who ever heard of a person going for a walk in the woods when they didn't feel well?

MARY. Oh, leave me alone. I came home because I was sick.

AGATHA. You look all right.

MARY. But I don't feel all right. (*Whining*) I can't even come home without everybody nagging at me.

AGATHA. Don't think you're fooling me, young lady. You might pull the wool over some people's eyes, but—I bet you've been up to something again. (*Stares suspiciously at* MARY, *who says nothing*) Well, you wait right here till I tell your grandmother. And if you feel so sick, you certainly won't want any dinner. A good dose of rhubarb and soda will fix you up. (*Exits Left.*)

(MARY *makes a face in the direction* AGATHA *has gone and stops sniffling. She looks nervously around the room, then goes to a low mirror and tries several experiments with her face in an attempt to make it look sick and haggard.*)

(MRS. TILFORD, *followed by* AGATHA, *enters Left.* MRS. TILFORD *is a large, dignified woman in her sixties, with a pleasant, strong face.*)

AGATHA (*to* MRS. TILFORD, *as she follows her into the room*). Why didn't you put some cold water on your chest? Do you want to catch your death of cold at your age? Did you have to hurry so?

MRS. TILFORD. Mary, what are you doing home?

(MARY *rushes to her and buries her head in* MRS. TILFORD'S *dress, crying.* MRS. TILFORD *lets her cry for a moment while she pats her head, then puts an arm around the child and leads her to a sofa.*)

MRS. TILFORD. Never mind, dear; now stop crying and tell me what is the matter.

MARY (*gradually stops crying, fondling* MRS. TILFORD'S

hand). It's so good to see you, Grandma. You didn't come to visit me all last week.

MRS. TILFORD. I couldn't, dear. But I was coming tomorrow.

MARY. I missed you so. (*Smiling up at* MRS. TILFORD) I was awful homesick.

MRS. TILFORD. I'm glad that's all it was. I was frightened when Agatha said you were not well.

AGATHA. Did I say that? I said she needed a good dose of rhubarb and soda. Most likely she only came home for Wednesday night fudge cake.

MRS. TILFORD. We all get homesick. But how did you get here? Did Miss Karen drive you over?

MARY. I—I walked most of the way, and then a lady gave me a ride and—(*Looks timidly at* MRS. TILFORD.)

AGATHA. Did she have to walk through the woods in her very best coat?

MRS. TILFORD. Mary! Do you mean you left without permission?

MARY (*nervously*). I ran away, Grandma. They didn't know—

MRS. TILFORD. That was a very bad thing to do, and they'll be worried. Agatha, phone Miss Wright and tell her Mary is here. John will drive her back before dinner.

MARY (*as* AGATHA *starts toward telephone*). No, Grandma, don't do that. Please don't do that. Please let me stay.

MRS. TILFORD. But, darling, you can't leave school any time you please.

MARY. Oh, please, Grandma, don't send me back right away. You don't know how they'll punish me.

MRS. TILFORD. I don't think they'll be that angry. Come, you're acting like a foolish little girl.

MARY (*hysterically, as she sees* AGATHA *about to pick up the telephone*). Grandma! Please! I can't go back! I can't! They'll kill me! They will, Grandma! They'll kill me!

(MRS. TILFORD *and* AGATHA *stare at* MARY *in amazement. She puts her head in* MRS. TILFORD's *lap and sobs.*)

MRS. TILFORD (*motioning with a hand for* AGATHA *to leave the room*). Never mind phoning now, Agatha.

AGATHA. If you're going to let her—

(MRS. TILFORD *repeats the gesture.* AGATHA *exits Right, with offended dignity.*)

MRS. TILFORD. Stop crying, Mary.

MARY (*raising her head from* MRS. TILFORD's *lap*). It's so nice here, Grandma.

MRS. TILFORD. I'm glad you like being home with me, but at your age you can hardly—(*More seriously*) What made you say such a terrible thing about Miss Wright and Miss Dobie? You know they wouldn't hurt you.

MARY. Oh, but they would. They—I—(*Breaks off, looks around as if hunting for a clue to her next word; then dramatically*) I fainted today!

MRS. TILFORD (*alarmed*). Fainted?

MARY. Yes, I did. My heart—I had a pain in my heart. I couldn't help having a pain in my heart, and when I fainted right in class, they called Cousin Joe and he said I didn't. He said it was maybe only that I ate my breakfast too fast and Miss Wright blamed me for it.

MRS. TILFORD (*relieved*). I'm sure if Joseph said it wasn't serious, it wasn't.

MARY. But I did have a pain in my heart—honest.

MRS. TILFORD. Have you still got it?

MARY. I guess I haven't got it much any more, but I feel a little weak, and I was so scared of Miss Wright being so mean to me just because I was sick.

MRS. TILFORD. Scared of Karen? Nonsense. It's perfectly possible that you had a pain, but if you had really been sick your Cousin Joseph would certainly have known it. It's not nice to frighten people by pretending to be sick when you aren't.

MARY. I didn't *want* to be sick, but I'm always getting punished for everything.

MRS. TILFORD (*gently*). You mustn't imagine things like that, child, or you'll grow up to be a very unhappy woman. I'm not going to scold you any more for coming home this time, though I suppose I should. Run along upstairs and wash your face and change your dress, and after dinner John will drive you back. Run along.

MARY (*happily*). I can stay for dinner?

MRS. TILFORD. Yes.

MARY. Maybe I could stay till the first of the week. Saturday's your birthday and I could be here with you.

MRS. TILFORD. We don't celebrate my birthday, dear. You'll have to go back to school after dinner.

MARY. But—(*She hesitates, then goes up to* MRS. TILFORD *and puts her arms around the older woman's neck. Softly*) How much do you love me?

MRS TILFORD (*smiling*). As much as all the words in all the books in all the world.

MARY. Remember when I was little and you used to tell me that right before I went to sleep? And it was a rule nobody could say another single word after you finished? You used to say: "Wor-rr-ld," and then I had to shut my eyes tight.

MRS. TILFORD. And sometimes you were naughty and didn't shut them.

MARY. I miss you an awful lot, Grandma.

MRS. TILFORD. And I miss you, but I'm afraid my Latin is too rusty—you'll learn it better in school.

MARY. But couldn't I stay out the rest of this term? After the summer maybe I won't mind it so much. I'll study hard, honest, and—

MRS. TILFORD. You're an earnest little coaxer, but it's out of the question. Back you go tonight. (*Gives* MARY *a playful slap*) Let's not have any more talk about it now, and let's have no more running away from school ever.

MARY (*slowly*). Then I really have to go back there to-night?

MRS. TILFORD. Of course.

MARY. You don't love me. You don't care whether they kill me or not.

MRS. TILFORD. Mary.

MARY. You don't! You don't! You don't care what happens to me.

MRS. TILFORD (*sternly*). But I *do* care that you're talking this way.

MARY (*meekly*). I'm sorry I said that, Grandma. I didn't mean to hurt your feelings. (*Puts her arms around* MRS. TILFORD's *neck*) Forgive me?

MRS. TILFORD. What made you talk like that?

MARY (*in a whisper*). I'm scared, Grandma, I'm scared. They'll do dreadful things to me.

MRS. TILFORD. Dreadful? Nonsense. They'll punish you for running away. You deserve to be punished.

MARY. It's not that. It's not anything I do. It never is. They —they just punish me anyhow, just like they got something against me. I'm afraid of them, Grandma.

MRS. TILFORD. That's ridiculous. What have they ever done to you that is so terrible?

MARY. A lot of things—all the time. Miss Wright says I can't go to the boat-races and—(*Realizing the inadequacy of this reply, she breaks off, hesitates, hunting for a more telling reply, and finally stammers*) It's—it's after what happened today.

MRS. TILFORD. You mean something else besides your naughtiness in pretending to faint and then running away?

MARY. I *did* faint. I didn't pretend. They just said that to make me feel bad. Anyway, it wasn't anything that I did.

MRS. TILFORD. What was it, then?

MARY. I can't tell you.

MRS. TILFORD. Why?

MARY (*sulkily*). Because you're just going to take their part.

MRS. TILFORD (*a little annoyed*). Very well. Now run upstairs and get ready for dinner.

MARY. It was—it was all about Miss Dobie and Mrs. Mortar. They were talking awful things and Peggy and Evelyn heard them and Miss Dobie found out, and then they made us move our rooms.

MRS. TILFORD. What has that to do with you? I don't understand a word you're saying.

MARY. They made us move our rooms. They said we couldn't be together any more. They're afraid to have us near them, that's what it is, and they're taking it out on me. They're scared of you.

MRS. TILFORD. For a little girl you're imagining a lot of big things. Why should they be scared of me? Am I such an unpleasant old lady?

MARY. They're afraid you'll find out.

MRS. TILFORD. Find out what?

MARY (*vaguely*). Things.

MRS. TILFORD. Run along, Mary. I hope you'll get more coherent as you get older.

MARY (*slowly starting for door*). All right. But there're a lot of things. They have secrets or something, and they're afraid I'll find out and tell you.

MRS. TILFORD. There's not necessarily anything wrong with people having secrets.

MARY (*coming back in the room again*). But they've got funny ones. Peggy and Evelyn heard Mrs. Mortar telling Miss Dobie that she was jealous of Miss Wright marrying Cousin Joe.

MRS. TILFORD. You shouldn't repeat things like that.

MARY. But that's what she said, Grandma. She said it was unnatural for a girl to feel that way.

MRS. TILFORD. What?

MARY. I'm just telling you what she said. She said there was something funny about it, and that Miss Dobie had always been like that, even when she was a little girl, and that it was unnatural—

MRS. TILFORD. Stop using that silly word, Mary.

MARY (*vaguely realizing that she is on the right track, hurries on*). But that was the word *she* kept using, Grandma, and then they got mad and told Mrs. Mortar she'd have to get out.

MRS. TILFORD. That was probably not the reason at all.

MARY (*nodding vigorously*). I bet it was, because honestly, Miss Dobie does get cranky and mean every time Cousin Joe comes, and today I heard her say to him: "God damn you," and then she said she was just a jealous fool and—

MRS. TILFORD. You have picked up some very fine words, haven't you, Mary?

MARY. That's just what she said, Grandma, and one time Miss Dobie was crying in Miss Wright's room, and Miss Wright was trying to stop her, and she said that all right, maybe she wouldn't get married right away if—

MRS. TILFORD. How do you know all this?

MARY. We couldn't help hearing because they—I mean Miss Dobie—was talking awful loud, and their room is right next to ours.

MRS. TILFORD. Whose room?

MARY. Miss Wright's room, I mean, and you can just ask Peggy and Evelyn whether we didn't hear. Almost always Miss Dobie comes in after we go to bed and stays a long time. I guess that's why they want to get rid of us—of me—because we hear things.

That's why they're making us move our room, and they punish me all the time for—

MRS. TILFORD. For eavesdropping, I should think. (*She has said this mechanically. With nothing definite in her mind, she is making an effort to conceal the fact that* MARY'S *description of the life at school has shocked her*) Well, now I think we've had enough gossip, don't you? Dinner's almost ready, and I can't eat with a girl who has such a dirty face.

MARY (*softly*). I've heard other things, too.

MRS. TILFORD (*abstractedly*). What? What did you say?

MARY. I've heard other things. Plenty of other things, Grandma.

MRS. TILFORD. What things?

MARY. Bad things.

MRS. TILFORD. Well, what were they?

MARY. I can't tell you.

MRS. TILFORD. Mary, you're annoying me very much. If you have anything to say, then say it and stop acting silly.

MARY. I mean I can't say it out loud.

MRS. TILFORD. There couldn't possibly be anything so terrible that you couldn't say it out loud. Now either tell the truth or be still.

MARY. Well, a lot of things I don't understand. But it's awful, and sometimes they fight and then they make up, and Miss Dobie cries and Miss Wright gets mad, and then they make up again, and there are funny noises and we get scared.

MRS. TILFORD. Noises? I suppose you girls have a happy time imagining a murder.

MARY. And we've seen things, too. Funny things. (*Sees the impatience of her grandmother*) I'd tell you, but I got to whisper it.

MRS. TILFORD. Why must you whisper it?

MARY. I don't know. I just got to. (*Climbs on the sofa*

next to MRS. TILFORD *and begins whispering. At first the whisper is slow and hesitant, but it gradually works itself up to fast, excited talking. In the middle of it* MRS. TILFORD *stops her.*)

MRS. TILFORD (*trembling*). Do you know what you're saying? (*Without answering,* MARY *goes back to the whispering until the older woman takes her by the shoulders and turns her around to stare in her face*) Mary! *Are you telling me the truth?*

MARY. Honest, honest. You just ask Peggy and Evelyn and—(*After a moment* MRS. TILFORD *gets up and begins to pace about the room. She is no longer listening to* MARY, *who keeps up a running fire of conversation*) They know too. And maybe there're other kids who know, but we've always been frightened and so we didn't ask, and one night I was going to go and find out, but I got scared and we went to bed early so we wouldn't hear, but sometimes I couldn't help it, but we never talked about it much, because we thought they'd find out and— Oh, Grandma, don't make me go back to that awful place.

MRS. TILFORD (*abstractedly*). What? (*Starts to move about again.*)

MARY. Don't make me go back to that place. I just couldn't stand it any more. Really, Grandma, I'm so unhappy there, and if only I could stay out the rest of the term, why, then—

MRS. TILFORD (*makes irritated gesture*). Be still a minute. (*After a moment*) No, you won't have to go back.

MARY (*surprised*). Honest?

MRS. TILFORD. Honest.

MARY (*hugging* MRS. TILFORD). You're the nicest, loveliest grandma in all the world. You—you're not mad at me?

MRS. TILFORD. I'm not mad at you. Now go upstairs and get ready for dinner. (MARY *kisses her and runs hap-*

pily out Left. MRS. TILFORD *stands staring after her for a long moment; then, very slowly, she puts on her eyeglasses and crosses to the phone. She dials a number)* Is Miss Wright—is Miss Wright in? (*Waits a second, hurriedly puts down the receiver)* Never mind, never mind. (*Dials another number)* Dr. Cardin, please. Mrs. Tilford. (*She remains absolutely motionless while she waits. When she does speak, her voice is low and tense)* Joseph? Joseph? Can you come to see me right away? Yes, I'm perfectly well. No, but it's important, Joseph, very important. I must see you right away. I—I can't tell you over the phone. Can't you come sooner? It's not about Mary's fainting—I said it's not about Mary, Joseph; in one way it's about Mary— (*Suddenly quiet)* But will the hospital take so long? Very well, Joseph, make it as soon as you can. (*Hangs up the receiver, sits for a moment undecided. Then, taking a breath, she dials another number)* Mrs. Munn, please. This is Mrs. Tilford. Miriam? This is Amelia Tilford. I have something to tell you—something very shocking, I'm afraid —something about the school and Evelyn and Mary—

Curtain

SCENE II

SCENE: *The same as Scene I. The curtain has been lowered to mark the passing of a few hours.*

AT RISE: MARY *is lying on the floor playing with a puzzle.* AGATHA *appears lugging blankets and pillows across the room. Almost at the door, she stops and gives* MARY *an annoyed look.*

AGATHA. And see to it that she doesn't get my good quilt all dirty, and let her wear your green pajamas.

MARY. Who?

AGATHA. Who? Don't you ever keep your ears open? Rosalie Wells is coming over to spend the night with you.

MARY. You mean she's going to sleep *here?*

AGATHA. You heard me.

MARY. What for?

AGATHA. Do I know all the crazy things that are happening around here? Your grandmother phones Mrs. Wells all the way to New York, three dollars and eighty-five cents and families starving, and Mrs. Wells wanted to know if Rosalie could stay here until tomorrow.

MARY (*relieved*). Oh. Couldn't Evelyn Munn come instead?

AGATHA. Sure. We'll have the whole town over to enter·tain you.

MARY. I won't let Rosalie Wells wear my new pajamas.

AGATHA (*exits as the front door-bell rings*). Don't tell me what you won't do. You'll act like a lady for once in your life. (*Off-stage*) Come on in, Rosalie. Just go on in there and make yourself at home. Have you had your dinner?

ROSALIE (*off-stage*). Good evening. Yes'm.

AGATHA (*off-stage*). Hang up your pretty coat. Have you had your bath?

ROSALIE (*off-stage*). Yes, ma'am. This morning.

AGATHA (*off-stage*). Well, you better have another one.

(*She is climbing the stairs as* ROSALIE *comes into the room.* MARY, *lying in front of the couch, is hidden from her. Gingerly* ROSALIE *sits down on a chair.*)

MARY (*softly*). Whooooooo. (ROSALIE *jumps*) Whoooooooo. (ROSALIE, *frightened, starts hurriedly for the door.* MARY *sits up, laughs*) You're a goose.

ROSALIE (*belligerently*). Oh, so it's you. Well, who likes to hear funny noises at night? You could have been a werewolf.

MARY. A werewolf wouldn't want you.

ROSALIE. You know everything, don't you? (MARY *laughs.*
    ROSALIE *comes over, stands staring at puzzle*) Isn't it
    funny about school?

MARY. What's funny about it?

ROSALIE. Don't act like you can come home every night.

MARY. Maybe I can from now on. (*Rolls over on her back
    luxuriously*) Maybe I'm never going back.

ROSALIE. Am I going back? I don't want to stay home.

MARY. What'll you give to know?

ROSALIE. Nothing. I'll ask Mamma.

MARY. Will you give me a free T. L. if I tell you?

ROSALIE (*thinks for a moment*). All right. Lois Fisher told
    Helen that you were very smart.

MARY. That's an old one. I won't take it.

ROSALIE. You got to take it.

MARY. Nope.

ROSALIE (*laughs*). You don't know, anyway.

MARY. I know what I heard, and I know Grandma phoned
    your mother in New York to come and get you right
    away. You're just going to spend the night here. I wish
    Evelyn could come instead of you.

ROSALIE. But what's happened? Peggy and Helen and
    Evelyn and Lois went home tonight, too. Do you think
    somebody's got scarlet fever or something?

MARY. No.

ROSALIE. Do *you* know what it is? How'd you find out?
    (*No answer*) You're always pretending you know
    everything. You're just faking. (*Flounces away*) Never
    mind, don't bother telling me. I think curiosity is very
    unladylike, anyhow. I have no concern with your silly
    secrets.

MARY. Suppose I told you that I just may have said that
    you were in on it?

ROSALIE. In on what?

MARY. The secret. Suppose I told you that I *may have*
    said that you told me about it?

ROSALIE. Why, Mary Tilford! You can't do a thing like that. I didn't tell you about anything. (MARY *laughs*) Did you tell your grandmother such a thing?

MARY. Maybe.

ROSALIE. Did you?

MARY. Maybe.

ROSALIE. Well, I'm going right up to your grandmother and tell her I didn't tell you anything—whatever it is. You're just trying to get me into trouble and I'm not going to let you. (*Starts for door.*)

MARY. Wait a minute, I'll come with you.

ROSALIE. What for?

MARY. I want to tell her about Helen Burton's bracelet.

ROSALIE (*sits down suddenly*). What about it?

MARY. Just that you stole it.

ROSALIE. Shut up. I didn't do any such thing.

MARY. Yes, you did.

ROSALIE (*tearfully*). You made it up. You're always making things up.

MARY. You can't call me a fibber, Rosalie Wells. That's a kind of a dare and I won't take a dare. I guess I'll go tell Grandma, anyway. Then she can call the police and they'll come for you and you'll spend the rest of your life in one of those solitary prisons and you'll get older and older, and when you're very old and can't see anymore, they'll let you out maybe with a big sign on your back saying you're a thief, and your mother and father will be dead and you won't have any place to go and you'll beg on the streets—

ROSALIE. I didn't steal anything. I borrowed the bracelet and I was going to put it back as soon as I'd worn it to the movies. I never meant to keep it.

MARY. Nobody'll believe that, least of all the police. You're just a common, ordinary thief. Stop that bawling. You'll have the whole house down here in a minute.

ROSALIE. You won't tell? Say you won't tell.

MARY. Am I a fibber?

ROSALIE. No.

MARY. Then say: "I apologize on my hands and knees."

ROSALIE. I apologize on my hands and knees. Let's play with the puzzle.

MARY. Wait a minute. Say: "From now on, I, Rosalie Wells, am the vassal of Mary Tilford and will do and say whatever she tells me under the solemn oath of a knight."

ROSALIE. I won't say that. That's the worse oath there is. (MARY *starts for the door*) Mary! Please don't—

MARY. Will you swear it?

ROSALIE (*sniffling*). But then you could tell me to do anything.

MARY. And you'd have to do it. Say it quick or I'll—

ROSALIE (*hurriedly*). From now on, I, Rosalie Wells, am the vassal of Mary Tilford and will do and say whatever she tells me under the solemn oath of a knight. (*She gasps, and sits up straight as* MRS. TILFORD *enters.*)

MARY. Don't forget that.

MRS. TILFORD. Good evening, Rosalie, you're looking very well.

ROSALIE. Good evening, Mrs. Tilford.

MARY. She's getting fatter every day.

MRS. TILFORD (*abstractedly*). Then it's very becoming. (*Door-bell rings*) That must be Joseph. Mary, take Rosalie into the library. There's some fruit and milk on the table. Be sure you're both fast asleep by half past ten. (*Leans down, kisses them both.* ROSALIE *starts to exit Right, sees* MARY, *stops and hesitates.*)

MARY. Go on, Rosalie. (*Waits until* ROSALIE *reluctantly exits*) Grandma.

MRS. TILFORD. Yes?

MARY. Grandma, Cousin Joe'll say I've got to go back. He'll say I really wasn't—

(CARDIN *enters and she runs from the room.*)

CARDIN. Hello, Amelia. (*Looks curiously at the fleeing* MARY) Mary home, eh?

MRS. TILFORD (*watching* MARY *as she leaves*). Hello, Joseph. Sit down. (*He sits down, looks at her curiously, waits for her to speak*) Whisky?

CARDIN. Please. How are you feeling? Headaches again?

MRS. TILFORD (*puts drink on table*). No.

CARDIN. Those are good powders. Bicarbonate of soda and water. Never hurt anybody yet.

MRS. TILFORD. Yes. How have you been, Joseph?

CARDIN. My good health is monotonous.

MRS. TILFORD (*vaguely, sparring for time*). I haven't seen you the last few weeks. Agatha misses you for Sunday dinners.

CARDIN. I've been busy. We're getting the results from the mating-season right about now.

MRS. TILFORD. Did I take you away from a patient?

CARDIN. No. I was at the hospital.

MRS. TILFORD. How's it getting on?

CARDIN. Just the same. No money, badly equipped, a lousy laboratory, everybody growling at everybody else— Amelia, you didn't bring me here to talk about the hospital. We're talking like people waiting for the muffins to be passed around. What's the matter with you?

MRS. TILFORD. I—I have something to tell you.

CARDIN. Well, out with it.

MRS. TILFORD. It's a very hard thing to say, Joseph.

CARDIN. Hard for you to say to *me*? (*No answer*) Don't be worried about Mary. I guessed that she ran home to tell you about her faint. It was caused by nothing but bad temper and was very clumsily managed, at that. Amelia, she's a terribly spoilt—

MRS. TILFORD. I heard about the faint. That's not what is worrying me.

CARDIN (*gently*). Are you in some trouble?

MRS. TILFORD. We all are in trouble. Bad trouble.

CARDIN. We? Me, you mean? Nothing's the matter with me.

MRS. TILFORD. When did you last see Karen?

CARDIN. Today. This afternoon.

MRS. TILFORD. Oh. Not since seven o'clock?

CARDIN. What's happened since seven o'clock?

MRS. TILFORD. Joseph, you've been engaged to Karen for a long time. Are your plans any more definite than they were a year ago?

CARDIN. You can get ready to buy the wedding present. We'll have the wedding here, if you don't mind. The smell of clean little girls and boiled linen would worry me.

MRS. TILFORD. Why has Karen decided so suddenly to make it definite?

CARDIN. She has not suddenly decided anything. The school is pretty well on its feet, and now that Mrs. Mortar is leaving—

MRS. TILFORD. I've heard about their putting Mrs. Mortar out.

CARDIN. Putting her out? Well, maybe. But a nice sum for a trip and a promise that a good niece will support you the rest of your life is an enviable way of being put out.

MRS. TILFORD (*slowly*). Don't you find it odd, Joseph, that they want so much to get rid of that silly, harmless woman?

CARDIN. I don't know what you're talking about, but it isn't odd at all. Lily Mortar is not a harmless woman, although God knows she's silly enough. She's a nasty, tiresome, spoilt old bitch. If you're forming a Mortar Welfare Society, you're wasting your time. (*Gets up, puts down his glass*) It's not like you to waste your time. Now, what's it that's really on your mind?

MRS. TILFORD. You must not marry Karen.

CARDIN (*shocked, he grins*). You're a very impertinent

lady. Why must I—(*imitates her*) not marry Karen?

MRS. TILFORD. Because there's something wrong with Karen—something horrible.

(*The door-bell is heard to ring loud and long.*)

CARDIN. I don't think I can allow you to say things like that, Amelia.

MRS. TILFORD. I have good reason for saying it. (*Breaks off as she hears voices off-stage*) Who is that?

KAREN (*off-stage*). Mrs. Tilford, Agatha. Is she in?

AGATHA (*off-stage*). Yes'm. Come on in.

MRS. TILFORD. I won't have her here.

CARDIN (*angrily*). What are you talking about?

MRS. TILFORD. I won't have her here.

CARDIN (*picks up his hat*). Then you don't want me here either. (*Turns to face* KAREN, *who, with* MARTHA, *has rushed in*) Darling, what?—

KAREN (*stops when she sees him, puts her hand over her eyes*). Is it a joke, Joe?

MARTHA (*with great force to* MRS. TILFORD). We've come to find out what you are doing.

CARDIN (*kissing* KAREN). What is it?

KAREN. It's crazy! It's crazy! What did she do it for?

CARDIN. What are you talking about? What do you mean?

MRS. TILFORD. You shouldn't have come here.

CARDIN. What is all this? What's happened?

KAREN. I tried to reach you. Hasn't she told you?

CARDIN. Nobody's told me anything. I haven't heard anything but wild talk. What is it, Karen? (*She starts to speak, then dumbly shakes her head*) What's happened, Martha?

MARTHA (*violently*). An insane asylum has been let loose. How do we know what's happened?

CARDIN. What was it?

KAREN. We didn't know what it was. Nobody would talk to us, nobody would tell us anything.

MARTHA. I'll tell you, I'll tell you. You see if you can

make any sense out of it. At dinner-time Mrs. Munn's chauffeur said that Evelyn must be sent home right away. At half past seven Mrs. Burton arrived to tell us that she wanted Helen's things packed and that she'd wait outside because she didn't want to enter a place like ours. Five minutes later the Wells's butler came for Rosalie.

CARDIN. What was it?

MARTHA. It was madhouse. People rushing in and out, the children being pushed into cars—

KAREN (*quiet now, takes his hand*). Mrs. Rogers finally told us.

CARDIN. What? What?

KAREN. That—that Martha and I are—in love with each other. In love with each other. Mrs. Tilford told them.

CARDIN (*for a moment stands staring at her incredulously. Then he walks across the room, stares out of the window, and finally turns to* MRS. TILFORD). Did you tell them that?

MRS. TILFORD. Yes.

CARDIN. Are you sick?

MRS. TILFORD. You know I'm not sick.

CARDIN (*snapping the words out*). Then what did you do it for?

MRS. TILFORD (*slowly*). Because it's true.

KAREN (*incredulously*). You think it's true, then?

MARTHA. You fool! You damned, vicious—

KAREN. Do you realize what you're saying?

MRS. TILFORD. I realize it very well. And—

MARTHA. You realize nothing, nothing, nothing.

MRS. TILFORD. And that's why I don't think you should have come here. (*Quietly, with a look at* MARTHA) I shall not call you names, and I will not allow you to call me names. It comes to this: I can't trust myself to talk about it with you now or ever.

KAREN. What's she talking about, Joe? What's she mean?

What is she trying to do to us? What is everybody doing to us?

MARTHA (*softly, as though to herself*). Pushed around. We're being pushed around by crazy people. (*Shakes herself slightly*) That's an awful thing. And we're standing here— (CARDIN *puts his arm around* KAREN, *walks with her to the window. They stand there together*) We're standing here taking it. (*Suddenly with violence*) Didn't you know we'd come here? Were we supposed to lie down and grin while you kicked us around with these lies?

MRS. TILFORD. This can't do any of us any good, Miss Dobie.

MARTHA (*scornfully imitating her*). "This can't do any of us any good." Listen, listen. Try to understand this: you're not playing with paper dolls. We're human beings, see? It's our lives you're fooling with. *Our* lives. That's serious business for us. Can you understand that?

MRS. TILFORD (*for the first time she speaks angrily*). I can understand that, and I understand a lot more. *You've* been playing with a lot of children's lives, and that's why I stopped you. (*More calmly*) I know how serious this is for you, how serious it is for all of us.

CARDIN (*bitterly*). I don't think you do know.

MRS. TILFORD. I wanted to avoid this meeting because it can't do any good. You came here to find out if I had made the charge. You've found out. Let's end it there. *I don't want you in this house.* I'm sorry this had to be done to you, Joseph.

CARDIN. I don't like your sympathy.

MRS. TILFORD. Very well. There's nothing I mean to do, nothing I want to do. There's nothing anybody can do.

CARDIN (*carefully*). You have already done a terrible thing.

MRS. TILFORD. I have done what I had to do. What they are may possibly be their own business. It becomes a great deal more than that when children are involved.

KAREN (*wildly*). It's not true. Not a word of it is true; can't you understand that?

MRS. TILFORD. There won't be any punishment for either of you. But there mustn't be any punishment for me, either—and that's what this meeting is. This—this thing is your own. Go away with it. I don't understand it and I don't want any part of it.

MARTHA (*slowly*). So you thought we would go away?

MRS. TILFORD. I think that's best for you.

MARTHA. There must be something we can do to you, and, whatever it is, we'll find it.

MRS. TILFORD. That will be very unwise.

KAREN. You are right to be afraid.

MRS. TILFORD. I am not afraid, Karen.

CARDIN. But you *are* old—and you *are* irresponsible.

MRS. TILFORD (*hurt*). You know that's not true.

KAREN (*goes to her*). I don't want to have anything to do with your mess, do you hear me? It makes me feel dirty and sick to be forced to say this, but here it is: there isn't a single word of truth in anything you've said. We're standing here defending ourselves—and against what? Against a lie. A great, awful lie.

MRS. TILFORD. I'm sorry that I can't believe that.

KAREN. Damn you!

CARDIN. But you can believe this: they've worked eight long years to save enough money to buy that farm, to start that school. They did without everything that young people ought to have. You wouldn't know about that. That school meant things to them: self-respect, and bread and butter, and honest work. Do you know what it is to try so hard for anything? Well, now it's gone. (*Suddenly hits the side of the table with his hand*) What the hell did you do it for?

MRS. TILFORD (*softly*). It had to be done.

CARDIN. Righteousness is a great thing.

MRS. TILFORD (*gently*). I know how you must feel.

CARDIN. You don't know anything about how I feel. And you don't know how they feel, either.

MRS. TILFORD. I've loved you as much as I loved my own boys. I wouldn't have spared them; I couldn't spare you.

CARDIN (*fiercely*). I believe you.

MARTHA. What is there to do to you? What can we do to you? There must be something—something that makes you feel the way we do tonight. You don't want any part of this, you said. But you'll get a part. More than you bargained for. (*Suddenly*) Listen: are you willing to stand by everything you've said tonight?

MRS. TILFORD. Yes.

MARTHA. All right. That's fine. But don't get the idea we'll let you whisper this lie: you made it and you'll come out with it. Shriek it to your town of Lancet. We'll *make* you shriek it—and we'll make you do it in a court room. (*Quietly*) Tomorrow, Mrs. Tilford, you will have a libel suit on your hands.

MRS. TILFORD. That will be very unwise.

KAREN. Very unwise—for you.

MRS. TILFORD. It is you I am thinking of. I am frightened for you. It was wrong of you to brazen it out here to-night; it would be criminally foolish of you to brazen it out in public. That can bring you nothing but pain. I am an old woman, Miss Dobie, and I have seen too many people, out of pride, act on that pride. In the end they punish themselves.

MARTHA. And you feel that you are too old to be punished? That we should spare you?

MRS. TILFORD. You know that is not what I meant.

CARDIN (*turns from the window*). So you took a child's word for it?

MARTHA (*looks at him, shakes her head*). I knew it, too.

KAREN. That is really where you got it? I can't believe— it couldn't be. Why, she's a child.

MARTHA. She's not a child any longer.

KAREN. Oh, my God, it all fits so well now. That girl has hated us for a long time. We never knew why, we never could find out. There didn't seem to be any reason—

MARTHA. There wasn't any reason. She hates everybody and everything.

KAREN. Your Mary's a strange girl, a bad girl. There's something very awful the matter with her.

MRS. TILFORD. I was waiting for you to say that, Miss Wright.

KAREN. I'm telling you the truth. We should have told it to you long ago. (*Stops, sighs*) It's no use.

MARTHA. Where is she? Bring her out here and let us hear what she has to say.

MRS. TILFORD. You cannot see her.

CARDIN. Where is she?

MRS. TILFORD. I won't have that, Joseph.

CARDIN. I'm going to talk to her.

MRS. TILFORD. *I won't have her go through with that again.* (*To* KAREN *and* MARTHA) You came here demanding explanations. It was I who should have asked them from you. You attack me, you attack Mary. I've told you I didn't mean you any harm. I still don't. You claim that it isn't true; it may be natural that you should say that, but I *know* that it is true. No matter what you say, you know very well I wouldn't have acted until I was absolutely sure. All I wanted was to get those children away. That has been done. There won't be any talk about it or about you—I'll see to that. You have been in my house long enough. Get out.

KAREN (*gets up*). The wicked very young, and the wicked very old. Let's go home.

CARDIN. Sit down. (*To* MRS. TILFORD) When two people come here with their lives spread on the table for you to cut to pieces, then the only honest thing to do is to give them a chance to come out whole. Are you honest?

MRS. TILFORD. I've always thought so.

CARDIN. Then where is Mary? (*After a moment she moves her head to door Right. Quickly* CARDIN *goes to the door and opens it*) Mary! Come here.

(*After a moment* MARY *appears, stands nervously near door. Her manner is shy and afraid.*)

MRS. TILFORD (*gently*). Sit down, dear, and don't be afraid.

MARTHA (*her lips barely moving*). Make her tell the truth.

CARDIN (*walking about in front of* MARY). Look: everybody lies all the time. Sometimes they have to, sometimes they don't. I've lied myself for a lot of different reasons, but there was never a time when, if I'd been given a second chance, I wouldn't have taken back the lie and told the truth. You're lucky if you ever get that chance. I'm telling you this because I'm about to ask you a question. Before you answer the question, I want to tell you that if you've l—, if you made a mistake, you must take this chance and say so. You won't be punished for it. Do you get all that?

MARY (*timidly*). Yes, Cousin Joe.

CARDIN (*grimly*). All right, let's get started. Were you telling your grandmother the truth this afternoon? The exact truth about Miss Wright and Miss Dobie?

MARY (*without hesitation*). Oh, yes.

(KAREN *sighs deeply*, MARTHA, *her fists closed tight, turns her back to the child.* CARDIN *smiles as he looks at* MARY.)

CARDIN. All right, Mary, that was your chance; you passed it up. (*Pulls up a chair, sits down in front of her*) Now let's find out things.

MRS. TILFORD. She's told you. Aren't you through?

CARDIN. Not by a long shot. You've started something, and I'm going to finish it for you. Will you answer some more questions, Mary?

MARY. Yes, Cousin Joe.

MARTHA. Stop that sick, sweet tone.

(MRS. TILFORD *half rises;* CARDIN *motions her back.*)

CARDIN. Why don't you like Miss Dobie and Miss Wright?

MARY. Oh, I do like them. They just don't like me. They never have liked me.

CARDIN. How do you know?

MARY. They're always picking on me. They're always punishing me for everything that happens. No matter what happens, it's always me.

CARDIN. Why do you think they do that?

MARY. Because—because they're—because they— (*Stops, turns*) Grandma, I—

CARDIN. All right, we'll skip that one. Did you get punished today?

MARY. Yes, and it was just because Peggy and Evelyn heard them and so they took it out on me.

KAREN. That's a lie.

CARDIN. Sssh. Heard what, Mary?

MARY. Mrs. Mortar told Miss Dobie that there was something funny about her. She said that she had a funny feeling about Miss Wright, and Mrs. Mortar said that was unnatural. That was why we got punished, just because—

KAREN. That was not the reason they got punished.

MRS. TILFORD (*to* MARTHA). Miss Dobie?

MARTHA. My aunt is a stupid woman. What she said was unpleasant; it was said to annoy me. It meant nothing more than that.

MARY. And, Cousin Joe, she said every time you came to the school Miss Dobie got jealous, and that she didn't want you to get married.

MARTHA (*to* CARDIN). She said that, too. For God's sake,

can't you see what's happening? This—this child is taking little things, little family things, and making them have meanings that— (*Stops, suddenly regards* MARY *with a combination of disgust and interest*) Where did you learn so much in so little time?

CARDIN. What do you think Mrs. Mortar meant by all that, Mary?

MRS. TILFORD. Stop it, Joseph!

MARY. I don't know, but it was always kind of funny and she always said things like that and all the girls would talk about it when Miss Dobie went and visited Miss Wright late at night—

KAREN (*angrily*). And we go to the movies at night and sometimes we read at night and sometimes we drink tea at night. Those are guilty things, too, Mrs. Tilford.

MARY. And there are always funny sounds and we'd stay awake and listen because we couldn't help hearing and I'd get frightened because the sounds were like—

MARTHA. Be still!

KAREN (*with violence*). No, no. You don't want her still now. What else did you hear?

MARY. Grandma, I—

MRS. TILFORD (*bitterly to* CARDIN). You are trying to make her name it, aren't you?

CARDIN (*ignoring her, speaks to* MARY). Go on.

MARY. I don't know; there were just sounds.

CARDIN. But what did you think they were? Why did they frighten you?

MARY (*weakly*). I don't know.

CARDIN (*smiles at* MRS. TILFORD). She doesn't know.

MARY (*hastily*). I saw things, too. One night there was so much noise I thought somebody was sick or something and I looked through the keyhole and they were kissing and saying things and then I got scared because it was different sort of and I—

MARTHA (*her face distorted, turns to* MRS. TILFORD). That child—that child is sick.

KAREN. Ask her again how she could see us.

CARDIN. How could you see Miss Dobie and Miss Wright?

MARY. I—I—

MRS. TILFORD. Tell him what you whispered to me.

MARY. It was at night and I was leaning down by the keyhole.

KAREN. *There's no keyhole on my door.*

MRS. TILFORD. What?

KAREN. There—is—no—keyhole—on—my—door.

MARY (*quickly*). It wasn't her room, Grandma, it was the other room, I guess. It was *Miss Dobie's* room. I saw them through the keyhole in Miss Dobie's room.

CARDIN. How did you know anybody was in Miss Dobie's room?

MARY. I told you, I told you. Because we heard them. Everybody heard them—

MARTHA. I share a room with my aunt. It is on the first floor at the other end of the house. It is impossible to hear anything from there. (*To* CARDIN) Tell her to come and see for herself.

MRS. TILFORD (*her voice shaken*). What is this, Mary? Why did you say you saw through a keyhole? *Can* you hear from your room?—

MARY (*starts to cry*). Everybody is yelling at me. I don't know what I'm saying with everybody mixing me all up. I did see it! I did see it!

MRS. TILFORD. *What* did you see? *Where* did you see it? I want the truth, now. The truth, whatever it is.

CARDIN (*gets up, moves his chair back*). We can go home. We are finished here. (*Looks around*) It's not a pleasant place to be.

MRS. TILFORD (*angrily*). Stop that crying, Mary. Stand up.

(MARY *gets up, head down, still crying hysterically.* MRS. TILFORD *goes and stands directly in front of her.*)

MRS. TILFORD. *I want the truth.*

MARY. All—all right.

MRS. TILFORD. What is the truth?

MARY. It was Rosalie who saw them. I just said it was me so I wouldn't have to tattle on Rosalie.

CARDIN (*wearily*). Oh, my God!

MARY. It *was* Rosalie, Grandma, she told us all about it. She said she had read about it in a book and she knew. (*Desperately*). You ask Rosalie. You just ask Rosalie. She'll tell you. We used to talk about it all the time. That's the truth, that's the honest truth. She said it was when the door was open once and she told us all about it. I was just trying to save Rosalie, and everybody jumps on me.

MRS. TILFORD (*to* CARDIN). Please wait a minute. (*Goes to library door*) Rosalie!

CARDIN. You're giving yourself an awful beating, Amelia, and you deserve whatever you get.

MRS. TILFORD (*stands waiting for* ROSALIE, *passes her hand over her face*). I don't know. I don't know, any more. Maybe it's what I do deserve. (*As* ROSALIE, *frightened, appears at the door, making bows to everybody, she takes the child gently by the hand, brings her down Center, talking nervously*) I'm sorry to keep you up so late, Rosalie. You must be tired. (*Speaks rapidly*) Mary says there's been a lot of talk in the school lately about Miss Wright and Miss Dobie. Is that true?

ROSALIE. I—I don't know what you mean.

MRS. TILFORD. That things have been said among you girls.

ROSALIE (*wide-eyed, frightened*). What things? I never--I—I—

KAREN (*gently*). Don't be frightened.

MRS. TILFORD. What was the talk about, Rosalie?

ROSALIE (*utterly bewildered*). I don't know what she means, Miss Wright.

KAREN. Rosalie, Mary has told her grandmother that certain things at school have been—er—puzzling you girls. You, particularly.

ROSALIE. History puzzles me. I guess I'm not very good at history, and Helen helps me sometimes, if that—

KAREN. No, that's not what she meant. She says that you told her that you saw certain—certain acts between Miss Dobie and myself. She says that once, when the door was open, you saw us kissing each other in a way that—(*Unable to bear the child's look, she turns her back*) women don't kiss one another.

ROSALIE. Oh, Miss Wright, I didn't, didn't, I didn't. I *never* said such a thing.

MRS. TILFORD (*grimly*). That's true, my dear?

ROSALIE. I never saw any such thing. Mary always makes things up about me and everybody else. (*Starts to weep in excitement*) I never said any such thing ever. Why, I never even could have thought of—

MARY (*staring at her, speaks very slowly*). Yes, you did, Rosalie. You're just trying to get out of it. I remember just when you said it. I remember it, because it was the day Helen Burton's bracelet was—

ROSALIE (*stands fascinated and fearful, looking at* MARY). I never did. I—I—you're just—

MARY. It was the day Helen's bracelet was stolen, and nobody knew who did it, and Helen said that if her mother found out, she'd have the thief put in jail.

KAREN (*puzzled, as are the others, by the sudden change in* ROSALIE'S *manner*). There's nothing to cry about. You must help us by telling the truth. Why, what's the matter, Rosalie?

MARY. Grandma, there's something I've got to tell you that—

ROSALIE (*with a shrill cry*). Yes. Yes. I did see it. I told Mary. What Mary said was right. I said it, I said it— (*Throws herself on the couch, weeping hysterically;* MARTHA *stands leaning against the door;* KAREN, CARDIN, *and* MRS. TILFORD *are staring at* ROSALIE; MARY *slowly sits down as the Curtain falls.*)

ACT THREE

SCENE: *The same as Act One. Living room of the school.*

AT RISE: *The room has changed. It is not dirty, but it is dull and dark and uncared for. The windows are tightly shut, the curtains tightly drawn.* KAREN *is sitting in a large chair, Right Center, feet flat on floor.* MARTHA *is lying on the couch, her face buried against the pillows, her back to* KAREN. *It is a minute or two after the rise of the curtain before either speaks.*

MARTHA. It's cold in here.

KAREN. Yes.

MARTHA. What time is it?

KAREN. I don't know. What's the difference?

MARTHA. None. I was hoping it was time for my bath.

KAREN. Take it early today.

MARTHA (*laughs*). Oh, I couldn't do that. I look forward all day to that bath. It's my last touch with the full life. It makes me feel important to know that there's one thing ahead of me, one thing I've *got* to do. You ought to get yourself something like that. I tell you, at five o'clock every day you comb your hair. How's that? It's better for you, take my word. You wake up in the morning and you say to yourself, the day's not entirely empty, life is rich and full: at five o'clock I'll comb my hair.

(*They fall back into silence. A moment later the phone rings. Neither of them pays the slightest attention to it. But the ringing becomes too insistent.* KAREN *rises, takes the receiver off, goes back to her chair and sits down.*)

KAREN. It's raining.

MARTHA. Hungry?

KAREN. No. You?

MARTHA. No, but I'd like to be hungry again. Remember how much we used to eat at college?

KAREN. That was ten years ago.

MARTHA. Well, maybe we'll be hungry in another ten years. It's cheaper this way.

KAREN. What's the old thing about time being more nourishing than bread?

MARTHA. Yeah? Maybe.

KAREN. Joe's late today. What time is it?

MARTHA (*turns again to lie on her side*). We've been sitting here for eight days asking each other the time. Haven't you heard? There isn't any time any more.

KAREN. It's been days since we've been out of this house.

MARTHA. Well, we'll have to get off these chairs sooner or later. In a couple of months they'll need dusting.

KAREN. What'll we do when we get off?

MARTHA. God knows.

KAREN (*almost in a whisper*). It's awful.

MARTHA. Let's not talk about it. (*After a moment*) What about eggs for dinner?

KAREN. All right.

MARTHA. I'll make some potatoes with onions, the way you used to like them.

KAREN. It's a week ago Thursday. It never seemed real until the last day. It seems real enough now, all right.

MARTHA. Now and forever after.

KAREN (*suddenly*). Let's go out.

MARTHA (*turns over, stares at her*). Where to?

KAREN. We'll take a walk.

MARTHA. Where'll we walk?

KAREN. Why shouldn't we take a walk? We won't see anybody, and suppose we do, what of it? We'll jus—

MARTHA (*slowly gets up*). Come on. We'll go through the park.

KAREN. They might see us. (*They stand looking at each other*) Let's not go. (MARTHA *goes back, lies down again*) We'll go tomorrow.

MARTHA (*laughs*). Stop kidding yourself.

KAREN. But Joe says we've got to go out. He says that all the people who don't think it's true will begin to wonder if we keep hiding this way.

MARTHA. If it makes you feel better to think there *are* such people, go ahead.

KAREN. He says we ought to go into town and go shopping and act as though—

MARTHA. Shopping? That's a sound idea. There aren't three stores in Lancet that would sell us anything. Hasn't he heard about the ladies' clubs and their meetings and their circulars and their visits and their—

KAREN (*softly*). Don't tell him.

MARTHA (*gently*). I won't. (*There are footsteps in the hall, and the sound of something being dragged*) There's our friend.

(*A* GROCERY BOY *appears lugging a box. He brings it into the room, stands staring at them, giggles a little. Walks toward* KAREN, *stops, examines her. She sits tense, looking away from him. Without taking his eyes from* KAREN, *he speaks.*)

GROCERY BOY. I knocked on the kitchen door but nobody answered.

MARTHA. You said that yesterday. All right. Thanks. Good-bye.

KAREN (*unable any longer to stand the stare*). Make him stop it.

GROCERY BOY. Here are the things. (*Giggles, moves toward* MARTHA, *stands looking at her. Suddenly* MARTHA *thrusts her hand in the air.*)

MARTHA. I've got eight fingers, see? I'm a freak.

GROCERY BOY (*giggling*). There's a car comin' here. (*Get. no answer, starts backing out of door, still looking. Familiarly*) Good-bye. (*Exits.*)

MARTHA (*bitterly*). You still think we should go into town?

KAREN. I don't know. I don't know about anything any more. (*After a moment*) Martha, Martha, Martha—

MARTHA (*gently*). What is it, Karen?

KAREN. What are we going to do? It's all so cold and unreal and—. It's like that dark hour of the night when, half awake, you struggle through the black mess you've been dreaming. Then, suddenly, you wake up and you see your own bed or your own nightgown and you know you're back again in a solid world. But now it's all the nightmare; there is no solid world. Oh, Martha, *why* did it happen? *What* happened? What are we doing here like this?

MARTHA. Waiting.

KAREN. For what?

MARTHA. I don't know.

KAREN. We've got to get out of this place. I can't stand it any more.

MARTHA. You'll be getting married soon. Everything will be all right then.

KAREN (*vaguely*). Yes.

MARTHA (*looks up at the tone*). What is it?

KAREN. Nothing.

MARTHA. There mustn't be anything wrong between you and Joe. Never.

KAREN (*without conviction*). Nothing's wrong. (*As footsteps are heard in the hall, her face lights up*) There's Joe now.

(MRS. MORTAR, *small suitcase in hand, stands in the doorway, her face pushed coyly forward.*)

MRS. MORTAR. And here I am. Hello, hello.

MARTHA (*she has turned over on her back and is staring*

at her aunt. She speaks to KAREN). The Duchess, isn't it? Returned at long last. (*Too jovially*) Come on in. We're delighted to see you. Are you tired from your journey? Is there something I can get you?

MRS. MORTAR (*surprised*). I'm very glad to see you both, and (*looks around*) I'm very glad to see the old place again. How is everything?

MARTHA. Everything's fine. We're splendid, thank you. You're just in time for tea.

MRS. MORTAR. You know, I should like some tea, if it isn't too much trouble.

MARTHA. No trouble at all. Some small sandwiches and a little brandy?

MRS. MORTAR (*puzzled finally*). Why, Martha.

MARTHA. Where the hell have you been?

MRS. MORTAR. Around, around. I had a most interesting time. Things—

MARTHA. Why didn't you answer my telegrams?

MRS. MORTAR. Things have changed in the theater—drastically changed, I might say.

MARTHA. *Why didn't you answer my telegrams?*

MRS. MORTAR. Oh, Martha, there's your temper again.

MARTHA. Answer me and don't bother about my temper.

MRS. MORTAR (*nervously*). I was moving around a great deal. (*Conversationally*) You know, I think it will throw a very revealing light on the state of the new theater when I tell you that the Lyceum in Rochester now has a toilet back-stage.

MARTHA. To hell with the toilet in Rochester. Where were you?

MRS. MORTAR. Moving around, I tell you.

KAREN. What difference does it all make now?

MRS. MORTAR. Karen is quite right. Let bygones be bygones. As I was saying, there's an effete something in the theater now, and that accounts for—

MARTHA (*to* KAREN). Isn't she wonderful? (*To* MRS.

MORTAR) Why did you refuse to come back here and testify for us?

MRS. MORTAR. Why, Martha, I didn't refuse to come back at all. That's the wrong way to look at it. I was on a tour; that's a moral obligation, you know. Now don't let's talk about unpleasant things any more. I'll go up and unpack a few things; tomorrow's plenty of time to get my trunk.

KAREN (*laughs*). Things have changed here, you know.

MARTHA. She doesn't know. She expected to walk right up to a comfortable fire and sit down and she very carefully waited until the whole thing was over. (*Leans forward, speaking to* MRS. MORTAR) Listen. Karen Wright and Martha Dobie brought a libel suit against a woman called Tilford because her grandchild had accused them of having what the judge called "sinful sexual knowledge of one another." (MRS. MORTAR *holds up her hand in protest, and* MARTHA *laughs*) Don't like that, do you? Well, a great part of the defense's case was based on remarks made by Lily Mortar, actress in the toilets of Rochester, against her niece, Martha. And a greater part of the defense's case rested on the telling fact that Mrs. Mortar would not appear in court to deny or explain those remarks. Mrs. Mortar had a moral obligation to the theater. As you probably read in the papers, we lost the case.

MRS. MORTAR. I didn't think of it that way, Martha. It couldn't have done any good for all of us to get mixed up in that unpleasant notoriety— (*Sees* MARTHA'S *face. Hastily*) But now that you've explained it, why, I do see it your way, and I'm sorry I didn't come back. But now that I am here, I'm going to stand shoulder to shoulder with you. I know what you've gone through, but the body and heart *do* recover, you know. I'll be here working right along with you and we'll—

MARTHA. There's an eight o'clock train. Get on it.

MRS. MORTAR. Martha.

MARTHA. You've come back to pick the bones dry. Well, there aren't even bones anymore. There's nothing here for you.

MRS. MORTAR (*sniffling a little*). How can you talk to me like that?

MARTHA. Because I hate you. I've always hated you.

MRS. MORTAR (*gently*). God will punish you for that.

MARTHA. He's been doing all right.

MRS. MORTAR. When you wish to apologize, I will be temporarily in my room. (*Starts to exit, almost bumps into* CARDIN, *steps back with dignity*) How do you do?

CARDIN (*laughs*). Look who's here. A little late, aren't you?

MRS. MORTAR. So it's you. Now, I call *that* loyal. A lot of men wouldn't still be here. They would have felt—

MARTHA. Get out of here.

KAREN (*opening door*). I'll call you when it's time for your train.

(MRS. MORTAR *looks at her, exits.*)

CARDIN. Now, what do you think brought her back?

KAREN. God knows.

MARTHA. I know. She was broke.

CARDIN (*pats* MARTHA *on the shoulder*). Don't let her worry you this time, Martha. We'll give her some money and get rid of her. (*Pulls* KAREN *to him*) Been out today, darling?

KAREN. We started to go out.

CARDIN (*shakes his head*). Feel all right?

(KAREN *leans over to kiss him. Almost imperceptibly he pulls back.*)

KAREN. Why did you do that?

MARTHA. Karen.

CARDIN. Do what?

KAREN. Draw back that way.

CARDIN (*laughs, kisses her*). If we sit around here much

longer, we'll all be bats. I sold my place today to Foster.

KAREN. You did what?

CARDIN. We're getting married this week. Then we're going away—all three of us.

KAREN. You can't leave here. I won't have you do this for me. What about the hospital and—

CARDIN. Shut up, darling, it's all fixed. We're going to Vienna and we're going quick. Fischer wrote that I can have my old place back.

KAREN. No! No! I'm not going to let you.

CARDIN. It's already done. Fischer can't pay me much, but it'll be enough for the three of us. Plenty if we live cheap.

MARTHA. I couldn't go with you, Joe.

CARDIN. Nonsense, Martha, we're all going. We're going to have fun again.

KAREN (*slowly*). You don't want to go back to Vienna.

CARDIN. No.

KAREN. Then why?

CARDIN. Look: I don't want to go to Vienna; I'd rather have stayed here. But then you don't want to go to Vienna; you'd rather have stayed here. Well, to hell with that. We *can't* stay here, and Vienna offers enough to eat and sleep and drink beer on. Now don't object any more, please, darling. All right?

KAREN. All right.

MARTHA. I can't go. It's better for all of us if I don't.

CARDIN (*puts his arm around her*). Not now. You stay with us now. Later on, if you want it that way. All right?

MARTHA (*smiles*). All right.

CARDIN. Swell. I'll buy you good coffee cakes and take you both to Ischl for a honeymoon.

MARTHA (*picking up grocery box, she starts for door*). A big coffee cake with a lot of raisins. It would be nice to like something again. (*Exits.*)

CARDIN (*with a slightly forced heartiness*). I'll be going back with a pretty girl who belongs to me. I'll show you off all over the place—to Dr. Engelhardt, and the nurse at the desk, and to the fat gal in the cake shop, and to Fischer. (*Laughs*) The last time I saw him was at the railroad station. He took me back of the baggage car. (*With an imitation of an accent*) "Joseph," he said, "you'll be a good doctor; I would trust you to cut up my Minna. But you're not a great doctor, and you never will be. Go back where you were born and take care of your sick. Leave the fancy work to the others." I came home.

KAREN. You'll be coming home again some day.

CARDIN. No. Let's not talk about it. (*After a moment*) You'll need some clothes?

KAREN. A few. Oh, your Dr. Fischer was so right. This is where you belong.

CARDIN. I need an overcoat and a suit. You'll need a lot of things—heavy things. It's cold there now, much colder than you'd expect—

KAREN. I've done this to you. I've taken you away from everything you want.

CARDIN. But it's lovely in the mountains, and that's where we'll go for a month.

KAREN. They—*they've* done it. They've taken away every chance we had. Everything we wanted, everything we were going to be.

CARDIN. And we've got to stop talking like that. (*Takes her by the shoulder*) We've got a chance. But it's just one chance, and if we miss it we're done for. It means that we've got to start putting the whole business behind us now. *Now*, Karen. What you've done, you've done—and that's that.

KAREN. What *I've* done?

CARDIN (*impatiently*). What's been done to you.

KAREN. What did you mean? (*When there is no answer*)

What did you mean when you said: "What you've done"?

CARDIN (*shouting*). Nothing. Nothing. (*Then very quietly*) Karen, there are a lot of people in this world who've had bad trouble in their lives. We're three of those people. We could sit around the rest of our lives and exist on that trouble, until in the end we had nothing else and we'd want nothing else. That's something I'm not coming to and I'm not going to let you come to.

KAREN. I know. I'm sorry. (*After a moment*) Joe, can we have a baby right away?

CARDIN (*vaguely*). Yes, I guess so. Although we won't have much money now.

KAREN. You used to want one right away. You always said that was the way you wanted it. There's some reason for your changing.

CARDIN. My God, we *can't* go on like this. Everything I say to you is made to mean something else. We don't talk like people any more. Oh, let's get out of here as fast as we can.

KAREN (*as though she is finishing the sentence for him*). And every word will have a new meaning. You think we'll be able to run away from that? Woman, child, love, lawyer—no words that we can use in safety any more. (*Laughs bitterly*) Sick, high-tragic people. That's what we'll be.

CARDIN (*gently*). No, we won't, darling. Love is casual— that's the way it should be. We must find that out all over again. We must learn again to live and love like other people.

KAREN. It won't work.

CARDIN. What?

KAREN. The two of us together.

CARDIN (*sharply*). Stop talking like that.

KAREN. It's true. (*Suddenly*) I want you to say it now.

CARDIN. I don't know what you're talking about.

KAREN. Yes, you do. We've both known for a long time. I knew surely the day we lost the case. I was watching your face in court. It was ashamed—and sad at being ashamed. Say it now, Joe. Ask it now.

CARDIN. I have nothing to ask. Nothing— (*Quickly*) All right. Is it—was it ever—

KAREN (*puts her hand over his mouth*). No. Martha and I have never touched each other. (*Pulls his head down on her shoulder*) That's all right, darling. I'm glad you asked. I'm not mad a bit, really.

CARDIN. I'm sorry, Karen, I'm sorry. I didn't mean to hurt you, I—

KAREN. I know. You wanted to wait until it was all over, you really never wanted to ask at all. You didn't know for sure; you thought there might be just a little truth in it all. (*With great feeling*) You've been good to me and loyal. You're a fine man. (*Afraid of tears, she pats him, walks away*) Now go and sit down, Joe. I have things to say. They're all mixed up and I must get them clear.

CARDIN. Don't let's talk any more. Let's forget and go ahead.

KAREN (*puzzled*). Go ahead?

CARDIN. Yes, Karen.

KAREN. You believe me, then?

CARDIN. Of course I believe you. I only had to hear you say it.

KAREN. No, no, no. That isn't the way things work. Maybe you believe me. I'd never know whether you did or not. You'd never know whether you did, either. We couldn't do it that way. Can't you see what would happen? We'd be hounded by it all our lives. I'd be frightened, always, and in the end my own fright would make me—would make me hate you. (*Sees slight movement he makes*) Yes, it would; I know it would. I'd hate you for what I thought I'd done to you. And

I'd hate myself, too. It would grow and grow until we'd be ruined by it. (*Sees him about to speak*) Ah, Joe, you've seen all that yourself. You knew it first.

CARDIN (*softly*). I didn't mean it that way; I don't now.

KAREN (*smiles*). You're still trying to spare me, still trying to tell yourself that we might be all right again. But we won't be all right. Not ever, ever, ever. I don't know all the reasons why. Look, I'm standing here. I haven't changed. (*Holds out her hands*) My hands look just the same, my face is the same, even my dress is old. We're in a room we've been in so many times before; you're sitting where you always sit; it's nearly time for dinner. I'm like everybody else. I can have all the things that everybody has. I can have you and a baby, and I can go to market, and we can go to the movies, and people will talk to me and— (*Suddenly notices the pain in his face*) Oh, I'm sorry. I mustn't talk like that. That couldn't be true any more.

CARDIN. It could be, Karen. We'll make it be like that.

KAREN. No. That's only what we'd like to have had. It's what we can't have now. Go home, darling.

CARDIN (*with force*). Don't talk like that. No matter what it is, we can't leave each other. I can't leave you—

KAREN. Joe, Joe. Let's do it now and quick; it will be too hard later on.

CARDIN. No, no, no. We love each other. (*His voice breaks*) I'd give anything not to have asked questions, Karen.

KAREN. It had to be asked sooner or later—and answered. You're a good man—the best I'll ever know—and you've been better to me than— But it's no good now, for either of us; you can see that.

CARDIN. It can be. You say I helped you. Help me now; help me to be strong and good enough to— (*Goes toward her with his arms out*) Karen!

KAREN (*drawing back*). No, Joe! (*Then, as he stops*) Will you do something for me?

CARDIN. No. I won't—

KAREN. Will you—will you go away for two days—a day —and think this all over by yourself—away from me and love and pity? Will you? And then decide.

CARDIN (*after a long pause*). Yes, if you want, but it won't make any difference. We will—

KAREN. Don't say anything. Please go now. (*She sits down, smiles, closes her eyes. For a moment he stands looking at her, then slowly puts on his hat*) And all my heart goes with you.

CARDIN (*at door, leaving*). I'll be coming back. (*Exits, slowly, reluctantly, closing door.*)

KAREN (*a moment after he has gone*). No, you won't. Never, darling. (*Stays as she is until* MARTHA *enters Right.*)

MARTHA (*goes to lamp, lights it*). It gets dark so early now. (*Sits down, stretches, laughs*) Cooking always makes me feel better. Well, I guess we'll have to give the Duchess some dinner. When the hawks descend, you've got to feed 'em. Where's Joe? (*No answer*) Where's Joe?

KAREN. Gone.

MARTHA. A patient? Will he be back in time for dinner?

KAREN. No.

MARTHA (*watching her*). We'll save dinner for him, then. Karen! What's the matter?

KAREN (*in a dull tone*). He won't be back any more.

MARTHA (*speaking slowly and carefully*). You mean he won't be back any more tonight.

KAREN. He won't be back at all.

MARTHA (*quickly, walks to* KAREN). What happened? (KAREN *shakes her head*) What happened, Karen?

KAREN. He thought that we had been lovers.

MARTHA (*tensely*). I don't believe you.

(*Wearily* KAREN *turns her head away.*)

KAREN. All right.

MARTHA (*automatically*). I don't believe it. He's never said a word all these months, all during the trial— (*Suddenly grabs* KAREN *by the shoulder, shakes her*) Didn't you tell him? For God's sake, didn't you tell him it wasn't true?

KAREN. Yes.

MARTHA. He didn't believe you?

KAREN. I guess he believed me.

MARTHA (*angrily*). Then what have you done?

KAREN. What had to be done.

MARTHA. It's all wrong. It's silly. He'll be back in a little while and you'll clear it all up— (*Realizes why that can't be, covers her mouth with her hand*) Oh, God, I wanted that for you so much.

KAREN. Don't. I feel sick to my stomach.

MARTHA (*goes to couch opposite* KAREN, *puts her head in her arms*). What's happened to us? What's really happened to us?

KAREN. I don't know. I want to be sleepy. I want to go to sleep.

MARTHA. Go back to Joe. He's strong; he'll understand. It's too much for you this way.

KAREN (*irritably*). Stop talking about it. Let's pack and get out of here. Let's take the train in the morning.

MARTHA. The train to where?

KAREN. I don't know. Some place; any place.

MARTHA. A job? Money?

KAREN. In a big place we could get something to do.

MARTHA. They'd know about us. We've been famous.

KAREN. A small town, then.

MARTHA. They'd know more about us.

KAREN (*as a child would say it*). Isn't there anywhere to go?

MARTHA. No. There'll never be any place for us to go.

We're bad people. We'll sit. We'll be sitting the rest of our lives wondering what's happened to us. You think this scene is strange? Well, get used to it; we'll be here for a long time. (*Suddenly pinches* KAREN *on the arm*) Let's pinch each other sometimes. We can tell whether we're still living.

KAREN (*shivers, listlessly gets up, starts making a fire in the fireplace*). But this isn't a new sin they tell us we've done. Other people aren't destroyed by it.

MARTHA. They are the people who believe in it, who want it, who've chosen it. We aren't like that. We don't love each other. (*Suddenly stops, crosses to fireplace, stands looking abstractedly at* KAREN. *Speaks casually*) I don't love you. We've been very close to each other, of course. I've loved you like a friend, the way thousands of women feel about other women.

KAREN (*only half listening*). Yes.

MARTHA. Certainly that doesn't mean anything. There's nothing wrong about that. It's perfectly natural that I should be fond of you, that I should—

KAREN (*listlessly*). Why are you saying all this to me?

MARTHA. Because I love you.

KAREN (*vaguely*). Yes, of course.

MARTHA. I love you that way—maybe the way they said I loved you. I don't know. (*Waits, gets no answer, kneels down next to* KAREN) Listen to me!

KAREN. What?

MARTHA. *I have loved you the way they said.*

KAREN. You're crazy.

MARTHA. There's always been something wrong. Always —as long as I can remember. But I never knew it until all this happened.

KAREN (*for the first time looks up, horrified*). Stop it!

MARTHA. You're afraid of hearing it; I'm more afraid than you.

KAREN (*puts her hands over her ears*). I won't listen to you.

MARTHA. Take your hands down. (*Leans over, pulls KAREN's hands away*) You've got to know it. I can't keep it any longer. I've got to tell you how guilty I am.

KAREN (*deliberately*). You are guilty of nothing.

MARTHA. I've been telling myself that since the night we heard the child say it; I've been praying I could convince myself of it. I can't, I can't any longer. It's there. I don't know how, I don't know why. But I did love you. I do love you. I resented your marriage; maybe because I wanted you; maybe I wanted you all along; maybe I couldn't call it by a name; maybe it's been there ever since I first knew you—

KAREN (*tensely*). It's a lie. You're telling yourself a lie. We never thought of each other that way.

MARTHA (*bitterly*). No, of course *you* didn't. But who says I didn't? I never felt that way about anybody but you. I've never loved a man— (*Stops. Softly*) I never knew why before. Maybe it's that.

KAREN (*carefully*). You are tired and sick.

MARTHA (*as though she were talking to herself*). It's funny; it's all mixed up. There's something in you, and you don't know it and you don't do anything about it. Suddenly a child gets bored and lies—and there you are, seeing it for the first time. (*Closes her eyes*) I don't know. It all seems to come back to *me*. In some way I've ruined your life. I've ruined my own. I didn't even *know*. (*Smiles*) There's a big difference between us now, Karen. I feel all dirty and—(*Puts out her hand, touches KAREN's head*) I can't stay with you any more, darling.

KAREN (*in a shaken, uncertain tone*). All this isn't true. You've never said it; we'll forget it by tomorrow—

MARTHA. Tomorrow? That's a funny word. Karen, we

would have had to invent a new language, as children
do, without words like tomorrow.

KAREN (*crying*). Go and lie down, Martha. You'll feel
better.

MARTHA (*looks around the room, slowly, carefully. She
is very quiet. Exits Right, stands at door for a second
looking at* KAREN, *then slowly shuts the door behind
her*).

(KAREN *sits alone without moving. There is no sound in
the house until, a few minutes after* MARTHA'S *exit, a
shot is heard. The sound of the shot should not be too
loud or too strong. For a few seconds after the noise has
died out,* KAREN *does not move. Then, suddenly, she
springs from the chair, crosses the room, pulls open
door Right. Almost at the same moment footsteps are
heard on the staircase.*)

MRS. MORTAR. What was that? Where is it? (*Enters door
Center, frightened, aimlessly moving about*) Karen!
Martha! Where are you? I heard a shot. What was—
(*Stops as she sees* KAREN *reappear Right. Walks toward
her, still talking. Stops when she sees* KAREN'S *face*)
What—what is it? (KAREN *moves her hands, shakes her
head slightly, passes* MRS. MORTAR, *and goes toward
window.* MRS. MORTAR *stares at her for a moment,
rushes past her through door Right. Left alone,* KAREN
leans against the window. MRS. MORTAR *re-enters crying. After a minute*) What shall we do? What shall
we do?

KAREN (*in a toneless voice*). Nothing.

MRS. MORTAR. We've got to get a doctor—right away.
(*Goes to phone, nervously, fumblingly starts to dial.*)

KAREN (*without turning*). There isn't any use.

MRS. MORTAR. We've got to do something. Oh, it's awful.
Poor Martha. I don't know what we can do— (*Puts
phone down, collapses in chair, sobs quietly*) You think
she's dea—

KAREN. Yes.

MRS. MORTAR. Poor, poor Martha. I can't realize it's true. Oh, how could she—she was so—I don't know what—(*Looks up, still crying, surprised*) I'm—I'm frightened.

KAREN. Don't cry.

MRS. MORTAR. I can't help it. How can I help it? (*Gradually the sobs cease, and she sits rocking herself*) I'll never forgive myself for the last words I said to her. But I was good to her, Karen, and you know God will excuse me for that once. I always tried to do everything I could. (*Suddenly*) Suicide's a sin. (*No answer. Timidly*) Shouldn't we call somebody to—

KAREN. In a little while.

MRS. MORTAR. She shouldn't have done it, she shouldn't have done it. It was because of all this awful business. She would have got a job and started all over again—she was just worried and sick and—

KAREN. That isn't the reason she did it.

MRS. MORTAR. What—why—?

KAREN (*wearily*). What difference does it make now?

MRS. MORTAR (*reproachfully*). You're not crying.

KAREN. No.

MRS. MORTAR. What will happen to me? I haven't anything. Poor Martha—

KAREN. She was very good to you; she was good to us all.

MRS. MORTAR. Oh, I know she was, Karen, and I was good to her too. I did everything I could. I—I haven't any place to go. (*After a few seconds of silence*) I'm afraid. It seems so queer—in the next room. (*Shivers.*)

KAREN. Don't be afraid.

MRS. MORTAR. It's different for you. You're young.

KAREN. Not any more.

(*The sound of the door-bell ringing.* MRS. MORTAR *jumps.* KAREN *doesn't move. It rings again.*)

MRS. MORTAR (*nervously*). Who is it? (*The bell rings again*) Shall I answer it? (KAREN *shrugs*) I think we'd better. (*Exits down the hall through Center doors. Returns in a minute followed by* MRS. TILFORD's *maid,* AGATHA, *who stands in the door*) It's a woman. (*No answer*) It's a woman to see you, Karen. (*Getting no answer, she turns to* AGATHA) You can't come in now; we've had a—we've had trouble here.

AGATHA. Miss Karen, I've *got* to speak to you.

KAREN (*turns slowly, mechanically*). Agatha.

AGATHA (*goes to* KAREN). Please, Miss Karen. We've tried so hard to get you. I been phoning here all the time. Trying to get you. Phoning and phoning. Please, please let her come in. Just for a minute, Miss Karen. Please—

MRS. MORTAR. Who wants to come in here?

AGATHA. Mrs. Tilford. (*Looks at* KAREN) Don't you feel well? (KAREN *shakes her head*) You ain't mad at *me?*

MRS. MORTAR. That woman can't come in here. She caused all—

KAREN. I'm not mad at you, Agatha.

AGATHA. Can I—can I get you something?

KAREN. No.

AGATHA. You poor child. You look like you got a pain somewhere. (*Hesitates, takes* KAREN's *hands*) I only came cause she's so bad off. She's got to see you, Miss Karen, she's just got to. She's been sittin' outside in the car, hoping you'd come out. She can't get Dr. Joe. He—he won't talk to her any more. I wouldn't a come—I always been on your side—but she's sick. If only you could see her, you'd let her come for just a minute.

KAREN. I couldn't do that, Agatha.

AGATHA. I don't blame you. But I had to tell you. She's old. It's going to kill her.

KAREN (*bitterly*). Kill her? Where is Mrs. Tilford?

AGATHA. Outside.

KAREN. All right.

AGATHA (*presses* KAREN's *arm*). You always been a good girl. (*Hurriedly exits.*)

MRS. MORTAR. You going to allow that woman to come in here? With Martha lying there? How can you be so feelingless? (*She starts to cry*) I won't stay and see it. I won't have anything to do with it. I'll never let that woman— (*Rushes sobbing from the room.*)

(*A second after,* MRS. TILFORD *appears in the doorway Center. Her face, her walk, her voice have changed. She is feeble.*)

MRS. TILFORD. Karen, let me come in.

(*Without turning,* KAREN *bows her head.* MRS. TILFORD *enters, stands staring at the floor.*)

KAREN. Why have you come here?

MRS. TILFORD. I had to come. (*Stretches out her hand to* KAREN, *who does not turn. She drops her hand*) I know now; I know it wasn't true.

KAREN. What?

MRS. TILFORD (*carefully*). I know it wasn't true, Karen.

KAREN (*stares at her, shudders*). You know it wasn't true? I don't care what you know. It doesn't matter any more. If that's what you had to say, you've said it. Go away.

MRS. TILFORD (*puts her hand to her throat*). I've got to tell you.

KAREN. I don't want to hear you.

MRS. TILFORD. Last Tuesday Mrs. Wells found a bracelet in Rosalie's room. The bracelet had been hidden for several months. We found out that Rosalie had taken the bracelet from another girl, and that Mary—(*Closes her eyes*) that Mary knew that and used it to force Rosalie into saying that she had seen you and Miss Dobie together. I—I've talked to Mary. I've found out. (KAREN *suddenly begins to laugh, high and sharp*) Don't do that, Karen. I have only a little more to say. I've talked to Judge Potter. He will make all arrangements. There will be a public apology and an explanation. The damage suit will be paid to you in full and— and any more that you will be kind enough to take from me. I—I must see that you won't suffer any more.

KAREN. We're not going to suffer any more. Martha is dead. (MRS. TILFORD *gasps, shakes her head as though to shake off the truth, feebly falls into a chair, and covers her face.* KAREN *watches her for a minute*) So you've come here to relieve your conscience? Well, I won't be your confessor. It's choking you, is it? (*Violently*) And you want to stop the choking, don't you? You've done a wrong and you have to right that wrong or you can't rest your head again. You want to be "just," don't you, and you wanted us to help you be just? You've come to the wrong place for help. You want to be a "good" woman again, don't you? (*Bitterly*) Oh, I know. You told us that night you had to do what you did. Now you "have" to do this. A public apology and money paid, and you can sleep again and eat again. That done and there'll be peace for you. You're old, and the old are callous. Ten, fifteen years left for you. But what of me? It's a whole life for me. A whole God-damned life. (*Suddenly quiet, points to door Right*) And what of her?

MRS. TILFORD (*she is crying*). You are still living.

KAREN. Yes. I guess so.

MRS. TILFORD (*with a tremendous effort to control herself*). I didn't come here to relieve myself. I swear to God I didn't. I came to try—to try anything. I knew there wasn't any relief for me, Karen, and that there never would be again. (*Tensely*) But what I am or why I came doesn't matter. The only thing that matters is you and—You, now.

KAREN. There's nothing for me.

MRS. TILFORD. Oh, let's try to make something for you. You're young and I—I can help you.

KAREN (*smiles*). You can help me?

MRS. TILFORD (*with great feeling*). Take whatever I can give you. Take it for yourself and use it for yourself.

It won't bring me peace, if that's what's worrying you. (*Smiles*) Those ten or fifteen years you talk about! They will be bad years.

KAREN. I'm tired, Mrs. Tilford. (*Almost tenderly*) You will have a hard time ahead, won't you?

MRS. TILFORD. Yes.

KAREN. Mary?

MRS. TILFORD. I don't know.

KAREN. You can send her away.

MRS. TILFORD. No. I could never do that. Whatever she does, it must be to me and no one else. She's—she's——

KAREN. Yes. Your very own, to live with the rest of your life. (*For a moment she watches* MRS. TILFORD'S *face*) It's over for me now, but it will never end for you. She's harmed us both, but she's harmed you more, I guess. (*Sits down beside* MRS. TILFORD) I'm sorry.

MRS. TILFORD (*clings to her*). Then you'll try for yourself.

KAREN. All right.

MRS. TILFORD. You and Joe.

KAREN. No. We're not together anymore.

MRS. TILFORD (*looks up at her*). Did I do that, too?

KAREN. I don't think anyone did anything, any more.

MRS. TILFORD (*makes a half-movement to rise*). I'll go to him right away.

KAREN. No, it's better now the way it is.

MRS. TILFORD. But he must know what I know, Karen. You must go back to him.

KAREN (*smiles*). No, not any more.

MRS. TILFORD. You must, you must— (*Sees her face, hesitates*) Perhaps later, Karen?

KAREN. Perhaps.

MRS. TILFORD (*after a moment in which they both sit silent*). Come away from here now, Karen. (KAREN *shakes her head*) You can't stay with— (*Moves her hand toward door Right.*)

KAREN. When she is buried, then I will go.

MRS. TILFORD. You'll be all right?

KAREN. I'll be all right, I suppose. Good-bye, now.

(*They both rise.* MRS. TILFORD *speaks, pleadingly.*)

MRS. TILFORD. You'll let me help you? You'll let me try?

KAREN. Yes, if it will make you feel better.

MRS. TILFORD (*with great feeling*). Oh, yes, oh, yes, Karen.

(*Unconsciously* KAREN *begins to walk toward the window.*)

KAREN (*suddenly*). Is it nice out?

MRS. TILFORD. It's been cold. (KAREN *opens the window slightly, sits on the ledge.* MRS. TILFORD *with surprise*) It seems a little warmer, now.

KAREN. It feels very good.

(*They smile at each other.*)

MRS. TILFORD. You'll write me some time?

KAREN. If I ever have anything to say. Good-bye, now.

MRS. TILFORD. You will have. I know it. Good-bye, my dear.

(KAREN *smiles, shakes her head as* MRS. TILFORD *exits. She does not turn, but a minute later she raises her hand.*)

KAREN. Good-bye.

Curtain

DAYS TO COME

FOR

JULIA AND MAX HELLMAN

Days to Come was first produced at the Vanderbilt Theatre, New York City, on December 15, 1936, with the following cast:

(In the order of their appearance)

HANNAH	CLARE WOODBURY
LUCY	MURIEL GALLICK
CORA RODMAN	FRIEDA ALTMAN
HENRY ELLICOTT	NED WEVER
ANDREW RODMAN	WILLIAM HARRIGAN
JULIE RODMAN	FLORENCE ELDRIDGE
THOMAS FIRTH	JOSEPH SWEENEY
LEO WHALEN	BEN SMITH
SAM WILKIE	CHARLES DINGLE
MOSSIE DOWEL	JACK CARR
JOE EASTER	THOMAS FISHER

Produced and directed by HERMAN SHUMLIN

Settings designed by ALINE BERNSTEIN

ACT ONE

Living room of the Rodman house.
Late morning in October.

SCENE: *The living room of the Rodman house in Callom,*
Ohio, two hundred miles from Cleveland. The room is
deep and the Left stage window-wall is curved into
the room. All furniture gives the impression of being
arranged for the entrance doors which are on the Right
Center stage wall. On the backstage wall, on the ex-
treme Right, is a door leading into the library. On the
curved Left stage wall are two high windows. These
windows open on a circular porch and are used as an
entrance by people who know the house well. Between
the windows, and well out on the stage, is a large drum
table. There are chairs on each side of the table. Back
from the table is an antique flat topped table desk. Left
downstage is a high circular cabinet, unglassed, in
which there are many small figures of animals. Near
the cabinet is a couch. The room is beautiful, simple.
But the objects in the cabinet are too neatly placed and
the effect is rigid and bad.
Left and Right stage directions are always the audience's
Left and Right.

AT RISE: *A large vigorous woman is sitting on the floor in*
front of the window, comfortably arranging flowers in
several bowls. (The bowls and the flowers are on the
porch.) She has on a house dress, but is not in servant's
uniform. LUCY, *in uniform, is dusting. On a chair next*
to HANNAH *is a bowl of half shelled peas.*

LUCY (*finishes dusting the animals*). That's enough for them today.

HANNAH (*hands her a bowl of flowers and laughs*). Did you get your wages this morning? (*No answer*) Huh?

LUCY (*reluctantly*). Yes.

HANNAH (*cheerfully*). Then hand it over.

LUCY. I was going to. But Hannah, I got to keep five dollars out of it because I owe somebody the five dollars.

HANNAH. Is the five dollar somebody in this town?

LUCY. No.

HANNAH. Then don't pay 'em. The boys need it— (*Soberly*) and I got a hunch will need it more. (*As* LUCY *gives her the money from her apron pocket*) Thanks, Lucy. You're a nice kid. I'll tell them how it comes from you.

LUCY. But when's it going to be over? Seems funny, don't it?

HANNAH. I'm not laughing. (*She hands* LUCY *another bowl of flowers.* LUCY *takes it to a table near the couch and puts it very carefully in a certain spot*) I don't know when it's going to be over. But I guessed it was going to be. I haven't lived in this house twenty years for nothing. (HANNAH *has been watching* LUCY *place the bowl. She laughs and makes a this-way gesture with her hands*) Uh-uh. Bring it over.

LUCY (*as if this joke had been played before*). What's the use? Miss Cora will only— (*Makes imitative gestures on the table*) move it right back here.

HANNAH. I know. I like to see her do it.

LUCY. But Aunt Lundee says that all they do is sit around talking and that a man should be at work and that Uncle Jim and the rest should go on back and stop this crazy strike and—

HANNAH. Since when does anybody listen to your Aunt Lundee?

LUCY. I don't know.

HANNAH (*cheerfully*). Lucy, there were people made to think and people made to listen. I ain't sure either you or Lundee were made to do either.

LUCY (*pointing to the vase*). Miss Cora's been downtown already this morning. So was Mrs. Rodman, and when I came out of the butcher store there was Miss Cora standing on one side of the street, looking at Mrs. Rodman in the funniest way, and she didn't call to her, she just stood watching and not saying anything—

HANNAH. And *you* just stood watching and not saying anything, too, huh?

LUCY (*hurt*). What's wrong with that now?

HANNAH. Nothing. (*Then looks at her, half-seriously, half-teasingly*) As long as you just watch and don't say anything.

(CORA RODMAN *enters from the Center doors. She is a thin, nervous-looking woman of about forty-two. She has a small clay Chinese horse in her hand.* HANNAH *doesn't look up, but* LUCY *watches* CORA *as she crosses to the cabinet with the horse.*)

CORA. I brought this down. I'll take the elephant up for my desk. It will make a nice change.

LUCY. Yes'm.

CORA (*to* HANNAH). Did you make something sweet?

HANNAH (*to* CORA). Chocolate cake. All over.

CORA (*to* LUCY, *who has picked up carpet sweeper, rags, etc. and is exiting*). Well, don't cut me such a small piece. You didn't bring me enough butter on my tray this morning, and I had a roll left over.

LUCY. Yes'm. (*She exits.*)

CORA (*she crosses to flower bowl and, with the motions* LUCY *has imitated, moves it back to its particular spot*). Always seems to be something the matter with the breakfast tray. I read in the morning paper about a thirteen year old girl who had a baby in the county hospital. Why don't they watch those things?

HANNAH (*who has smiled maliciously as* CORA *moved the bowl*). Who's going to watch 'em?

CORA. It was a very dangerous Caesarian operation. Maybe that always happens when the mother is under age. What's the name of that man who boards with your sister?

HANNAH. Now you can go over and ask Doc Morris about the girl—and he can tell you, the way he did that time about cats, which you never gotten straight.

CORA. I asked you what is the name of that man.

HANNAH. I don't know which you mean. She's got five boarders regular.

CORA. He was walking up and down in front of the factory, the way they've been doing and wasting their time, and I said good morning and he didn't answer. I said it again and he walked to the other side. So I went right up and told him I didn't like rudeness—

HANNAH. That's Odave. He's only been here a year. Maybe that's not time enough to fall in love with the Rodman family. (*Thoughtfully*) You know, Miss Cora, they tell me that in places where there's a strike, the men forget sometimes to bow to the boss' sister.

CORA. There is never any need for rudeness.

HANNAH. She's getting a new boarder. Guess he's moved in by now. Leo Whalen.

CORA (*after a pause*). That's very wrong of your sister. And disloyal of you to let her. He's a bad character—

HANNAH. How do you know? You never spoke to him.

CORA. I know why he's here. That's enough. He's trying to make trouble and you know it. That's what he came here for—

HANNAH. Not my business. She's in the boarding house business and it's open to anybody who don't steal. (*Picks up bowl of peas and starts to exit*) Anyway, she likes him. Lots of people here like him. (*So casually that it has meaning*) Women, too, I guess.

(*She passes* HENRY ELLICOTT *who is entering. He has on a hat and overcoat. He is about forty, good-looking in a worldly kind of way.*)

ELLICOTT. Good morning. Did anyone call me, Cora?

CORA (*as he takes off his coat*). A woman called you about a month ago. I told you about that, although I don't see why she called you here.

ELLICOTT. You told me about that. Several times.

CORA. She hasn't called you since. I think I gave her to understand that you should conduct your affairs at your own house.

ELLICOTT. I'm not talking about women, Cora. I'm talking about my office.

CORA. *They* did *not* call.

HANNAH (*as* ELLICOTT *crosses to desk*). You be here for lunch? We got a good lunch.

CORA. Hannah, will you please allow *me* to invite Mr. Ellicott for lunch?

ELLICOTT. You, and you alone, may invite me to lunch.

CORA (*to* HANNAH). *I* have invited Mr. Ellicott to lunch. (HANNAH *nods, pleased at the effect she has had on* CORA, *then exits.*)

ELLICOTT. You put your foot down very firmly on that important matter. Where is Julie? (*He is moving around the room.*)

CORA (*holds out a small box*). Don't move around so. Want one? They're pepsin drops with chocolate. Doctor Morris says they're good for me. I'm going to get a dog this week. I've ordered it. A male this time. Females are too difficult to take care of during, er, during. I was reading only this morning about a thirteen year old girl who had a baby. You travel around. Have you ever seen that before?

ELLICOTT. I haven't actually seen it. But they tell me that in warm countries—

CORA. In *warm* countries. But not in Cleveland. (*He goes*

to the window, and after a second she says softly) Julie
is out, Henry.

ELLICOTT. Where is she?

CORA (*as if she had been waiting for it*). I don't know. I
don't spy on Julie.

ELLICOTT (*turns and looks at her*). You've such a pleasant
way of saying things. (*Then he looks at his watch and
goes to the telephone, dials a number*) This is Mr. Ellicott. Joe still there? (*To* CORA) Andrew around?

CORA. I suppose so. I shall have to move my room if he
doesn't stop walking up and down in the library all
night. I sleep badly enough anyway and if a pin drops
it wakes me. I've always been like that—

ELLICOTT (*into phone*). Joe? I've been waiting for you to
call. Everything all right? Good. (ANDREW RODMAN
*comes in through the library doors. He has a pleasant,
serious face. His motions are those of a man who is
puzzled and tired. He crosses to the desk and looks at
some papers, idly, as he listens to* ELLICOTT *on the
phone*) Take them off a few at a time. Then drive
Wilkie up to Mr. Rodman's. (*Gets up, to* ANDREW)
That's good. They'll be off the train about lunch time.
The train will come in on the siding. They won't be
noticed much.

ANDREW. Are these high-jinks necessary? As long as they're
coming, let them in at the station.

ELLICOTT. There's no sense walking into trouble.

ANDREW (*nods his head*). So you're admitting now that
there might be trouble? That they might not see it the
way—the way we do?

CORA. But why should there be any trouble? We can run
the factory when we want to. It's ours. I don't understand why there should be any trouble—

ELLICOTT (*sharply*). I didn't say there'd be any trouble.

CORA (*placatingly to* ANDREW). Now you see. Henry says
there won't be a bit of trouble.

ELLICOTT (*smiles, obviously irritated*). Andrew, do we
have to start this all over again now?

ANDREW. No. Don't pay any attention to me. We've made
up our minds and that's that.

ELLICOTT. And a damn good thing! The loan's o. k. now.
But Nelson says you couldn't've gotten a nickel in
Cleveland if you hadn't made this decision. He had to
swear to them that you wouldn't change your mind
again.

CORA. See? As long as you have to spend the money anyway, you should have hired these new workers weeks
ago. The way Henry and I told you to.

ANDREW. I didn't want to do it that way. I don't now.

CORA. No, of course you didn't. You thought kind talk and
reason would do it. Well, it didn't work, did it? Papa
would have known what to do. And without wasting
time and money. Papa would have known—

(*Her speech is interrupted by* JULIE RODMAN *who comes
in from the porch windows. She is a very attractive,
slim, slightly tired-looking woman of about thirty-two.
She is wearing a sweater and skirt, low shoes, a loose
tweed coat, no hat. Her clothes are expensive and
careless.*)

JULIE (*slowly, as if she didn't expect the room to be full:
as if thinking of something else*). Good morning.

CORA. The man was here about the tree planting. I told
him that you always did that. Forgetting about things.

JULIE. I did forget. You could have told him about the
planting.

CORA (*smugly*). You know my rules. Not to interfere.

JULIE. There are so many rules. It's hard to remember
them all. It's funny to go walking now. The Carlsen
kids were coming from school. (*Smiles*) They had a
bad minute wondering whether to say hello to me.
(ANDREW *has moved on her speech as if he knew what*

*she meant, and didn't like hearing it. She has gone to
the decanters on the table)* Sherry? It's cold.

ELLICOTT. Your walks take you in all directions, don't they?

JULIE *(without answering, turns to* ANDREW, *motions to
sherry glass)*. Andy? Do you good.

ANDREW. No, darling. *(As he gathers up papers)* I have
work to do before lunch.

ELLICOTT. Wilkie should be here soon.

ANDREW *(slowly, at door)*. I haven't forgotten.

JULIE *(gently)*. You look so tired.

CORA. Certainly he looks tired. He's worn himself out for
no reason. Papa would have settled this strike weeks
ago—

ANDREW *(at door, smiles, speaks slowly)*. Yes. I suppose
so. Maybe Papa was a better man than I am.

CORA *(gets up, gently to* JULIE). I will see about the trees.
Before my headache gets worse. *(JULIE begins to protest, but is interrupted by* CORA's *wheeling sharply on*
ELLICOTT *as if she had just thought of something)* Inci-
dentally, I hope you didn't touch my securities for this
loan? You are my lawyer. You must protect me—

ELLICOTT *(smiles)*. Certainly. Increased protection, increased fees.

CORA. I'm unmarried. It's different with me. I have no one
to support me. It's different when you're not married—

ELLICOTT. Unfortunately, in the business world there is
no reward for virginity. *(Sharply, quickly, as he sees
the question coming again)* No. Andrew wouldn't let
me take your securities. I don't know why—

CORA *(pleasantly now)*. Because I'm his sister.

ELLICOTT. Really? Is that the reason? *(Annoyed at her
sudden turn to good nature)* However, when it's
cleaned up, you will pay your part of the expenses.

CORA. I don't understand that.

ELLICOTT. Then it's not because I haven't tried to explain

it to you. You own as much of the factory as Andy does.
As you share the profits, you must share the losses.

CORA. Why should I pay for Andrew's mistakes? If we'd
been able to make him do this three weeks ago—

ELLICOTT. You will still be well this side of starvation.
You can have two pieces of cake instead of your usual
three.

CORA. I shall have to talk the losses business over with Andrew. I don't understand why— (*As if she had just
heard him*) And I shall eat just as much as I please.
Just as much as I please. (*She closes the door as ELLI-
COTT looks after her.*)

JULIE (*smiling, watching him*). Cora worries you too
much.

ELLICOTT. And you, happily, very little. She seems to be
watching you these days— (*As her face changes*) Or
am I imagining it? Where have you been, Julie?

JULIE. Walking.

ELLICOTT. In town?

JULIE. I must be getting old. I don't like autumn anymore. The river is full of leaves and it was too cold to
walk very far.

ELLICOTT. Weren't you in town?

JULIE (*very deliberate*). The storm broke the big elm.
The heavy branch is lying in the river. There's a big
lizard on the branch that looks as if it grew there—

ELLICOTT. You were near the strike office. I saw you. I
think Cora saw you, too.

JULIE (*annoyed*). Really? Were you both hiding?

ELLICOTT. That's the second time you've lied about being
in town. Why?

JULIE. Maybe because I like to lie. (*Quietly, looking at
him*) Maybe it's because I'm tired of your questions.

ELLICOTT (*quietly*). I don't like your being tired. (*After
a second*) I'm going down to White Sulphur when
things are cleared up here. Are you coming?

JULIE. No.

ELLICOTT (*suddenly, sharply*). I want to know where we stand, Julie. It's time for me to know.

JULIE (*lightly, kindly*). We stand nowhere. We've always stood nowhere. I knew about you—and you knew about me. (*Quickly*) Staying for lunch?

ELLICOTT. Yes, I knew about you. And what I didn't know our friends told me. (*Carefully*) But I find, more to my surprise than to yours, that you mean something to me. I think you have for a long time.

JULIE. I don't think so. (*Kindly*) Look. It doesn't mean anything to me—and that's where I've got to quit.

ELLICOTT. "And that's where I've got to quit." There isn't a man living who doesn't know about the woman who allows herself anything, but who invents the one rule that will keep her this side of what she thinks is respectable. She'll lie, but not on Thursdays. She'll sleep with you, but not immediately after lunch. Usually it's funny. In your case, for me, it's not so funny. (*Angrily*) What the hell did you expect me to mean to you?

JULIE (*puts her hand on his arm*). What did I expect you to mean to me? I don't know. I haven't any excuse, really. I've hoped for a very long time that everybody or anybody would mean something. (*Smiles*) Things start as hopes and end up as habits. (*Earnestly*) Look. Don't let's talk about it. You like civilized conversations about love too much, and I like them too little. One of the things that brings people like you and me together is the understanding that there won't be any talk about it at the end.

ELLICOTT. That's true. And it's too callous for me.

JULIE (*violently*). And for me, too. That's why I don't like it. I'm ashamed of its callousness—and I don't want any more of it. I don't mean to hurt you. (*She gets up, smiles, takes off her coat*) I asked you if you were staying for lunch.

ELLICOTT (*after a second, watching her*). Yes, I'm stay-·
ing. If you ever saw what you wanted, Julie, would you
know it?

JULIE (*quickly, unconsciously, very seriously, as if to herself*). Yes. I knew it. I knew about it quick.

ELLICOTT (*suddenly wheels about and takes her arm,
tightly*). That's foolish what you're saying. Too foolish
to believe. (*Tensely*) And what's more important, it's
dangerous. Don't start anything, Julie—

JULIE (*softly*). I don't know what you are talking about.

(*They stand for a second as they are. He does not release
her arm until the window-doors open and* THOMAS
FIRTH *followed by* LEO WHALEN *appear on the porch.
Then he quickly releases her arm and moves away.*
FIRTH *taps on the window-wood. He is a big, lean,
middle-aged American working-man. He is obviously
nervous and excited.* WHALEN *is attractive in a simple,
clean, undistinguished way. All his movements from
this moment until the end of the play show calmness,
and are the movements of a man who knows he can
take care of himself.*)

FIRTH. Mrs. Rodman.

JULIE. Oh. (*Then cordially*) Hello, Tom. (*To* WHALEN,
her tone changed and nervous) Hello, Mr. Whalen.
Come in.

ELLICOTT (*to both*). Good morning.

FIRTH. I want to see Andrew. I came to see him.

JULIE (*surprised at the tenseness of his tone*). Yes. But
come in, won't you? (*Abruptly* FIRTH *steps into the
room, standing straight and rigid.* WHALEN *moves in
casually*) I thought you were leaving us, Mr. Whalen.
I haven't seen you in town the last few days.

WHALEN. Leaving? (*Looks at* FIRTH, *smiles*) Not for a
while yet.

ELLICOTT (*to* FIRTH). Andrew's busy. Will I do?

FIRTH. No.

JULIE (*moves to the wall bell, presses it, speaks nervously to* WHALEN). I thought—I thought perhaps you would come and have dinner with us one night—

WHALEN (*laughs heartily*). The boss asks me for dinner. Well, that's very pleasant. It's never happened to me before. (*Looks at* FIRTH) But strange things happen in this town.

FIRTH. Mrs. Rodman, can I see Andrew now?

(LUCY *appears at the door.*)

JULIE. Tell Mr. Rodman that Tom Firth is here and wants to see him. (LUCY *disappears. To* WHALEN) Why should that be so strange? We don't get many visitors here and because you and my husband happen to be, well, happen to think differently, is no reason we can't eat together.

WHALEN (*pleasantly*). In my business it's a good reason.

ELLICOTT. Julie. Whalen is in the business of hating. It pays well, I imagine.

WHALEN. Very well. All labor organizers are racketeers, Mr. Ellicott, as you and I both know from the papers. (*He has started to roll a cigarette. Quickly* JULIE *offers him a box from the table*) But there's no hate *here*. The boss loves the workers, and the workers— (*To* FIRTH) the worker—loves the boss. In other towns I've heard that called something else.

FIRTH. Shut up.

(*There is a second's embarrassed silence.* WHALEN, *however, is pleased.*)

JULIE (*to* WHALEN). Old Mrs. Hicks tells me you like our river. That you walk there very often.

WHALEN. Yes. You've got a nice river. You've kept it clean.

JULIE (*to* WHALEN). When I first moved here I used to fish in it. Do you like to fish?

WHALEN. Yes. Very much. (*To* FIRTH) Maybe Mr. Rodman doesn't want to see you.

FIRTH. You don't have to wait.

ELLICOTT (*to* WHALEN). No. I'm sure you're busy—

WHALEN. I'll wait. (*To* JULIE) If it's all right.

JULIE (*smiles, warmly, quickly*). It's very all right. (*Still smiling, turns to* ELLICOTT) Mr. Ellicott is too concerned with your time.

FIRTH. You're staying to watch. I don't need you to watch me. You and nobody is going to make me act blind. You and nobody is going to make me hate a man who's been my friend.

ELLICOTT (*to* JULIE). He *is* in the business of hate. I was right.

WHALEN (*to* FIRTH). I don't give a damn who you hate and who you love. I'm trying to see that that Christian heart of yours doesn't do too much harm. (*To* ELLICOTT) You were right.

(*On* WHALEN's *words,* FIRTH *moves toward him angrily, and then turns and stands rigidly as* ANDREW *comes into the room.*)

ANDREW (*slowly*). Hello, Tom. (*Less friendly*) Hello, Mr. Whalen.

FIRTH. Andrew, I went out on strike with the rest. That was my duty. But I stood by you in a lot of ways.

WHALEN (*unpleasantly*). He did. I can vouch for it.

FIRTH. We've all been trying to see it from both our sides and we've been friends about it—

WHALEN. Ask your question.

FIRTH. He says that a trainload of strikebreakers came through Callom Junction this morning. And I said I didn't believe it. I said you didn't know no more about things like that than we did, and that I knew you—

ANDREW. Tom, I wanted to talk to you this afternoon.

ELLICOTT (*looking at his watch*). Which would still be wisest. This afternoon.

FIRTH. I'm here. I don't want to wait. Talk to me now. (*After a second's silence, speaks to* WHALEN *over his shoulder*) Read him that fool thing.

WHALEN (*takes a telegram from his pocket, reads it in a pleasant, unconcerned way*). "Wilkie on way probably fifty sixty of the boys including Gans Easter Malloy which gives you rough idea stop Easter just out of jail with toothache so watch your heart and anything else." That's from a friend of mine in Cleveland. He's a wit.

FIRTH. I don't know about these people he's talking about. And neither do you. That's why I know it's got to be wrong. (*Watches* ANDREW, *gets no answer, then slowly, firmly*) Andrew. It's got to be wrong.

ANDREW. Tom, I've tried to explain. I tried from the first day you came to me. (*Touches a paper on the desk, looks at it*) The figures are here. They're as much yours to see as they are mine.

FIRTH. I don't have to see 'em again.

ANDREW. You don't. But I have to see them again and again and again. We've got to sell the brushes we make.

WHALEN. Some places make what they can sell.

ANDREW (*sharply*). Yes. They make them cheaper than we do— (*Slowly*) and they make them cheaper because they cost less. You know that Partee cut salaries two years ago—

FIRTH. I know that. I told you to cut us a little. That we'd take a little for you. And I told you to make three, four model brushes, not eighteen—

ANDREW. I can't, against the others.

WHALEN. Then make them the way they make them.

ANDREW. You mean cheaper brushes? Ask Tom what he thinks of that.

FIRTH. We make the best brush in America.

WHALEN (*laughs*). There. You've hit on something. That'll pay your rent. You can eat fine on that.

ANDREW (*to* FIRTH). You tell me a way out, I'll take it. Seven years ago we were making a lot of money. (*Touches the paper*) I can't stay in business losing it this way. We'd be out in another year.

WHALEN. You haven't been answering his question, Mr. Rodman.

ANDREW. I'm doing my best to answer him. (*After a second*) I knew the cuts had to come. I tried hard to keep them off as long as I could. I thought you'd see that the only way you could stay working and I could stay working was if we took the bad times together. I couldn't do anything else.

FIRTH. And I know we can't live on forty-cent piece work. I told you it was too big a cut. And I told you they wouldn't take it.

ANDREW. Do you think I want to cut you that way? It's just for a little while—

FIRTH. And who's going to pay our bills for the little while?

ANDREW (*shakes his head*). I know. I don't blame you. But you mustn't blame us, either.

FIRTH (*quickly*). Who's us?

ANDREW. Me, I mean. That's the story. I wish I'd known what else to do.

(*Slowly* WHALEN *rises, smiling.* FIRTH *turns and looks at him, looks around the room, and then crosses quickly to* ANDREW *as if he didn't believe the answer had been made.*)

FIRTH. All right. We knew all that. That's what I been saying to myself, and I ain't got the answer for either of us. (*Hits the table*) But that's something between us to settle. We ain't foreigners. Our people came here with your people, and worked along with them and helped them, too. In twelve when they came and tried to make a union, we threw 'em out. There ain't never been any trouble here, Andrew—

ELLICOTT (*to* ANDREW). It's late.

ANDREW. Let him say what he wants to say.

FIRTH. I ain't believing that you're bringing foreigners—

ANDREW (*slowly*). You've been out three weeks. The place
had to start running again.

FIRTH (*slowly*). You mean you're giving away our jobs.
You mean other people are taking our work— (*Breaks
off sharply and stands staring at* ANDREW, *shaking his
head.*)

WHALEN (*rises, smiles to* JULIE). Sad to grow up, isn't it?
(*To* FIRTH) Well, come on. Cry at home. You've wasted
enough time now. The world is a bad place and you're
a big boy.

ELLICOTT (*to* FIRTH). You could have talked this over
with me. It may be all right for you to walk out, but it
is also all right for Andrew to keep his own machines
going his own way.

FIRTH (*shouting*). And this was his way of keeping 'em
going, eh? I could've known you had a hand in it.

ELLICOTT (*sharply*). He's got to start making brushes
again. If you've made up your mind not to make them,
then somebody else has to.

WHALEN. No? You're kidding. (*To* ANDREW) Who sold
you the idea Wilkie's boys can run machines? (*Makes
the motion of pointing a pistol*) That's the kind they
meant. That's the kind you'll get run—and they do that
fine. (*To* FIRTH) And be sure you're there to make
speeches about the boat your grandfather came over
on, and God is love, and your heart's breaking. Turn
the other cheek, and crawl back. It hurts less that way,
I guess.

FIRTH (*slowly*). I told the boys we'd be settling it like
friends. I was wrong. (*To* WHALEN) I won't be turning
the other cheek. I won't be crawling back. Nobody
else will either. (*Without turning to look at* ANDREW,
he moves quickly to the window and out.)

ANDREW (*quietly, to* JULIE). He's been a good friend. For
a long time.

ELLICOTT (*slowly, to* WHALEN). We don't want trouble

here. We're sorry that you do want it. But I suppose
that's your job.

WHALEN (*getting up*). Sometimes it is. Sometimes it isn't.
But what you and I want won't make much difference.
When the guns start popping and the skulls start crack-
ing, they won't be thinking about us.

ANDREW (*angrily*). There won't be any guns here—on
either side.

ELLICOTT. Unless you have them.

WHALEN. I? No, sir. I'm scared to death of them. (*To
ANDREW, moving toward the window*) I hope you're
right, Mr. Rodman.

(*As WHALEN moves toward the window the front door
bell starts to ring, steadily, loudly. They have all turned,
startled by it. HANNAH, calm, quiet, appears in the
door.*)

JULIE. What is it, Hannah?

HANNAH. Lucy's watching my oven so the things don't
burn.

ANDREW (*looking at her*). Then you answer it, Hannah.

HANNAH. No, Mr. Andrew. If what I heard is right, that's
one bell I ain't going to answer. I can't help what other
people do, but I don't have to help 'em out.

JULIE. Hannah—

HANNAH. And Lucy can't answer because she's watching
my oven so the things don't burn, if she's got the sense.
(*ELLICOTT, quickly, angrily, moves past HANNAH and
out into the hall. To WHALEN*) Like boarding at my
sister's?

WHALEN. Sure. It's a good place. (*Smiles at her warmly*)
I'm no boarder, I'm charity.

HANNAH. She can afford it. But watch her. She don't always like to get the dust from under things. (*She exits.*)

(*WHALEN, in the first quick motion he has made, moves
to ANDREW's desk, leans over it, speaks tensely, hurriedly.*)

WHALEN. Rodman. It's hard to believe, but I'm believing
it. You don't know. (*He points toward Center doors*)
about things like this. I do. This is a nice town. I hate
to see it hurt. (*Then quietly*) Give them their sixty-
cent hour. Give them their union. They'll be back to
work in ten minutes.

ANDREW. They can have any union they want. But I can't
pay the salaries. I want to—and I can't. I don't know
what you've seen in the past. But there won't be any
trouble here. I won't let there be. I hope you won't
either.

(ELLICOTT, *followed by* SAMUEL WILKIE, *comes in from
the hall.* WILKIE *is of medium height, heavy. He looks
like any husky business man. Directly behind him are*
MOSSIE DOWEL *and* JOE EASTER. MOSSIE *is fat and pleasant-looking.* EASTER *is thin, nervous, tough.* MOSSIE *and*
EASTER *stand stiffly at the door.*)

WILKIE. Mr. Rodman. I'm Samuel Wilkie. (*He bows to*
JULIE) How do you do?

ELLICOTT (*as* WILKIE *looks at* WHALEN). This is Mr. Whalen. You'll meet, I think.

WHALEN (*pleasantly*). I've heard of Mr. Wilkie.

WILKIE. Seems I've heard of you, too. (*To the others*)
We're in the same line, you might say.

WHALEN. You knew my friend Cliff Taylor?

WILKIE. I knew who he was.

WHALEN (*conversationally to the others*). Taylor was an
organizer. He had his throat cut last year in Gainesville.

WILKIE. They tell me he was a nice guy.

WHALEN. Yeah. And they tell me a side-burn guy did it.
He worked for you, I think, and he played with knives
a lot.

WILKIE (*thoughtfully*). No. I don't think he worked for
me. But you can't tell. Lot of people come in and out
of the office. Were you in Gainesville?

WHALEN (*laughs*). No. (*Touches his throat*) Fortunately, I was in Akron.

WILKIE. Now we're talking. That's the job I wanted. That's money for you. But they pieced it out in New York. You been here long?

WHALEN. About two weeks. I haven't done much. How many men you got?

WILKIE. Fifty-two, three. (WHALEN *says "um"*) Yes. That's what I say. I been trying to tell these gentlemen that it isn't enough. Better to spend it now than later. (*Hastily, as he sees* ELLICOTT's *face*) But they're paying, and they should know.

ANDREW. The men with you are good brush makers?

MOSSIE (*unconsciously*). Huh?

WILKIE (*puzzled, turns to look at* WHALEN, *who is smiling*). Good? Well, we'll hope so.

WHALEN (*laughs*). They are also skilled motormen, miners, car loaders, longshoremen—and anything you like. They're the best.

WILKIE (*laughs*). Now that's the kind of recommendation we want. (*To* WHALEN) How many men you signed? What kind?

ANDREW. What I need, and what I ordered, were brush workers.

WILKIE (*looks at him*). We'll see how it works out.

WHALEN. Hundred and ninety-two men and not bad for a new union. Decent and—(*Looks at* WILKIE) peaceful, the right way.

WILKIE (*heartily*). And that's the way we like it.

WHALEN (*laughs*). Yes. That's the way we like it.

ELLICOTT. If you gentlemen are finished with your conference, perhaps, Wilkie—

WHALEN. Certainly. I talk too much. (*Moves toward windows, and as he passes* JULIE) And if I promise not to talk at all, may I still walk by your river?

JULIE (*smiles*). Yes. But I hope you will talk. I like to listen.

(*As he exits, he collides with* CORA, *who is coming in from the porch.*)

WHALEN. Oh. Sorry.

JULIE. This is Mr. Whalen, Cora. (CORA *looks up at him, then lowers her eyes, says "Hum," and marches past him into the room.* WHALEN *looks at her, amazed, then grins and runs off the porch.* JULIE, *violently, to* CORA) Don't ever do that in my house again.

CORA. What? What did you say to me?

JULIE. I said you were never to do that in my house again.

LUCY (*at door*). Lunch is ready, Mrs. Rodman.

ELLICOTT (*looks at* JULIE, *smiles*). You're very upset, aren't you?

CORA. How dare you talk to me that way—

JULIE (*to* ANDREW, *touching his arm*). I'm sorry, Andy.

ANDREW. There's nothing to be sorry for, darling. Cora acted like a fool.

CORA (*to* JULIE). So it's *your* house now? My father built it, but it's your house now.

JULIE. Please. I'm sorry.

CORA. You've thought that all these years. It's very strange that you waited to tell me until something happened about *that* man—

ANDREW (*sharply*). Stop that silly shouting.

JULIE. I don't want lunch, Andy. Go in without me.

(*She pats his arm and exits quickly through library door.* CORA *sits down and begins to sniffle.* ANDREW *and* ELLICOTT *stare after* JULIE.)

WILKIE (*after a moment*). Um.

ELLICOTT (*turns*). It's late. You'd better have lunch here, Wilkie. It'll save time.

ANDREW (*has turned and is looking at* MOSSIE *and* JOE). Who are these gentlemen, Mr. Wilkie?

WILKIE. Mr. Easter, Mr. Dowel. I'll be staying at the hotel. They'll be here with you. (*To* ELLICOTT) Thank you. Can I wash up?

ANDREW. Staying here? Why should they be staying here? (*To* CORA, *who is sniffling and arranging the figures in the cabinet*) Please stop that, Cora.

WILKIE. They're here to take good care of you and your family, Mr. Rodman. You won't have anything to worry about.

ANDREW (*carefully*). I don't think I understand what you are talking about. Neither I nor my family need any taking care of.

WILKIE. I hope not. I believe not. But I don't like taking chances with people who pay my bills.

ANDREW (*to* ELLICOTT). What kind of nonsense is this? (*To* WILKIE) They'll stay at the hotel.

CORA. It's not nonsense. It's not nonsense. I'm paying my share of this and it's my house, too, and if Julie is going to have people like that around—(*Motions toward window*) in and out of the house, we will all need protection. She treats that man like—

ELLICOTT (*sharply*). Cora.

CORA. I insist on my rights. If you don't care what happens to me, then *I* must care—

WILKIE (*pleasantly to* ANDREW). If you'd prefer the boys stay at the hotel—?

ANDREW (*wearily*). My sister needs protection. It makes no difference. (*Starts slowly for the door.*)

LUCY (*back at door*). Lunch is getting cold.

ANDREW (*at door, over his shoulder to* ELLICOTT). I don't want lunch. Go ahead.

ELLICOTT (*stares after him for a moment. Then to* CORA). We're a small party. But that will leave more food for you. Let's go in now. You can take up the hysterics again after lunch. (CORA *rises, sweeps past him, exits.*

ELLICOTT, *as he starts out, to* WILKIE) Miss Rodman is a nervous lady.

WILKIE. Yes. They're all nervous, aren't they?

⟨*Without answering,* ELLICOTT *exits.*⟩

MOSSIE. It's like a society picture, what they were doing. (*Touches his throat*) They talk so high. (*Watches* WILKIE *who is standing in the middle of the room*) You look like you're puzzling something, boss. What's a brush worker? (*He cracks his knuckles.*)

WILKIE (*laughs*). I don't know. Somebody who makes a brush, I guess.

EASTER (*suddenly, as* MOSSIE *cracks knuckles again*). For Christ's sake quit that. You're getting me crazy.

WILKIE (*turns*). Sit down. Both of you. Try to act like you've been in a house with a bathroom before. (*Looks at* EASTER) I don't want to have to worry about your nerves this time. (*He exits.*)

MOSSIE (*sits down near cabinet*). I couldn't follow what they were saying. They talk fast, don't they? (EASTER *has wandered over to desk. Idly he looks at papers on it, examines a few things on it*) They were mad. I got that. But it don't sound bad when you talk high. (*He cracks his knuckles.*)

EASTER. I liked it for myself in Cleveland. Fifty of us. What kind of piker job is this? That Wilkie goes crazy when he smells a dollar. Always has.

MOSSIE. I don't get what he's doing. The boys sit in the factory and we sit here, huh? What's that for?

EASTER. Something he made up. We're going to get a lot extra sitting here.

MOSSIE (*cheerfully*). Well, we're eating on him. (MOSSIE *cracks his knuckles.*)

EASTER. Just keep that up for a few days, hear me? I can feed myself. I told him that.

MOSSIE (*laughs*). Yeah. But it tastes better when somebody else buys it.

EASTER. There might be street car trouble on the coast next month. I found out. I told him about it. So would he stay and wait and play for big stuff? No. He's got to take this, 'cause they let him smell a dollar bill first.

MOSSIE (*thoughtfully*). Well, he ain't working for us. He don't care about us. Car stuff, huh? Who's going to get it?

EASTER. How do I know? (MOSSIE *cracks his knuckles*) Stop it.

MOSSIE. Jesus Christ. Passing up street car work. He made enough money in New Orleans to keep him for a year.

EASTER. So did you.

MOSSIE. And so did you. More'n me, with the dice. I got some of mine yet. I took a little insurance for my mother. That's what you should've done. Instead of that sucker diamond Phil walked you in to—

EASTER (*irritated*). You said that before. (*Looks at his watch*) What do we do? Cook our food in here?

MOSSIE. They couldn't invite us to eat inside. We're out here protecting her. (*Cracks his knuckles. During his next speech* EASTER *has idly started to play with a cigarette lighter on the desk. After the second light, it stops working. He picks up a paper-knife and begins fixing it.* MOSSIE *looks down at his hand, smiles*) Everybody's got a habit. That's a good one. Protecting her. Bet there ain't even an inch anymore to protect. But the other one looks good. You can't tell about people like this. They say, in the papers, talking fine, what they wouldn't do, and then they sneak off and take a shot in bed at the first thing that comes along— (*He has cracked his knuckles again. Quickly,* EASTER *throws the paper-knife at him.* MOSSIE *ducks, the knife misses him and knocks over a vase on a small table. Slowly,* MOSSIE *adjusts his chair, shakes his head, stares at the vase*) Starting it again, huh? When you get time, Joe, you ought to take a rest cure. Ain't natural to be so nervous with knives. (*Shakes his head, looking at the vase*) You certainly ain't neat with other people's things.

Curtain

ACT TWO

SCENE I

Four weeks later.

AT RISE: MOSSIE DOWEL *is seated and* JOE EASTER *is standing at the table between the windows. They are playing
two-handed poker.* MOSSIE *has his chair turned.* WILKIE,
*in hat and overcoat, is sitting on the arm of a chair,
looking idly out of the window. The radio is playing
softly. For a few seconds after the rise of the curtain
there are no sounds but the shuffling of cards, the sound
of money on the table, the radio.*

EASTER (*after a second, sharply*). All right. All right. Show
'em. Stop flirting with 'em.

(MOSSIE *puts his hand down, smiles, rakes in the center
money.* EASTER *puts down his cards, crosses to radio,
angrily snaps it off.*)

MOSSIE. Funny. Losers never like music. It's good luck
for me, on the contrary. (*To* WILKIE) It's after nine.
Must be something big keeping you out of bed.

EASTER. I guess. It's got to be money to keep him out of
those woolen nightgowns.

WILKIE. It's pay day, or it should be. That always gives
me insomnia. (*They have started to play again*) Ellicott been here?

EASTER. Nope.

MOSSIE. He's coming. Always is. Looking for Mrs. Rodman
with the legs.

EASTER (*to* WILKIE, *pointing upstairs*). You think Rodman
knows about 'em?

113

WILKIE (*unpleasantly*). What do you know?

MOSSIE. What does he know? He's guessing. He sees it everywhere. It comes from watching the flies go to it on cell doors.

WILKIE (*sharply, to* EASTER). I'd get the shakedown out of my head, if I were you.

EASTER. You think I'm crazy? (MOSSIE *cracks his knuckles*) Deal 'em. And stop that cracking. (*He wins a small hand and begins to shuffle the cards. Maliciously, casually to* WILKIE) So things ain't going so good, huh?

MOSSIE (*cheerfully*). It's nice and easy here. I like a rest job once in a while.

WILKIE. Another few weeks like this and you'll get a long rest.

MOSSIE. It ain't our fault, Sam.

EASTER. When you got nothing to do, we can't do it for you.

MOSSIE. Finger tried a fight. Eddie tried a fight. I even had Sig chase the old guy Firth's girl around. (*Puzzled*) Any guy'd protect his thirteen year old kid.

EASTER. Three sevens.

MOSSIE. But nobody'll fight. No matter what you do, they don't fight. Must be some kind of new religion, maybe. (*Turns up his hand, cracks his knuckles*) Three nines easy.

EASTER (*through his teeth*). They *are* running pretty easy the last two days, huh? (*To* WILKIE) I'm crazy for this place. Losing to him and following that dame around.

WILKIE. Just keep on doing it. I'll tell you when you're fit for anything else.

(ELLICOTT *appears at the Center doors. He looks around the room, then after a second, coldly.*)

ELLICOTT. Good evening. I hear you were looking for me today. You're active on pay day, aren't you?

WILKIE. Yes, sir. (*Pointing to desk*) The account's over there.

ELLICOTT (*as he passes* MOSSIE *and* JOE). I'm glad to see that nothing has disturbed your game, gentlemen. (*Picks up the sheet*) Yes. It's a very full account. Well, you're right to get it while you can. I'm not so sure how many more pay days there are going to be. You do nothing and your bills get bigger.

WILKIE. That's the way it seems to have worked out.

ELLICOTT. The Cincinnati Herald is crying its eyes out tonight over model town being over-run with toughs. None of that helps any. (*Looking at* MOSSIE *and* JOE) Do you think they could have meant these gentlemen and the other friends you brought with you?

WILKIE. I read the papers. (*Looks speculatively at* MOSSIE *and* JOE) They don't look like anything Oscar Wilde would have wanted, do they? But no job's ever paid me enough to have their faces pushed pretty. (*Gets up*) Well, I know I haven't done too much, and I like it less than you. We're in hunting country. You didn't tell me that.

ELLICOTT. What?

WILKIE. The people around here hunt. In the season, I mean. That right?

ELLICOTT. What's that got to do with it?

WILKIE. It's got a lot to do with it. Every man for five miles owns a gun. Flintlocks, maybe, but clean. But they won't use 'em on me. They won't use 'em at all. You know why? Because somebody in Cleveland made a mistake and sent down a smart organizer. He won't let 'em use 'em. There hasn't even been a nose bleed for me to stop. I can't work with nothing.

ELLICOTT. We didn't bargain to cut the plan out for you. That's your business, and you've done a bad job of it.

WILKIE (*coldly, still pleasantly*). Now, now. It's not all my fault. Even if there had been something to do, I couldn't have done it. Because I'm working for a man who doesn't want me to do anything. I'm working for a man who doesn't want me to work for him. That's a bad set-up, Mr. Ellicott.

ELLICOTT (*starting to exit, slowly*). You'd better come up and see Mr. Rodman. (*Looks up at him*) As a lawyer, I have found that for my client's own good, it is often wise not to ask his permission on little details.

(WILKIE *has turned to stare at him as he reaches the door and passes* CORA, *who is entering.*)

CORA (*to* ELLICOTT). Don't you ever stay in your own house anymore? There are people who can never stay quietly at home and read a book. (*He exits without answering her*) Good evening. Rain. Rain. Rain. Are there several types of detectives, Mr. Wilkie?

WILKIE. Only one kind, Miss Rodman. Lousy.

CORA. I mean, very funny things are happening here. Things are missing from the pantry— (*Coquettishly*) Or is that too unimportant work for you?

WILKIE. Not at all. I don't seem to be doing much else.

CORA (*goes to cabinet*). On Thursday, I was taking my weekly supply list. Just as a matter of routine. Mrs. Rodman was out—

WILKIE. Mrs. Rodman is out a good deal, isn't she?

CORA. Yes, Mrs. Rodman always manages to go off by herself. Well, when I looked in the closet I was amazed to find that at least eight or ten dollars' worth of canned goods—

WILKIE (*rises, politely*). Mr. Dowel is a specialist at just such detection. He's at your service, Miss Rodman. I'll be down later and we can lay our trap. (*He exits.*)

MOSSIE (*giggles*). Sure. Who, me? Sure.

CORA. I like to see a nice little card game. Do you know that night club singer who got killed in the paper this morning?

MOSSIE. No ma'am. I don't know ladies who get into trouble.

EASTER (*motioning to the cards*). Beat the straight.

MOSSIE. Easy. (*He rakes in the money as* EASTER *stares at him.*)

CORA (*to* EASTER). My. You were beaten. Are you playing for money?

(HANNAH *enters with a tray of drinks which she puts on the other side of the room.* CORA *watches her as she empties ash trays into a saucer.*)

HANNAH (*slamming ash tray on table, pointing to the floor*). Ain't it *more* trouble to lean over the ash trays to get the ashes on the rug? Pigs.

MOSSIE. My Ma used to say ashes were good for rugs.

HANNAH. Your Ma never saw a rug.

CORA. Hannah. We were just talking about the things that were stolen from the pantry.

HANNAH. Were you now? Anybody in jail?

CORA. It's ridiculous that you shouldn't know where they've disappeared to—

HANNAH (*has picked up* JOE'S *cigarette which is lying on the table, and carefully placed the lighted end nearer the wood*). Put it like this. It'll burn the table faster.

EASTER (*angrily, under his breath, as she starts to exit*). Mind your business.

CORA. Hannah! You haven't been listening to a word I've said— (ANDREW *enters from the rear library door. Goes to desk*) Henry and Mr. Wilkie are upstairs. Henry's been here three times today. In, out. In, out.

ANDREW (*as* EASTER *has noisily slammed down his cards*). Would you play in the other room, please?

MOSSIE (*softly, not paying any attention and not moving*). Yes sir.

CORA (*as* HANNAH *goes to the door*). Andrew. It's time for you to know that groceries have been missing from the kitchen. Regularly. Hannah refuses to tell me who's been doing it and I can't allow it to go on. I have asked Mr. Wilkie to take a hand.

HANNAH (*turning*). Have you? (*Laughs. The noise of the*

*game, the words, the raking in of the money has be-
come sharp once more.*)

ANDREW. *Get out of this room.* (*They turn, surprised. Then
slowly, without hurry, they gather up their things and
move out.*)

CORA (*after a second*). Andrew. I was telling you that—

HANNAH (*crossing to him quickly*). Miss Cora was telling
you that food's been missing. It has. I've been taking
it. I wish I could've taken more. (*Motions with her hand
toward windows*) I don't know what you feel, but I
don't like to see the boys go hungry. Do what you want
about it, Mr. Andrew.

ANDREW (*slowly, staring at her*). I don't want to do anything about it, Hannah.

(HANNAH *without answering exits. She passes* JULIE, *in
hat and coat, entering. For a fraction,* JULIE *draws back
when she sees the room is not empty.*)

CORA. Sometimes I think you're crazy. And sometimes I
think you are doing things just to humiliate me.

ANDREW. It's raining, darling.

JULIE. I know. But I'd like a walk anyway.

CORA. I say one thing. You say another. Telling her it's all
right to steal. What *right* have you to humiliate me in
front of servants?

JULIE (*gently*). Cora, do stop nagging at Andy—

CORA. Nagging at him. Nagging at him. He's gone crazy—

ANDREW. I like my wife. Could I ever, anymore, be alone
with her? For just a few minutes? And then you can
start with me all over again.

CORA (*at door*). Certainly you can be alone. I daresay
you have a great many things to ask.

JULIE. She has one of her bad headaches. She's upset.
(ANDREW *smiles, shakes his head. She looks around the
room*) How messy this room looks.

ANDREW (*comes up to her as he speaks*). Our friends have
been using it as a club. I don't blame you for wanting

to go out. (*Leans down, kisses her hair*) But not tonight,
Julie. It's cold and it's raining, and—

JULIE (*slowly*). I want to go.

ANDREW (*moves away from her to chair*). And I'm lonely.

JULIE (*on the "want to go" she has moved again to the
window. On his speech she turns, looks at him, puzzled*). You? Lonely?

ANDREW (*smiles*). Yes. I. Lonely. I always thought loneli-
ness meant alone, without people. It means something
else.

JULIE (*softly*). That's a late discovery. You're lucky.

ANDREW (*laughs*). Why do people always think it's lucky
to find out the simple things long after one should have
known them?

JULIE. Because each year you can put off knowing about
them gives you one more year of peace.

ANDREW. I don't think so. Unless you can put it off forever.
(*Smiles*) I think that's what I was trying to do. But
I'm at a bad age to start looking at the world, to start
looking at myself. (*Very simply*) It confuses me, Julie.
I am mixed up.

JULIE. I know. I've guessed. But I'm no one to help. I'm
more mixed up than you.

ANDREW. I've walked up and down this room so much
for so many nights, that I'm (*Angrily*) sick of it and
sick of myself. I try to tell myself that I can think
things straight, and every night I start the same way,
—by taking stock of this house. Bums walking in and
out, followed by Henry, as undisturbed and as anxious to get down to White Sulphur as always; Hannah,
trying to make me into the villain she wants me to be.
And Cora. Taking up one unpleasant sentence where
she left off the last. (*Softly*) And you. I've missed you.

JULIE. Missed me?

ANDREW (*looks at her, laughs*). You're embarrassed.
Strange. We've lived together so long it seems almost

indecent to talk about ourselves. We used to talk about ourselves. Remember?

JULIE (*smiles*). Yes. When we were young. We belonged to the time when talk was part of the marriage ceremony. Such cynical, smooth talk, about marriage and life and freedom. Not you. Me, I mean.

ANDREW. I suppose. I remember I used to be a little puzzled by it. But that's what we were then. (*Affectionately*) You always hate yesterday, don't you, Julie?

JULIE. Yes. (*She moves again to window and then turns back suddenly*) Andy. We haven't talked about it much. I knew you didn't want to. But the strike, these people here—it's wrong for you. I know it's so wrong for you. Settle it now. It doesn't make any difference who wins—

ANDREW (*sharply*). I don't care who wins. If it were that simple, it would be fine. But it isn't that simple. (*Leans forward, slowly*) I can't fit the pieces together. That's what is happening to me. I suddenly don't know where my place in the whole thing is. Don't tell me that's one of the things I was lucky to worry about late. That doesn't do any good. I've only loved two things in my whole life: you and this town. Papa never loved it. He just wanted to be boss and get to Carlsbad for the season. But my grandfather loved it. I think the way I do. Remember how I never wanted to go to Europe or to any place else,—even when you went? This was my home, these were my people, I didn't want much else. (*With feeling*) But that's been changed. I don't know how. And I don't know where I stand anymore.

JULIE (*softly*). Try to set it right again.

ANDREW. I wish I knew how. I worked well because I worked one way, without thinking about any other. They worked one way, without thinking about any other. How do I set that right again? Don't you see? It would be like us. If anything ever happened to us we could come together again and pretend it had never happened. But what good would that be if it had really happened, and we couldn't be the same anymore? (*Laughs suddenly*) Well, I'm not the strong man Papa was, and Cora will be down in a minute to remind me of it.

JULIE (*after a second, she kneels on the floor in front of him*). Andy. Look at me. You've talked because you wanted help. You wanted me to help you, about yourself. I can't do that. I need help myself. It's a mean thing I'm saying: that I can't stay and listen, because I want to talk myself. I want help, too.

ANDREW (*after a second he nods, smiles, pats her head*). Where are you going, Julie? Down by the river in the rain?

JULIE. I don't know. Probably the river. I always do. (*Then suddenly, softly*) And perhaps not.

ANDREW (*rises*). Good night, darling.

JULIE (*quietly*). Good night, Andy.

(*He watches her move toward the window and exit. He stands for a moment looking after her as* MOSSIE *opens the library door.*)

MOSSIE. Mr. Ellicott says he's waiting for you. (ANDREW, *his eyes on the window, pays no attention to* MOSSIE, *who, after a minute*) Mr. Ellicott's waiting.

(*For a second longer,* ANDREW *stands looking out of the window. Then slowly, without looking at* MOSSIE, *he exits from Center doors.* MOSSIE *comes into the room, idly, pushes the door shut with his foot as he turns on the radio. The radio is playing something banal and loud. Then he sits down—the corner near the cabinet has no light on it—comfortably leans back to listen to the music. After a second,* EASTER *comes slowly in from the library door. He has a pack of cards in his hand and is playing with them. He crosses to the large table and lays out six or seven of them, face-down on the table.*)

MOSSIE. Funny how a lot of rich people don't like noise.

I like that. I once took piano lessons for two months. (*No answer*) What you doing, Joe?

EASTER (*through his teeth*). Playing solitaire. (*As he leans very close to look at the backs of the cards*) A new way. (*As* MOSSIE *cracks his knuckles*) You doing it worse today. *Stop it.*

MOSSIE (*looks at cabinet*). Screwy. The way she plays with these things. And the other one. Walking up and down, up and down. Tim says she's had him crazy trying to follow her. Bet she's doing it tonight, in the rain. She just went out.

EASTER (*looks up*). Your finger nails need cutting, Mossie.

MOSSIE (*looks at him, laughs*). Yeah. You buying me a manicure?

EASTER. That'd be better than having you wear them down making marks on the back of these cards—and it wouldn't cost me as much.

MOSSIE. You're nuts.

EASTER (*straightens up*). Put the sixty-five bucks you won over here on the table, Mossie.

MOSSIE. *You* got the cards out of *that* drawer. My God, Joe, you don't mean to tell me you think rich people like this would fool around with wrong cards—Jesus, Joe, I been telling you you'd better take a rest cure. Books and milk and just laying in a bed. You're getting too nervous about nothing. You're seeing things. Rodman fixing the cards— (*Laughs, then quietly*) Was it Rodman's dice you made that killing with at Phil's? Joe, you're getting good and batty.

EASTER. The cards are scratched. Put that money on the table.

MOSSIE (*slowly, as he cracks his knuckles, turns toward the radio*). You don't want to get so excited, Joe. You don't want to come over here and get the dough, Joe, and I don't blame you. So stay over there and quiet

yourself. Sit down and whittle yourself some straight
dice.

EASTER (*slowly*). For the last time. Put the money on the
table.

MOSSIE (*quietly*). No.

(*As he turns back to the radio,* EASTER, *pressing the spring
of his knife, lets it fly through the air.* MOSSIE *screams
softly, pushes with his feet from the ground as he top-
ples from the chair. He falls noisily to the floor. For a
second* EASTER *stands watching him, listening to the two
soft groans. The groans cease and* EASTER *suddenly begins to move. His movements are quick but aimless, as
if he didn't know what to do first. He turns out the
lamp nearest him, shuts the library door, and moves to
Center doors. As he starts to turn the key, the door is
violently pushed open by* WILKIE. EASTER *steps back,
frightened.*)

WILKIE. What's it? (EASTER *looks out in the hall for a second, then quickly closes the door, nods his head toward*
MOSSIE *and the chair.* WILKIE *crosses quickly, leans
down, looks at* MOSSIE. *Then quickly, he moves toward*
EASTER, *grabs the lapel of his coat with one hand as he
hits him in the face with the other*) You tough guy. You
God damned tough guy.

EASTER (*hoarsely*). I couldn't help it, Sam—he had his
gun out.

WILKIE. Yeah, out in his pocket. O. K. the hell with you.
(*Lets go his lapels and shoves him.*)

EASTER. Sam. Give me some money. Please. Sam. Please.

WILKIE. I'll give you money—to get your hair waved for
the chair.

EASTER. I'm telling you, I'm telling you. What could I do?
He tried the gun. I'm telling you— (*Hysterically, as he
watches* WILKIE *move toward telephone*) Sam. Sam.
What are you doing—

WILKIE. I'm trying to think which cop would like to have you most. (*Turning on him violently*) This whole damn job wasn't lousy enough. You got to make it better. That boy scout upstairs you got to spell words in front of is going to like this in his house. I can sit in the office now and knit for a year—until they forget you worked for me. (*Picks up telephone*) Well, I'll take you in myself and make a pretty speech about how I didn't know your record, and the only dope who'll believe that is some guy milking a cow, and I'd never have worked for him anyway. You tough guy.

EASTER. No. No. Sam. No—

WILKIE (*as he starts to dial*). You son of a bitch. I can't get a nose bleed where I want it, but you've got to start carving— (*His last words have become slower, as if he were thinking. Then he looks up at* EASTER, *and slowly puts the receiver back on the hook. Stands at the table, staring at it, as* EASTER *watches him. After a long silence*) This way you'd hang during the warm weather. My way might keep you alive for the winter—maybe. (*Comes over and stands in front of* EASTER) Take that knife out of him. Take him out and dump him. (*Carefully*) Dump him in the right place—with no fancy work. Do you hear me? (EASTER *nods quickly, and as he starts to move,* WILKIE *jerks him back*) Remember, I don't promise you anything. If it goes wrong, you slob, it goes wrong for you. I'll turn you in myself if I have to—and with plenty of story to keep me in the clear. Do you understand me? (*Waits, gets no answer*) Do you understand me?

EASTER (*very quietly*). Yes.

Curtain

SCENE II

*The same evening. The time is immediately following
Scene I.*

SETTING: *A bare, clean office-room, the empty side of a
store. The office is in an alley. The entrance is Left
stage. There is a desk, a few chairs, a filing cabinet, a
typewriter, a mimeographing machine, an electric stove.*

AT RISE: WHALEN *is sitting at the desk chair, leaning over
to hammer on a box.* FIRTH *is sitting by the window,
staring idly out into the alley. Neither of them speaks
for a minute after the curtain rises. Then* FIRTH *gets
slowly to his feet and goes to the chair on which his hat
and raincoat are lying.*

FIRTH. Well. Want to come to my house for a bowl of
something hot?

WHALEN (*shakes his head, points to a cardboard container
on his desk*). Odave treated me to a pint of whisky. It
tastes like he made it on the picket line.

FIRTH. Bad for your stomach.

WHALEN. Don't worry about my stomach. It'll last another
few years. (*Waves toward the window*) Worry about
the stomachs out there.

FIRTH. I been worrying enough.

WHALEN. How much we got?

FIRTH. Enough, maybe. Hannah brought down canned
stuff and Richmondville sent over a pig.

WHALEN. That's enough for a month, if you take a little
caviar with it.

FIRTH. Well, it ain't enough. I don't say anybody's starving, but it's tough to watch kids not get enough. It ain't
only my kid, it's kids.

WHALEN. Yep!

FIRTH. I had a hundred sixty-two dollars left in my savings bank. Clyde needed it. Nobody's got much left. Clyde coughs too much.

WHALEN. Didn't anybody ever tell you that Christians aren't supposed to act like Christians?

FIRTH. Funny. All the boys had a little something. But we were talking last night how you work all your life to save it, then it runs out fast. Funny.

WHALEN. Very funny.

FIRTH (*suddenly, as if he had been thinking of it all along*). I couldn't tell her what they meant. I was so ashamed for the kid. (*Violently*) I'll kill 'em if they ever go near my girl again. I'll kill 'em—

WHALEN (*looks at him, slowly, calmly*). That's just what they want you to do. You boys were hot stuff Thursday. You couldn't take a little pushing around. You got to push back. So what? So it winds up Wilkie gets half his boys sworn in as deputy sheriffs. They're law and order now and you're un-American.

FIRTH. There's some things you can't take. Nobody can. Nobody.

WHALEN. Speak for yourself. There's not much I can't take, if I have to. (*Slowly*) You gave me your word that you wouldn't fight again, and that you'd keep the boys from fighting.

FIRTH. And I've kept my word. But it gets too much—

WHALEN (*wearily*). We've been over all this before. Try to believe that I'm telling you the truth. The longer you're quiet the sooner you'll win. Wilkie's been in this business for a long time. They've all got one gag—to make you fight. And no matter what *they* do to start it, you'll be surprised to read in the paper, and to hear from the police, that *you* started it. (*Slowly, with force*) And once they start a real fight here, you're lost.

FIRTH. You don't believe we can take care of ourselves, do you? You don't—

WHALEN. No. I don't believe it. There are men in your spot who know what it's about and who can take what's coming. I believe in *their* fighting, but not *you*. Your idea of fighting is not to hit below the waist— (*Laughs*) And that's no good. Now be good. And don't let your kid or anybody else go out alone.

FIRTH (*shakes his head, passes his hand over his face wearily, and begins to put on his coat*). Hannah says Andrew don't like things much. Might be a good sign. He's an easy going man. I don't believe he'd have ever got us into this if it hadn't been for the others.

WHALEN (*smiles*). That's the stuff. That kind of talk will do you a lot of good.

FIRTH (*sighs*). I don't know how much longer we can hold out here, when kids aren't getting enough. (*As he turns he looks at* WHALEN, *who is paying no attention to him*) I wouldn't be the one to know. What do you think?

WHALEN. I told you what I thought. Wilkie wants a fight, and as long as we're not giving him one we're sitting not bad. Now go on home. And if they cut your grandmother in half, don't lift a hand. Wait'll they cut her in slices and then maybe, but I don't promise, I'll let you take a sock at one of 'em.

FIRTH. That ain't what I meant. That ain't telling me how much longer we can feed. You ain't never told me.

WHALEN (*finally irritated*). And I'm never going to. That may be part of my job, too, but it's not for me. You pick your own minute. You'll get no speeches from me about the beauty of starving for what you think. I don't mind doing it for myself, but I don't do it for other people. (*Gets up*) Because it's a waste of time, and I'm busy. I guess you'll hold out as long as you've got the guts to. That I can't put in you.

FIRTH (*angrily*). We don't need you to tell us about guts—

WHALEN (*smiles*). That's all right. I'm no hero-worshiper.

FIRTH. We've got more guts around here than you'll ever see. Our folks have always had. We—

WHALEN (*wearily, goes back to his desk and starts working again on the box*). Go on home and boast to your wife.

(FIRTH *stands watching him. After a second he sighs, moves toward the door.*)

FIRTH (*softly*). I could bring you back something hot.

WHALEN (*affectionately*). Good night, Tom.

FIRTH (*affectionately*). Don't worry about the boys here. We'll be all right when you're crying for a rotten apple.

(*He exits.* WHALEN *watches him, smiling. Then with a few loud hammerings, he finishes with the box and gets up, carrying it to the other side of the room. He goes to a basin, washes his hands, dabs at his face, lights a cigarette, pours himself a drink. He stands smoking as the door opens and* JULIE RODMAN *comes slowly in. She stands away from the door, waiting for him to speak.*)

WHALEN (*turns, looks at her, then after a moment's silence, says loudly, as if he is talking for somebody outside*). Please close the door, Mrs. Rodman—unless there is somebody with you.

JULIE (*closing the door, without turning*). There is nobody with me. (*She stands waiting for him to speak*) I—I— Can't I come in?

WHALEN (*slowly, pleasantly*). I'm guessing. But I want to save you time. You can go back and tell them that I don't want any bribes—and that the gag is too stale.

JULIE (*crosses to him. Intensely*). No. No. Really, no. I haven't come for any reason—I mean, any reason except my own. Really, really, Mr. Whalen—

WHALEN (*picks up two cheap glasses from the window sill*). Well, whatever your reason, you look cold. Like

a drink? (*She nods, shy, embarrassed, watching him*)
It's filthy, but it's a drink. (*He hands her a glass, sits
down at desk, smiles, pours himself a drink*) Don't listen
to the doctors. Cheap whisky is good for you. Why did
you come, Mrs. Rodman?

JULIE. I—er—I— (*Looks up at him*) It won't sound like
the truth. I wanted to talk to you. Just talk to you. Not
about anything. I just wanted to talk to you—

WHALEN (*looks at her, then after a pause*). Well. That
sounds too pleasant. Don't you know that you're not
supposed to feel friendly enough for a visit and—
(*Slowly, seriously*) and that I'm not supposed to let
you make the visit?

JULIE (*rises, softly*). Yes, I suppose I knew it. I'm sorry. I
just wanted to talk to you.

WHALEN (*kindly*). What did you want to say?

JULIE. I don't know. Although I've thought about it a lot.
(*Turns to him and smiles*) You don't remember, but I
do. The first evening you came here, you talked to me.

WHALEN. I do remember. I didn't know who you were.

JULIE. I've walked past your alley often. Tonight I didn't
think. I just came in. (*Quickly*) Haven't you ever
wanted to talk to somebody you thought knew more
about things than you did, and you just hoped the talk
would start, and—(*Smiles*) there wouldn't be any questions about why you came?

WHALEN (*pours himself another drink*). Yes. Once. When
I was in college. I thought that Lafayette— (*Bows*)
Lafayette, of all people—was a fake and I wanted to
know about it. But the professor was eating his dinner,
and he thought Lafayette was fine. It never seems to
work out very well.

JULIE (*without snobbishness*). College?

WHALEN (*laughs*). Yes, ma'am. No, it's not as good as it
sounds. I only went to college for seven months. That

cost four hundred dollars. (*Bows*) Almost half of what my father could earn in a year. The old story. (*Leans forward, nastily*) My mother sacrificed herself.

JULIE. I went to college, too. But it cost more than that. (*Smiles*) And it wasn't any sacrifice for my mother.

WHALEN. No? You shouldn't have denied her that. My mother found great happiness in it, crowing over our half-starved neighbors. My mother hated what she was and what she came from. None of that love of beauty stuff in my mother. I was to become a priest.

JULIE (*smiling*). I'd have guessed that.

WHALEN (*smiles*). You would have been wrong. When that failed, she just wanted me to get rich enough to hate what I was and what I came from. (*Leans over to light a cigarette*) I fooled her. I hated her instead. I always had. I kind of liked my father, and that four hundred bucks would have been plenty of carfare for him. He had rheumatism bad and the places where they could pay a gardener were in the suburbs and he had to walk most of the way. He'd come home at night and it would hurt him to take his pants off and he'd sit in a chair and hold them out from his legs so the goods couldn't touch the skin. He wasn't much. But he was nice. Anyway, what for? Four years of dopes and faking that I had as much as they had. I quit. (*Stops, leans over to look at her, then slowly*) What is your reason for coming here?

JULIE (*puts up her hand, as if to detail him, softly*). In a minute. In a minute. (*Then politely, loudly*) What did you do then?

WHALEN (*sits back, looks at her, then after a second*). Nothing. I hoboed. Once in a while I'd work. But not when I could help it. Then one day, or one month, or one year, I began to get worried. I couldn't understand about things, and it scared hell out of me. (*Laughs, pours himself out a drink, pours her one*) When you don't feel yourself anything, I mean any part of anything, that's when you get scared. I was that way for a long time.

JULIE (*softly*). My husband said he felt that.

WHALEN. I imagine he would. Well it took me a long time. I had listened too much to what was wrong with the world from every louse from New Orleans to Seattle. I was sick of it all. I hated the rich. I hated the poor. I couldn't figure either of them. (*Smiles at her*) I'm not bright, but I'm stubborn. And I came out with something. (*Slowly, seriously*) I've been working ever since.

JULIE. Then you didn't hate. Not the poor anyway. You loved them.

WHALEN (*laughs*). Love them? No. Do you think you can love the smell that comes from dirty skin, or the scum on dishes, or the holes in the floor with the bugs coming through— (*Sharply*) Or the meanness and the cowardice that comes with poverty? (*Leans forward*) I hate the poor, Mrs. Rodman. But I love what they could be. (*Then lightly*) Do you hate the poor, Mrs. Rodman?

JULIE. No. And I don't know what they could be.

WHALEN. Not even hate? You've never thought that much about them?

JULIE (*simply*). No. I've never seen many poor people.

WHALEN. Some bright Sunday you must lift your hem from the mud and have a try.

JULIE. I'd like to.

WHALEN. I imagine one of the ladies' charities would be delighted to let you peep over the fence. (*Nastily*) It would not be unpleasant, since the poor *they* will show you will lick your boots—in gratitude for nothing. Or rather for the gift of seeing a handsome, clean lady who can eat three meals every day. The people *they* will show you haven't the— (*Uses the word carefully*) dignity to want those things for themselves. The church has taught them to be grateful that *you* have them. When you have left, with your empty bag of groceries, they will tell themselves that it is easier for a camel to go through the eye of a needle, than for a rich lady to enter the Kingdom of God. That has consoled them for a long time.

JULIE (*angrily*). That's not what I am. That's not what I want to see. You have no reason for thinking it is.

WHALEN. Perhaps not. But people like me always make symbols of people like you.

JULIE. I never wanted to see a selected world: I never knew how to see any other. I think that is one of the reasons I wanted to talk to you.

WHALEN (*laughs mockingly*). Are you in a hurry? Or can I show you my world in fifteen minutes? I'm not a teacher, Mrs. Rodman. (*Looks at her*) And I believe that if one wants to see the world, one knows where to find it. It's all about you. They tell me you've been married here a long time and that they don't know you very well.

JULIE. No, they don't. They're a hard people with strangers —as you've probably found out.

WHALEN (*smiles*). Yes.

JULIE. But it's really my fault. I've been busy. Busy, like you, finding out. (*Bitterly*) I was finding out about myself. That took all my time.

WHALEN. A psychoanalyst?

JULIE (*begins to be angry, then laughs*). No.

WHALEN. Oh. I thought that was the rich man's gin. What were you finding out?

JULIE. I don't know. When I was young, I guess I was looking for something I could do. Then for something I could be. (*Smiles*) Finally, just for something to want, or to think, or to believe in. I always wanted somebody to show me the way.

WHALEN (*smiles*). Certainly. That's what we all want. It's easy. Were you lucky?

JULIE. Lucky in finding them? No.

WHALEN (*looks at his watch, begins to put papers away in desk*). Then you should try for yourself. That works sometimes.

JULIE. No. I decided a long time ago that there were people who had to learn from other people. I'm one of them. (*Gets up, slowly*) That's why I wanted to talk to you.

WHALEN (*looks up at her, laughs, shakes his head*). To me? Is that why you came?

JULIE (*slowly*). Yes. And I'd like to stay.

WHALEN (*slowly, puzzled*). To stay?

JULIE. Sounds crazy, doesn't it? It isn't crazy for me. I know the things you're going to say about a silly, rich woman. But I've thought about it too much, and I know it isn't that. I have no right to come here and talk to you like this—

WHALEN (*gets up, looks at her*). What are you talking about, Mrs. Rodman?

JULIE (*angrily*). I've told you. I've told you. (*Then softly, quietly*) I want to stay, I want to stay here. I mean, I—

WHALEN (*there is a second's silence. Then he moves to her quickly, takes her roughly by the arm*). All right. Now go back and tell Wilkie this isn't a new one either. (*She draws her face away from him, sharply*) Don't look so hurt. What am I supposed to think?

JULIE. I've told you the truth. I don't care what you think. (*He looks at her, drops her arm, moves back to desk, turns to look at her again.*)

WHALEN. Who have you told this nonsense to?

JULIE (*carefully*). I haven't told this—this nonsense to anybody.

WHALEN (*angrily*). What the hell do you think I am?

JULIE. I don't blame you for anything you think. I know what a fool I've sounded. But it's been the truth. (*Softly*) I've never in my life talked that way before. (*To herself*) I should have known that when I did, I wouldn't be believed.

WHALEN. And if I do believe you, then you are a silly rich woman who doesn't know what to do with her life and who sees the solution for it in the first man she meets who doesn't stutter: sick of your own world, aren't you, and you think I know another? What do you think mine is? A new game to be learned in an evening and played for a week? (*Takes her arm*) I don't like that kind of playing, Mrs. Rodman.

JULIE (*after a second, slowly, carefully*). Maybe what you've said is true. Maybe it isn't. But I'm not playing —and you don't think I am.

WHALEN (*stares at her, as if he were thinking of something else*). You could blow me out of here with this. (*Carefully*) Please. Don't mention your—don't mention your coming here.

JULIE (*softly*). I won't. (*Her face hurt and tight, she begins to move toward the door. As she passes the desk, he stops her.*)

WHALEN. I'd like to say something kind. But I'm worrying about my job. (*Smiles*) I'm tired and I've got a lot of work to do.

JULIE (*without turning*). Do you think I'm pretty?

WHALEN (*as he starts to speak, there is the noise of a car outside, and he stops to listen. When he hears nothing more, he smiles*). No. Better than pretty. (*Looks at her, nods*) Yes, that I feel. Sure. I feel a lot of that. You'd be fun. If you ever feel like it, and I'm not working, you bring your maids, and your trunks, and your cars, and—

JULIE (*simply*). No.

WHALEN (*laughs*). All right. (*Pleasantly*) And now, good
   night.
(*As she walks toward the door, the noise of a car, the
   grinding of gears, becomes very sharp and close. She
   stops, and he looks quickly toward the door and window. Then, as if he is wondering whether the noise
   means anything to her, he looks at her. Quickly, he
   moves toward the door, jerks it open, runs out, as she
   draws back into the room. A minute later he returns,
   stands staring as if unconscious that she was there.*)

JULIE. What is it?

WHALEN (*slowly, looking at her*). It's a big night for me.
   Your friends have been playing tricks.

JULIE. What do you mean?

WHALEN. I mean that the dead body of that fat thug who
   was living in your house has just been planted in the
   alley.

JULIE. Dead? He's dead? I don't understand—

WHALEN. It's very simple. You heard the car. He was put
   there to get somebody in trouble. (*Stops, thinks*) Yep.
   (*Moves quickly to the telephone. Into phone*) Corley?
   Run next door and get me Tom Firth. Quick. (*Puts
   phone down. Crosses back to her*) Go out the other
   end of the alley, Mrs. Rodman. Please don't let anybody see you.

JULIE. But you—

WHALEN (*quickly, firmly*). Good night. (*She turns, stares
   at him, hesitates, and begins to run out of the door. He
   watches her, shuts the door, moves quickly back to the
   telephone*) Tom. One of Wilkie's boys is outside in the
   alley, dead. They planted him there. I don't know. For
   me or you or anybody else. Listen to me. I'm going to
   be in jail in a few minutes, sleeping tight. (*Sharply*)
   Stay where you are and don't worry about me. I don't
   know what he's going to start, but I know he's going to

start something. Stop worrying about me, and listen. (*Very carefully*) No matter what he starts, let him alone. *Don't fight with him.* (*Loudly*) Do you hear me? Let him do what he wants and don't fight with him. (*Pleasantly*) Just get ready to do nothing. That'll take all the guts you've got. No. I'll be all right. Good night. (*He hangs up, sits quietly for a second, then gets up and takes his hat and coat from the floor behind the desk, puts them on, sits down again, turns his chair to face the door, lights a cigarette. A second later there is a loud knocking on the door. He smiles, starts to rise, as the curtain falls.*)

Curtain

SCENE III

Same as Act One.

AT RISE: *The living room of the Rodman house. Some of the lamps have been turned off, as if to keep attention off the room.* WILKIE *has moved a large chair to face the Center doors. A second after the curtain rises, there is the noise of someone descending the hall stairs.* WILKIE *lights a cigarette, slowly, and leans forward.*

WILKIE. Mr. Ellicott.

ELLICOTT (*coming into the room, putting on his overcoat*). I thought you'd gone home long ago. (*Slowly*) What are you doing here, Wilkie?

WILKIE (*shakes his head, gets up, waits, then slowly, nodding his head toward card table*). My man Dowel was found knifed, dead, down near strike headquarters.

ELLICOTT. Oh. (*After a second, puzzled*) But he was here—

WILKIE (*watching him*). He went out.

ELLICOTT (*carefully*). You think they killed him?

WILKIE (*looks at him, amused, laughs*). I think so.

ELLICOTT. Why?

WILKIE. Whalen was there. Any of the others could have been there, too.

ELLICOTT (*carefully*). They got into a fight and killed him—

WILKIE (*smiles*). Maybe. Or maybe they thought he was snooping around and jumped him.

ELLICOTT. Well?

WILKIE. Well. That gives us a little job of law enforcement to do. The boys we had sworn in as deputy sheriffs last week will have to pass up their crap game, and— (*Smiles broadly*) go to work for justice.

ELLICOTT (*sharply, irritated*). What do you intend to do?

WILKIE. Find the guy who put the knife in Mossie, and find the guys he did it for.

ELLICOTT. And where does that lead?

WILKIE. Well, we'll hope it leads somewhere. (*Casually*) Is this Judge Alcott a good enough friend of yours that I can count on his not getting up out of bed to issue any silly court orders that could get in my way?

ELLICOTT (*slowly*). Yes.

WILKIE. And could you ask your marshal to go home and go to bed?

ELLICOTT (*carefully*). Rodman isn't going to stand for your making any trouble here, Wilkie.

WILKIE. I'm not going to make any and I'm going to leave it to you to tell him what's happened and to make him see it right.

ELLICOTT. I'll talk to him. (*Starts for door, stops, turns back to look at* WILKIE) You needn't wait. I should think you'd be needed downtown.

WILKIE. My boys know what to do. I'm waiting for Mrs. Rodman.

ELLICOTT (*after a second*). Why are you waiting for Mrs. Rodman?

WILKIE. Your guess should be pretty good. (*Looks at his watch*) She's taking a long time.

ELLICOTT (*after a second*). Where's Whalen?

WILKIE. In jail, I hope.

ELLICOTT. You think he—

WILKIE. I don't know. I'm only thinking for a little while. It don't hurt to have him in jail while I'm thinking. That—

(*The window doors open and* JULIE *comes quickly in. She looks as if she has been running. She starts for the door, ignores* WILKIE, *speaks to* ELLICOTT.)

JULIE. Where's Andy?

WILKIE. Mrs. Rodman. (*Sharply, as she does not turn*) Mrs. Rodman. (*Crosses in front of her*) I think Mr. Rodman's gone to bed. But I've been waiting for you. I thought you'd like to talk to me first.

JULIE. Yes. I'd like to talk to you. (*To* ELLICOTT) Do you know what's happened? (*He nods, slowly*) Do you know that he had that man's body put in the alley—

ELLICOTT (*sharply*). Julie. Those are dangerous guesses.

JULIE. They're not guesses. I was there.

ELLICOTT. I knew where you were. So your adventures finally carried you to an unpleasant place at an unpleasant hour? I—

WILKIE. I'd like to talk to Mrs. Rodman. (*Looks toward the hall*) Will you—?

ELLICOTT (*exiting*). Yes.

JULIE (*suddenly, furiously*). How dare you think you can do a thing like this in Mr. Rodman's name?

WILKIE. Mr. Ellicott was right. You are making very dangerous guesses.

JULIE. I am making no guesses. I was there to see and hear.

WILKIE. So you're going to tell your husband where you were?

JULIE (*staring at him*). Of course. (*She starts again for door.*)

WILKIE. I thought you would. That's why I waited. You're a noble lady, and I'm frightened of noble ladies. They usually land the men they know in cemeteries. (*As she opens the door*) And that's where you're getting ready to land Leo Whalen. (*She takes her hand off the door, stands without turning*) You're throwing a monkey-wrench, Mrs. Rodman, and it's going to hit both Whalen and Mr. Rodman.

JULIE (*softly, without turning*). What did you mean about —about Whalen?

WILKIE (*casually, sits down on arm of chair*). I meant several things. Now you tell me that you're going up-stairs to tell your husband that Whalen couldn't have had anything to do with Mossie, because you were with him?

JULIE. Yes.

WILKIE. And that's too bad. Right this minute Whalen's probably playing checkers— (*Smiles*) somewhere. But your way, he won't be for long.

JULIE. I don't know what you're talking about.

WILKIE. Then it's because you haven't thought about it. (*Pleasantly*) You see, Mrs. Rodman, *your husband* might believe you, *I* might believe you, but the police might take your noble gesture not as an alibi— (*Softly, as she turns*) but as a motive. It sounds foolish, since you and I know better, but they might think that— (*Makes a mocking gallant stop*) that Mossie caught you together and Whalen killed him for it. (*She has been staring at him. Then she moves past him, as if she were thinking*) That's my guess, and I've been in the busi-ness a long time. And even if my guess is wrong—and there's always a good chance that police will be boobs —he'll be through anyway. When the strikers found out he'd been carrying on with the boss's wife—

JULIE (*furiously*). He was not carrying on—

WILKIE (*smiles*). It's going to look like a sell out, and if he gets out all in one piece he's lucky.

JULIE (*defiance gone from her voice*). Why do you care what happens to him?

WILKIE. I don't. But I'm working for your husband. It's my job to keep him— (*Slowly*) and his wife out of trouble. (*Looks at his watch*) For a little while.

JULIE (*sits down slowly, then after a second*). Have you been telling me the truth? Will he be—

WILKIE. Oh, some of it's the truth, and some of it isn't. (*As he speaks,* CORA *opens the library door and comes in. She has on a warm woolen robe.*)

CORA (*crossing to bell, ringing it*). My milk and fruit aren't upstairs. We can't help it if he got killed. Whatever we do now isn't going to do him any good.

WILKIE (*to* JULIE). Yes. He'll be all right.

CORA. Henry just told me. He puts everything so badly, that it came as a shock. (HANNAH *appears carrying milk and a small plate of fruit*) Yes. You forgot it, didn't you?

HANNAH (*looking at* WILKIE, *curiously*). I didn't think you'd starve. (*Watches* CORA *drink the milk*) Funny how you drink it just like you need it— (*Motions to the window*) And those kids down town don't say anything.

CORA (*hysterical, childish voice*). Take it. Take it. Everything is begrudged me.

HANNAH (*to* JULIE, *gruffly, kindly*). Do you want something Mrs. Rodman?

JULIE (*softly, without looking up*). No, thank you, Hannah.

(ANDREW *and* ELLICOTT *enter from the Center doors.* ANDREW *comes directly into the room,* ELLICOTT *stands at the door.* JULIE *gets up as if she were going to turn to* ANDREW, *then slowly turns away again.*)

ANDREW (*to* WILKIE). I'm sorry about Dowel, Wilkie.

(*Then slowly*) But I won't pretend that I am not more sorry that murder happened in this town. We're not a tough people here, and we're not used to it.

WILKIE. Somebody was tough enough.

ANDREW. Yes. That's true, and that shocks me most. But that means that I pushed them into it, and that I'm responsible for it. I know these people here.

CORA. Do you know that they won't come around to murder us, too?

ANDREW (*to* WILKIE). This murder is for the police. Not for you and me. Your bill will be paid for the week, of course. Wilkie, I want you and your people out of here tonight.

JULIE (*turns quickly*). Yes. Yes. That's right for you, Andy—

CORA. Are you crazy?

ELLICOTT. I told you upstairs that the decision wasn't entirely up to you.

ANDREW (*to* ELLICOTT). But my part *is* up to me. (*To* WILKIE) I know I've been a hard man to work for. I didn't want you here, and I was right. We can't undo what's been done. But we can stop any further trouble.

WILKIE (*quietly*). I want the people who did it, Mr. Rodman.

ANDREW. I understand. The police will do that for you.

WILKIE (*pleasantly*). I don't think you do understand. I'm not talking about Mossie. I'm not crying about that. That was his job. He got paid for it. But somebody's been killed and that somebody worked for me. If I'm going to stay in business I can't let people get the idea they can slice up my folks. (*Less pleasantly*) And I won't. I can't make you let me keep this job. But I can't leave tonight. I'm the police here, Mr. Rodman, and if I wasn't worrying about finishing a job I was hired for, I'd have to think of that.

ANDREW (*with force*). *I won't have any more trouble.*

WILKIE. That's just what I'm trying to avoid for you. I want the guns and the knives and the bricks cleaned out, and no more murders. That's what you want too, isn't it? When the guns get put away in a nice, safe spot you and your boys can talk things over. But before I leave here, they're going to be put away. (*Gets up, looks at his watch*) That's the way it'll have to be, Mr. Rodman. No reason why things shouldn't be swell and peaceful. All I want is the guns, and if they don't intend to use 'em, they should be glad to give 'em up.

CORA. That's right. That's the nice way to do it—

ANDREW (*furiously*). No. That's not what I want done. No—

HANNAH. You can't let him do that. They can't walk in a house and take anything. Maybe the government can take things, but you— (*Motioning to the others in the room*) you can't take them. Why you let him go near one of their houses and they'll think you're crazy. You ain't got any rights they haven't got. They could come in here and take from you—

ELLICOTT. Andrew. We want this thing finished. It's gone on for weeks now. We've got to get it over soon—

JULIE (*to* ELLICOTT). Andy's right. There's been trouble enough.

CORA (*to* ANDREW). I don't know why you're so worried about *them*. You should protect us—

JULIE (*to* CORA). What are you talking about? How can you talk that way about people you went to school with, people you've known all your life—

HANNAH (*bitterly*). She never liked them. I know. I remember the school days.

ANDREW (*sharply*). Stop it. (*To* ELLICOTT) I won't have any more trouble.

ELLICOTT. He's told you there won't be any trouble—

(*As he speaks, there is the sudden, distant sound of firing. They all turn slowly to stare at the window.* WILKIE *puts*

his watch back into his pocket, moves toward his over-
coat, as the firing starts again, this time four or five shots
in rapid succession.)

WILKIE (*shakes his head*). That's too bad. Too bad. (*Starts*
for door) Rest easy, Miss Cora, the law will protect you.
(*He exits as they stand stiff and silent. Then suddenly,*
HANNAH *bursts into tears and begins to run from the*
room. The others do not move until CORA *rises, brushes*
off her robe, starts for the door.)

CORA. It is too bad. Well, all this excitement has made me
very tired and nervous. We all get far too worked up
about everything. (*As she gets to door*) Mr. Wilkie
knows more about these things than we do.

Curtain

ACT THREE

The same as Act One. Seven-thirty the next morning.

AT RISE: JULIE *is sitting in a chair, wrapped in a coat, her head thrown back. Several of the lamps are still lit, although the dull early light of a rainy morning is beginning to come through. The room is as it was at the end of the second act, but it has the mussed, unaired look of a morning-after living room. A few seconds after the rise of the curtain,* ANDREW, *in an overcoat, opens the Center doors. He comes in slowly, tired. Automatically, he puts the bunch of front door keys back into his pocket.*

JULIE (*without looking up*). It stopped a little while ago. Thank God. (*She shudders, looks up at him*) Are you all right, Andy?

ANDREW (*slowly*). Remember the last time we went riding early in the morning? Well, when we came to the high point on Tucker's Road, I thought that I didn't like to ride much anymore. When you don't know anything about poetry, you know how you feel sometimes when you see things? That's the way I always felt about the high point, because I could look down on the town and that made me happy. It always looks so scrubbed and clean and I thought the way I used to, when I was a kid: that I could stop in any house and have a good breakfast and they'd be glad to see me. (*Violently*) It doesn't look so pretty this morning. And they wouldn't be glad to have me for breakfast. (*Turns away, then quickly*) Yes, I'm all right. The partnership of Ellicott

144

and Wilkie practically locked me in the office. They
were busy and I'd only have been a nuisance.

JULIE (*again*). It stopped a while ago. Why did it stop?
Did you stop it?

ANDREW (*bitterly*). No. Not me. I didn't stop it. (*Slowly*)
People got hurt. I guess that's why it stopped.

JULIE (*gets up, starts to turn out lamps*). I've been using
guns all my life— (*Turns*) Who got hurt?

ANDREW. But the guns sound different when they're not
for fun, don't they? I don't know who got hurt. There
was some fuss around Corley's house and— (*Softly*)
around Firth's.

JULIE (*carefully*). Was Whalen—was Leo Whalen—was
he hurt?

ANDREW. He's in jail.

JULIE (*sharply*). In jail? What for? Wilkie told me—

ANDREW (*wearily*). I don't know. Something about that
fat man. They think he got into a fight with him and—
(*Sits down suddenly*) My God, I'm tired.

JULIE. He can't—I can't— (*She stands watching him, then
turns away as if she had changed her mind.*)

ANDREW. I tried to get down to Firth's, but they wouldn't
let me.

JULIE (*as if she were thinking of something else*). Maybe
it was just a fight. Maybe no one was hurt.

ANDREW. Maybe. Maybe.

JULIE (*suddenly, violently*). Why didn't you stop it? Why
did you let it go on like this? They talked you into it.
Why did you let them?

ANDREW (*smiles*). You make me sound like a child. And
you're right.

JULIE. You didn't want any of this. Why did you ever
have to start it? Then why didn't you stop it?

ANDREW. You asked me that before. (*Slowly, with force*)
There are a lot of reasons. The reason I tell myself is
that I couldn't stop anything. I owe money. A lot of

money. (*Bitterly*) I've been borrowing it for a long
time. I've borrowed on the factory and on this house
and on how many brushes I thought I could make in
five years—

JULIE. Oh. (*Carefully*) From Henry?

ANDREW. Oh, from everybody. From banks, from dealers—
Mostly from Henry.

JULIE. But why did you borrow it? We didn't need it—

ANDREW. Oh, I got pushed and pushed until—until I
couldn't help myself. (*Looks up at her, smiles*) Don't
worry about it. If I were another kind of man, I guess I
wouldn't have let that make any difference.

JULIE. I didn't know any of that. (*After a second*) There
are a lot of things we don't know about each other.

ANDREW. I suppose so, darling. That's the way with most
marriages, I guess.

JULIE. Andy. He can't stay in jail. He had nothing to do
with that man. I was with him last night when it happened. With Whalen.

ANDREW (*there is a pause. Then he slowly raises his head
to look at her, speaks quietly, carefully*). Then you
shouldn't let him stay in jail, Julie. That's not right.
(*Sharply*) Why are you acting so strange? Why didn't
you say so and get him out? There's nothing to be
ashamed of— (*She looks at him, nods, starts for windows*) Julie! (*She turns*) Never mind. I'll do it. (*He
rises as she watches him go to telephone. Into phone*)
Operator, call Judge Alcott's house. (*To* JULIE) Didn't
you know he'd been arrested?

JULIE. No. I'd been told—

ANDREW (*through her last words, into phone*). Jim? This
is Andrew Rodman. I want you to let Leo Whalen out
of jail immediately. We—er—I know where he was last
night. I'll be down later and explain. (*Sharply*) Jim. I
don't give a damn what anybody said. Let him out.
(*Wearily*) Yes. Yes. Thanks. No. Everything's all right.

JULIE. Thank you, Andy.

ANDREW. What are you thanking me for? (*As if for himself*) It's not important. You don't have to thank me.

JULIE (*quietly*). We've been dealing with people shrewder than we are.

ANDREW. Yes, I suppose so. I suppose that's it.

(*He passes his hand over his eyes. She makes a half motion toward him, changes her mind, turns away. A second later,* FIRTH *appears in the Center doors. He is dirty, bruised and tired-looking. In his hand is a gun. It is hanging at his side, as if he had forgotten it. Through all his speeches, through his exit, he holds the gun, unconscious that he has it. He stands in the doorway as they both look up.*)

FIRTH (*aimlessly*). The front door's open. The rain's coming in. (*Then shakes his head, bewildered*) I don't know what to do with you, Andrew.

JULIE (*in a whisper*). What is it, Tom? What is it?

(ANDREW *is standing by the desk, staring at* FIRTH.)

FIRTH. When you can't have a kid, that's bad. It makes a man feel funny, like he can't do anything, and not the way it should be. Specially a big man. You feel like you can't do what you're here for. (*Directly to* ANDREW) Remember once when you were at that college and you came home for Christmas and you came to a meal and after Miriam went up, I told you about it. I cried. Remember? (ANDREW *stares, nods slowly*) They hit her here. (*Puts his hand on the back of his head*) They said she threw a brick. A little kid threw a brick. They broke something.

ANDREW (*horror in his voice*). Where's Morris? Where is he?

FIRTH (*shakes his head as if he were drunk*). It's worse, I guess, when it's an adopted kid. You like it better that way. It makes up for the other thing and you like it better— (*Quietly*) Doc Morris? He's down there. Talking. Telling me what broke. Telling me why it happened. Talking and talking. Talking won't make her live again.

JULIE (*in a whisper*). Oh my God.

ANDREW (*looks up, softly*). They killed her. (*He nods slowly, puts his hand to his mouth, comes to* FIRTH, *takes him by the arm, then lets him go suddenly.*)

FIRTH. I don't know what to do. I beat everybody up for a while like crazy, telling myself what I was going to do to you. (*Violently, shaking his finger at* ANDREW) But I know you. I know you. It's better to tell you. It'll do worse for you. (*Suddenly, quietly*) I can't touch you, Andrew. I'm too tired. (*He sits down, as if he couldn't stand any longer. Then, as if it were an old familiar position between them,* ANDREW *sits opposite him. For a second, neither of them speaks. To* JULIE, *without looking up*) Once she saw you coming home from school and she told me you were pretty and I told her that you weren't half as pretty as her, and not an ounce as pretty as she'd grow to be. She laughed and got red and said she wasn't pretty and that I just liked her— (*Quietly, but with passion*) How can I go home? How can I live? How can I sit and eat with Miriam when only yesterday the kid sat between us—

JULIE (*choking, desperately, to* ANDREW). Do something for him.

ANDREW (*looks up at her in surprise*). What is there to do?

FIRTH. There's nothing to do. And I wouldn't let you do it. Ain't it funny how everything's changed? (ANDREW *nods*) I've known you all your life. All my life I worked for your father, or for you. I liked you more—more than anybody except my own, I guess. (*Puzzled*) I guess you can't know anybody. You must have been bad all along.

ANDREW (*leans over to touch his arm, nods*). I must have been.

JULIE. Tom, Andrew didn't know. He didn't know anything bad would happen—

FIRTH (*shakes his head*). That does a lot of good. (*Slowly*) If my kid had—had died any other way, you'd been the first I'd come to. I guess I never knew you. I don't understand that.

ANDREW (*simply*). I don't understand it, either.

FIRTH. Well, I can't fight anymore. I wouldn't know how. We ain't used to things like last night. Lundee got his hand shot off— (ANDREW *gets up and turns away sharply*) they burnt Carlsen's house all to pieces. We always used to play penny-ante there. We had to drag Berthe out, she was half crazy. She got burnt a little. (On *the next speech*, WHALEN *appears in the open Center doors.* EASTER *has him by the arm. All three people see him, and all three stare at him.* FIRTH's *voice becomes defiant, and the next speech is meant for* WHALEN, *but is said directly to* ANDREW) I don't know, but I guess I can speak for most of 'em. We can't fight you when you fight like this. It's our town more'n it's yours. Our folks came and built it. We can't watch it go like this. (*Gets up, wearily, quietly*) You call off your dogs. Keep 'em away from us, so there won't be no more killing. Get 'em out of here. I guess we'll have to go back to work.

EASTER. I picked him up trying to shove in the front door. There wouldn't been any door in a minute. He's in jail.

ANDREW (*to* EASTER). Get out of here.

EASTER. Oh. (*Looks at him and begins to exit.*)

WHALEN (*to* EASTER). What's Wilkie do? Keep you for the knife work? (*Motions toward hall*) Don't let you in the rough fights, huh? (EASTER *looks at him, exits.* WHALEN *comes into the room, smiles pleasantly*) Somebody got soft and let me out of jail. (*To* FIRTH) They told me where you were. I could have guessed.

FIRTH. They killed my kid.

WHALEN. I got all the news.

FIRTH. I feel bad. I can't fight anymore.

WHALEN. I heard you.

FIRTH (*angrily*). It wasn't your kid.

WHALEN (*angrily*). Didn't I tell you to give them what they wanted? Didn't I tell you not to fight?

FIRTH (*quietly*). You were right.

WHALEN (*looks at* FIRTH *and then at* RODMAN, *and laughs*). You both look the same kind of surprised. What are you surprised at? What the hell did you think he was after— (*To* ANDREW) Or do you still believe he came down to make brushes for you?

ANDREW (*slowly*). No.

WHALEN (*to* FIRTH). He wanted you to fight. He's been trying to make you fight for weeks. So as soon as he gets me out of the way for a couple of hours, you give him the fight he's been waiting for.

FIRTH. I couldn't do anything. When they come in talking and shoving, you don't think. Then they hit my kid— (*As if he hadn't said it before*) My girl's dead.

WHALEN (*shouting*). All right. She's dead. What are you trying to do, make Joan of Arc out of her? You wanted to fight—till the time came. Well, here's your time. If they killed my kid, I wouldn't come crawling back to any lousy job—

JULIE. There's been enough trouble. Don't let's make any more.

FIRTH. I don't want any more. We ain't used to this. We're tired. We don't care so much who wins, like you—

WHALEN (*quietly*). You *will* care. More than I do. For me, you're only one of a thousand fights. But you've only got one fight. This one. And someday you're going to have to settle it.

FIRTH. There's no use arguing. I'm trying to tell you why and what and you don't understand. (*Gets up, wearily.*)

WHALEN. Your why and what aren't any good to me.

FIRTH. I can't seem to say what I'm getting at. All I'm saying is that it came too quick. We didn't know about the things you know about. Everybody's got to see for themselves, I guess.

WHALEN. You haven't seen anything. They didn't scratch the surface here.

FIRTH (*nods his head*). Yeah? Well, maybe you were right, when you said that all the time. Wouldn't make any sense to hold out now. There wouldn't be any spirit to hold out with. I guess I'm worse than anybody, because of my kid. We'll go on back, make the best of it. (*Turns, quietly*) And if the time comes again, we'll be different. We'll know. I don't like him now. He killed my kid. They don't like him, either. We won't forget.

ANDREW (*with force, to* WHALEN). That's the truth. He's telling you the truth. They won't forget.

WHALEN (*to* FIRTH). He didn't kill your kid. Don't start that, or you'll get the wrong answer again. He hasn't much to do with it. He's got to go his way, and you've got to go yours. And they're not the same way.

FIRTH (*softly*). We used to be good friends.

WHALEN. I know. And you're as good as he is. It says so in the book. Until the time comes. Look. You're on one side. He's on the other. That's lesson number one. Don't let 'em tell you that because your grandfather voted for Jefferson, you're any different from some Polack in Pittsburgh whose grandfather couldn't write his name. You're on the same side the Polack is, and that's where you belong.

FIRTH. Well, maybe we'll try again some day.

WHALEN (*smiles, as if he were pleased*). I hope so. And the guy they send in my place, you give him a better chance.

FIRTH (*starts for door*). You coming? They'd like to see you.

WHALEN (*shakes his head*). No. I'm going to be busy for a while.

ANDREW (*softly*). Tom, would you let me do anything for you and Miriam and the others?

FIRTH (*without turning, puzzled*). What? (*Laughs, then quietly*) Stay away from downtown, Andrew. For a while. (JULIE, *watching the effect of this on* ANDREW, *moves to him, puts a hand on his sleeve.* FIRTH *speaks to* WHALEN) Well, if it comes again, I hope they'll be sending you.

WHALEN (*simply, sincerely*). I hope so, too. (FIRTH *exits. No one speaks for a second*) Well, it's time for me to see whether your pink-cheeked policeman is holding me for murder or because I've got two legs. He's having a tough time deciding. (*He has started for door.*)

JULIE (*quickly*). Wait. You don't have to go back there. They won't hold you— (*On her speech, he has turned.*)

ANDREW (*who is still looking at the door, as if he were thinking of* FIRTH). I've spoken to Judge Alcott. There's no need for you to go back. Everything will be straightened out.

WHALEN (*carefully*). Straightened out, Mr. Rodman?

JULIE (*after a second, softly*). I've told my husband that I was in your office last night when it happened.

WHALEN (*has turned to look at* ANDREW, *and then back to* JULIE). Is that what you are going to say?

JULIE. Yes. (*Not looking at him*) I wanted to before. But —but I was told that you weren't in any trouble, and that I'd be doing you harm.

WHALEN (*quietly*). You were told right. (*Looks quickly at them both*) Please. Don't do that. They've got nothing on me, and they know it. A few days of nuisance, maybe, and that's all. That's my job. I don't want trouble for myself, ever, but when it comes it's part of my work.

JULIE (*looking at him*). Why don't you want any help from us? From me?

WHALEN. It's not my job to take help from the boss, or—
(*Slowly*) the boss's wife. I can't take chances on anybody thinking I do.

(WILKIE *comes in through Center doors.*)

WILKIE. Good morning. (*To* ANDREW) Glad to see you
here. We were worried about you. (*To* WHALEN) Good
morning.

WHALEN. Had a good breakfast?

WILKIE. Pretty good. I'm like the English, I eat big in the
mornings.

WHALEN. I thought so. You look like you've been licking
the cream.

WILKIE. You need some breakfast?

WHALEN (*laughs*). No, thank you. I'm eating on the
county. With the marshal.

WILKIE (*looking toward* JULIE, *then back to* WHALEN).
That. Oh. That's yokel stuff. They got nothing to hold
you on.

WHALEN. They held me long enough to make it easy for
you.

WILKIE. My break this time. Maybe yours the next.

(ELLICOTT *appears in the hall. Comes in, throws his coat
and hat on a chair.*)

ELLICOTT (*looking at* JULIE *and* ANDREW, *quietly*). Good
morning.

WHALEN (*to* WILKIE). Your spick outside looks like a knife
thrower to me. What do you think?

WILKIE (*seriously*). I don't know. Maybe so. You can't
keep track of everybody. I don't like to see a man get
buried without finding who did it— If you know anything—

WHALEN (*laughs*). I don't know anything. Some other
time. (*Crosses to* JULIE *and says kindly, with meaning*)
Don't worry about last night. There's no honor involved
in any of it. And if there was it wouldn't be practical

to remember it. (*Holds out his hand to her*) Good-bye, Mrs. Rodman.

JULIE (*touches his hand, speaks softly*). Good-bye.

WHALEN (*to* ANDREW). Good-bye.

ANDREW. Good-bye.

(WHALEN *exits.*)

ELLICOTT (*to* JULIE). You look tired. (*No answer. He looks at his watch*) Almost eight o'clock. I haven't been up this early in a long time.

WILKIE. Does you good sometimes.

JULIE (*to* ANDREW). What are they talking about? What are they cheerful about?

ANDREW (*slowly*). I don't know.

JULIE (*to* ELLICOTT). Did you have a good time? Was it more exciting than being at the club? Is it fun to see a killing?

ELLICOTT (*sharply*). Stop it. (*After a second*) We've been fighting your husband's battles for him.

ANDREW. Yes. That's quite true. The delicate prince in his ivory tower— (*Carefully*) was carefully protected from the dust and din of battle. You are noble warriors and you've done a noble night's work. (*Sharply to* ELLICOTT) I'll see to it that when the history is written, it won't be mentioned that you were fighting for yourself, too.

ELLICOTT. I knew nothing about the child until Morris told me.

WILKIE. I knew you were going to feel this way, Mr. Rodman. But nobody wanted any trouble. Sometimes these things can't be helped. I understand it's going to be settled now and I'm glad for you, and glad for me. (*Smiles*) I don't like to take money for losing, and for a while—

ANDREW. Send us your bill. We'll mail you a check.

WILKIE. Yes, sir. (*Goes to him, puts out his hand*) Thank you, Mr. Rodman—

ANDREW (*ignores the hand*). That's all. Good-bye.

WILKIE (*looks down at his hand, laughs*). Well, that's your business. But I want to tell you, I've worked for a lot of men, some of them deacons of the church who were breaking strikes for the good of America, but I never worked for a man before who believed I could come in, run his factory, and break his strike without walking on anybody's toes. You actually believed that. I come in to break strikes. That's my business. It's *not* a tea room business. You ought to have known that. Well, I break your strike and now you're sitting on the right hand of Jesus, crying because it doesn't smell of violets.

ELLICOTT (*sharply*). Does this speech go on your bill?

WILKIE. No. I'm giving it free of charge. If you didn't like what I was doing, you should have stopped it. But you didn't stop it, and that doesn't leave you in any place to call names. The boys standing in your shoes need the boys standing in mine. But the next time I have to waste weeks acting like it was a tea party, the next time I have to nurse along a blind man— (*Laughs carefully*) a blind man who calls the turns when they're over—I'm going to charge extra. (*Picks up his hat as he passes* ELLICOTT) There'll be expense items on my bill.

ELLICOTT. You'll get your check.

WILKIE. Good morning.

(*There is a long silence.* ELLICOTT *lights a cigarette, looks at* JULIE, *moves uncomfortably about the room.*)

ELLICOTT. Well, Andy— (*No answer*) What's the matter with you?

ANDREW (*unpleasantly*). Very little. I'm over here thinking how I don't like being a murderer. You are fortunate. You don't seem to mind so much.

ELLICOTT (*angrily*). I knew nothing about the child. But I did know there had to be trouble. (*Carefully*) And I'm not willing to act the saint about it now.

ANDREW. That's wise for you. I hope the little trouble last night won't keep you from White Sulphur.

ELLICOTT. It won't. I'm going tonight.

ANDREW. I wish you a happy journey, and I hope that your dreams are free.

ELLICOTT (*angrily*). If it makes you feel better to enjoy your conscience, go ahead. There was a lot of truth in what that bum just said.

ANDREW. Yes. There was. But did he know that *you* were also his employer? You own so much of me now— (JULIE *has turned to look at them as* ANDREW *breaks off.* ANDREW *sees her, and speaks as if he had been thinking of her all along*) Why were you with Whalen last night?

(ELLICOTT *turns quickly to look at her.*)

JULIE. You don't want to hear about it, Andy.

(ANDREW *begins to speak as* LUCY *comes into the room, carrying a small table with breakfast on it. She is followed by* CORA, *in a bathrobe.*)

CORA. The noise that's been going on here this morning. (*Puts up a commanding hand*) Now. Please. Please. Don't tell me about last night. I've heard all about it. Lucy had it from Morris' nurse, and insisted upon telling it to me. It's awful. Simply awful. (*Leans over, smells the chocolate pot. Then to* LUCY) Did Hannah make this chocolate? Take it back.

LUCY. No, ma'am. I made it. Hannah's out.

CORA. Out? At this time of the morning? (*To everybody as* LUCY *exits*) What do you think of that? Out at this time of the morning.

ELLICOTT. Do you have to have your breakfast here? In this room?

CORA (*as she starts to eat*). Mind your business. I've had it here for thirty years. I shall continue—

ANDREW (*who has been staring at* JULIE, *paying no attention to* CORA). Julie! Why were you in Whalen's office?

JULIE (*desperately*). Andy, I don't want to— Don't let's talk about it now.

ANDREW. Julie. Answer me.

JULIE. I wanted to go away with him. I wanted to tell him that.

(ANDREW *rises from his chair, and then, slowly, sits down again.* CORA *puts down her spoon suddenly.*)

ELLICOTT. My God, you're a foolish woman.

JULIE (*quietly*). That wasn't foolish. It was what I wanted. It would have been right for me.

CORA (*looking around the room, in a daze*). Is she crazy?

ELLICOTT. But he didn't want you to go away with him?

JULIE. No.

ANDREW. Leave her alone.

CORA (*springing from her chair*). Look at you. So you're just finding out about your wife, are you? Then you're the only one who is. She's been doing this for years.

ELLICOTT. Cora. Cora—

CORA (*ignoring the interruption, to* ANDREW). Now she's decided to tell you, finally. (*With great scorn*) "Leave her alone" you tell him. How can he leave her alone? All that's his business, too.

ELLICOTT (*furiously*). Cora, I tell you—

JULIE (*quietly*). Let her say it. She's wanted to for a long time.

CORA. Yes. I could have told you about them a long time ago. She's just as much Henry's business as she is yours. Just as much. I knew. I made it my business to know. He's crazy about her. (*Shrieking*) You fool. You fool. All these years—

ANDREW (*he has been staring at her, then as if he were speaking to an insane person*). Control yourself. Get away from my desk. Go back to your breakfast.

CORA (*to* JULIE). You were never fooling me. Never for a minute fooling me.

JULIE. I'm glad.

ELLICOTT (*after a long silence, while* CORA *paces around restlessly*). Well, it's a nasty story, Andy. Your best friend and—

CORA. And his wife.

ANDREW (*looks up at* ELLICOTT, *smiles*). In what strange ways you think of things. Did you read somewhere that it was wicked to sleep with your best friend's wife? Was it a vulgar book you read it in? Or does the fact that it was *my* wife make it more sinful, and therefore more pleasant?

CORA (*to* JULIE). I knew what you were doing to my brother. I knew every bit of it.

JULIE (*comes toward* ANDREW, *slowly*). I wasn't doing anything to you. Not the way she means. (*She sits down, opposite him*) Andy. I wasn't in love with you when I married you. That was what I did to you. The rest had only to do with me. I didn't want to get married. I didn't want to live here. I wanted to make something for myself, something that would be right for me. I told you all that when we were young. I thought marriage would be all that for me. But it wasn't. (*Gets up*) And when I found it wasn't, I took the wrong way. I knew I should have stopped. But I thought someday I might find somebody who—

ELLICOTT. You found him, didn't you?

JULIE (*to* ANDREW). Yes. I found him. It didn't do me any good. I was going to tell you that, Andy. That I thought you ought to know. But the rest—the rest was just me and just exactly as shabby as she's made it sound. (*Leans across the desk, suddenly*) Darling, I told you the truth. I wasn't in love with you when we were married. I'm not in love with you now. But I love you. Not the way I want to. But another way. More than anybody I've ever known.

ANDREW (*softly*). Julie. Julie. (*Motioning toward* CORA

and ELLICOTT) Don't listen to what they say. I know what you mean. You have done nothing to me.

CORA. No? That's a strange way of looking at it. Done nothing to you. She's broken you, that's what she's done. She's why you owe money— (JULIE *has turned and is staring at her*) to Henry and to everybody else. She's why—

ELLICOTT (*violently*). Is that your business, too?

CORA. No, thank you. It's not my money he's lost. But you needn't think I didn't know. I knew where it was going. The year her family lost their money and how her mother had to have the best doctors and how her brother had to go to Paris to study, and how she always had to have trips and clothes, and a year in Europe— (*With scorn*) to make her happy. Thousands and thousands he had to borrow for it—

JULIE (*suddenly, her voice hysterical*). I didn't know that. I swear I didn't. We always had so much. Why didn't you tell me?

ANDREW. It wasn't your business. It isn't now. I wanted it that way. I suppose, underneath, I always knew. I wanted to keep you. That was my way of trying. You had nothing to do with it. Nothing at all.

CORA. And didn't it ever occur to you that was *why* Henry lent you the money. That *she* was the reason he lent you the money? Why shouldn't he—

ELLICOTT (*quietly*). That's not true.

ANDREW. No. It's not true. He made a good investment in my business. And he protected his investment, last night.

JULIE (*in a whisper*). That's why you couldn't stop— that's why—

ANDREW. That's the reason I tell myself. It's not a good one. (*Suddenly starts to laugh. They all watch him. Then, after a second, he leans on his desk, smiles, talks to* JULIE) Isn't it strange? The three of us— (*Pointing*

to CORA *and* ELLICOTT) have known each other since
we were born. My sister— (*Bows*) my best friend—
my best friend. We grew up in this town knowing all
about each other. Henry and I, for example, know that
Cora, all her life—

CORA. Be still.

ANDREW. All her life has been, well, slightly ill. Then
Cora and I know all about Henry, the rich and worldly
Henry, and all the very legal manipulating he does with
his money and with his life. They, on the other hand,
Cora and Henry know all about me. They've always
thought me a soft, weak man and they've always had
contempt for me. Hannah shares the secrets of all of us.
That's why Cora can't get rid of her, isn't it, Cora? Ten
years ago you married me and came here, and so you
were one of us, too. Our married life always had an
audience—my sister and my best friend and my cook.
All the things we knew about each other, all the things
that accumulate through a lifetime, or through ten
years, sat quietly, waiting for us, while we lived politely
and tried, like most people, to push them out of sight.
Polite and blind, we lived.

JULIE (*softly*). And then early one morning, it all blew up.

ANDREW. You don't understand. It blew up last night. All
the things we know, were there to know a long time
ago. But we were polite. We were doing our best to live
happily. Well, there's no need for being polite anymore.
You were my wife. (*To* ELLICOTT) You and I and Cora
made me a murderer. (*To* CORA) You hate me and I
hated you from the day I was old enough to think about
you. You hate my wife and you have always hated her.
(*To* ELLICOTT) Since we were old enough to play together, you've never had anything but toleration for
me—and I've never had anything but contempt for
you. That's a lot of hate, isn't it? It was all there before.
(*Pleasantly*) It can be said now.

ELLICOTT (*after a moment's silence*). I'm sorry all this had to come now, Andy. That's straight. (*Motioning toward* CORA) And I'm sorry it had to come from Cora.

CORA (*calmly*). I think both of you are drunk.

ELLICOTT (*to* JULIE). Do you want me to stay?

JULIE. What? Oh no. (*He looks at her for a second and then exits quickly. After his exit, nobody speaks. Then after a second,* JULIE *says softly*) What do you want me to do, Andy?

ANDREW (*after a second, puzzled*). What do you mean?

JULIE. Do you want me to go away? Do you want a divorce?

ANDREW (*quietly, sadly, reproachfully*). Oh, Julie. Even you haven't understood. I'm not sitting here in tears for you or me. A year ago, a month ago, what you told me about you, about us, would have broken my heart. It will again, but not now. Because last night I lost the place and the land where I was born. (*Laughs bitterly*) I can't go downtown, he said. It isn't safe. It isn't safe for *me* to go into that town. You see what I mean. I lost what I thought I was. (*Softly*) I lost Firth his child. (*Suddenly, violently*) Murder is worse than lost love. Murder is worse than a broken heart.

JULIE (*softly*). It is. Yes.

ANDREW. They said it would come again. I think they're right. I'll be hardened to it by then, I guess, and I won't mind what happens. In a little while I'll think about us. About how I lost you, and how I never had you, and how much I loved you. But now it seems so small beside what else has happened here. (*Smiles*) And it seems almost right that it should be this way and that you should have told me this morning. It was right that it should have come. I don't know what you should do, Julie. Go to White Sulphur, if you like.

JULIE. That would be what I deserved.

ANDREW. That's foolish. You don't deserve anything. Go

anywhere you like. Or nowhere. Whatever is left here
is as much yours as it is mine. *That's* your punishment—
if you're looking for it. For the rest of your life, my wife,
for all the days to come— (*Laughs*) You can have half
of all this. Half of me. I'm sorry for you. (*He has mo-
tioned with his arm around the room, toward* CORA.
*Suddenly his face is dead and heavy, and he sits down
in the desk chair.*)

JULIE (*turns and stares curiously at* CORA's *cabinet. She
rises*). Your animals weren't touched, Cora. They're
still all right. (*She exits.*)

CORA (*after a long silence, she pours herself some chocolate, and speaks timidly*). Things went entirely too far.
It comes from everybody getting too excited. Now, you
go get some sleep and nothing will seem as bad when
you wake up. (*No answer. She takes a bite of toast*)
People said a lot of things they didn't mean, Andy.
(*Consolingly*) A lot of things they didn't mean. I'm
sure of that.

ANDREW (*doesn't answer for a minute. Then he raises his
head and with great force*). Take your breakfast out of
here. (*She rises hurriedly, frightened*) Get out. (*As
she moves toward the door*) Get out.

Curtain

THE LITTLE FOXES

"Take us the foxes, the little foxes,
that spoil the vines; for our vines
have tender grapes."

FOR

ARTHUR KOBER AND LOUIS KRONENBERGER

WHO HAVE BEEN MY GOOD FRIENDS

The Little Foxes was first produced at the National Theatre, New York City, on February 15, 1939, with the following cast:

(In order of their appearance)

ADDIE	ABBIE MITCHELL
CAL	JOHN MARRIOTT
BIRDIE HUBBARD	PATRICIA COLLINGE
OSCAR HUBBARD	CARL BENTON REID
LEO HUBBARD	DAN DURYEA
REGINA GIDDENS	TALLULAH BANKHEAD
WILLIAM MARSHALL	LEE BAKER
BENJAMIN HUBBARD	CHARLES DINGLE
ALEXANDRA GIDDENS	FLORENCE WILLIAMS
HORACE GIDDENS	FRANK CONROY

Produced and staged by HERMAN SHUMLIN

Settings designed by HOWARD BAY

Costumes designed by ALINE BERNSTEIN

SCENE

The scene of the play is the living room of the Giddens house, in a small town in the South.

ACT ONE
The Spring of 1900, evening.

ACT TWO
A week later, early morning.

ACT THREE
Two weeks later, late afternoon.

There has been no attempt to write Southern dialect. It is to be understood that the accents are Southern.

ACT ONE

SCENE: *The living room of the Giddens home, in a small town in the deep South, the spring of 1900. Upstage is a staircase leading to the second story. Upstage, right, are double doors to the dining room. When these doors are open we see a section of the dining room and the furniture. Upstage, left, is an entrance hall with a coat-rack and umbrella stand. There are large lace-curtained windows on the left wall. The room is lit by a center gas chandelier and painted china oil lamps on the tables. Against the wall is a large piano. Downstage, right, are a high couch, a large table, several chairs. Against the left back wall are a table and several chairs. Near the window there are a smaller couch and tables. The room is good-looking, the furniture expensive; but it reflects no particular taste. Everything is of the best and that is all.*

AT RISE: ADDIE, *a tall, nice-looking Negro woman of about fifty-five, is closing the windows. From behind the closed dining-room doors there is the sound of voices. After a second,* CAL, *a middle-aged Negro, comes in from the entrance hall carrying a tray with glasses and a bottle of port.* ADDIE *crosses, takes the tray from him, puts it on table, begins to arrange it.*

ADDIE (*pointing to the bottle*). You gone stark out of your head?

CAL. No, smart lady, I ain't. Miss Regina told me to get out that bottle. (*Points to bottle*) That very bottle for the mighty honored guest. When Miss Regina changes orders like that you can bet your dime she got her reason.

ADDIE (*points to dining room*). Go on. You'll be needed.

CAL. Miss Zan she had two helpings frozen fruit cream and she tell that honored guest, she tell him that you make the best frozen fruit cream in all the South.

ADDIE (*smiles, pleased*). Did she? Well, see that Belle saves a little for her. She like it right before she go to bed. Save a few little cakes, too, she like—

(*The dining room doors are opened and quickly closed again by* BIRDIE HUBBARD. BIRDIE *is a woman of about forty, with a pretty, well-bred, faded face. Her movements are usually nervous and timid, but now, as she comes running into the room, she is gay and excited.* CAL *turns to* BIRDIE.)

BIRDIE. Oh, Cal. (*Closes door*) I want you to get one of the kitchen boys to run home for me. He's to look in my desk drawer and— (*To* ADDIE) My, Addie. What a good supper! Just as good as good can be.

ADDIE. You look pretty this evening, Miss Birdie, and young.

BIRDIE (*laughing*). Me, young? (*Turns back to* CAL) Maybe you better find Simon and tell him to do it himself. He's to look in my desk, the left drawer, and bring my music album right away. Mr. Marshall is very anxious to see it because of his father and the opera in Chicago. (*To* ADDIE) Mr. Marshall is such a polite man with his manners and very educated and cultured and I've told him all about how my mama and papa used to go to Europe for the music— (*Laughs. To* ADDIE) Imagine going all the way to Europe just to listen to music. Wouldn't that be nice, Addie? Just to sit there and listen and— (*Turns and steps to* CAL) *Left* drawer, Cal. Tell him that twice because he forgets. And tell him not to let any of the things drop out of the album and to bring it right in here when he comes back.

(*The dining-room doors are opened and quickly closed by* OSCAR HUBBARD. *He is a man in his late forties.*)

CAL. Yes'm. But Simon he won't get it right. But I'll tell him.

BIRDIE. Left drawer, Cal, and tell him to bring the blue book and—

OSCAR (*sharply*). Birdie.

BIRDIE (*turning nervously*). Oh, Oscar. I was just sending Simon for my music album.

OSCAR (*to* CAL). Never mind about the album. Miss Birdie has changed her mind.

BIRDIE. But, really, Oscar. Really I promised Mr. Marshall. I—

(CAL *looks at them, exits.*)

OSCAR. Why do you leave the dinner table and go running about like a child?

BIRDIE (*trying to be gay*). But, Oscar, Mr. Marshall said most specially he *wanted* to see my album. I told him about the time Mama met Wagner, and Mrs. Wagner gave her the signed program and the big picture. Mr. Marshall wants to see that. Very, very much. We had such a nice talk and—

OSCAR (*taking a step to her*). You have been chattering to him like a magpie. You haven't let him be for a second. I can't think he came South to be bored with you.

BIRDIE (*quickly, hurt*). He wasn't bored. I don't believe he was bored. He's a very educated, cultured gentleman. (*Her voice rises*) I just don't believe it. You always talk like that when I'm having a nice time.

OSCAR (*turning to her, sharply*). You have had too much wine. Get yourself in hand now.

BIRDIE (*drawing back, about to cry, shrilly*). What am I doing? I am not doing anything. What am I doing?

OSCAR (*taking a step to her, tensely*). I said get yourself in hand. Stop acting like a fool.

BIRDIE (*turns to him, quietly*). I don't believe he was

bored. I just don't believe it. Some people like music and like to talk about it. That's all I was doing.

(LEO HUBBARD *comes hurrying through the dining-room door. He is a young man of twenty, with a weak kind of good looks.*)

LEO. Mama! Papa! They are coming in now.

OSCAR (*softly*). Sit down, Birdie. Sit down now. (BIRDIE *sits down, bows her head as if to hide her face.*)

(*The dining-room doors are opened by* CAL. *We see people beginning to rise from the table.* REGINA GIDDENS *comes in with* WILLIAM MARSHALL. REGINA *is a handsome woman of forty.* MARSHALL *is forty-five, pleasant-looking, self-possessed. Behind them comes* ALEXANDRA GIDDENS, *a very pretty, rather delicate-looking girl of seventeen. She is followed by* BENJAMIN HUBBARD, *fifty-five, with a large jovial face and the light graceful movements that one often finds in large men.*)

REGINA. Mr. Marshall, I think you're trying to console me. Chicago may be the noisiest, dirtiest city in the world but I should still prefer it to the sound of our horses and the smell of our azaleas. I should like crowds of people, and theaters, and lovely women— *Very* lovely women, Mr. Marshall?

MARSHALL (*crossing to sofa*). In Chicago? Oh, I suppose so. But I can tell you this: I've never dined there with *three* such lovely ladies.

(ADDIE *begins to pass the port.*)

BEN. Our Southern women are well favored.

LEO (*laughs*). But one must go to Mobile for the ladies, sir. Very elegant worldly ladies, too.

BEN (*looks at him very deliberately*). Worldly, eh? *Worldly*, did you say?

OSCAR (*hastily, to* LEO). Your uncle Ben means that worldliness is not a mark of beauty in any woman.

LEO (*quickly*). Of course, Uncle Ben. I didn't mean—

MARSHALL. Your port is excellent, Mrs. Giddens.

REGINA. Thank you, Mr. Marshall. We had been saving that bottle, hoping we could open it just for you.

ALEXANDRA (*as* ADDIE *comes to her with the tray*). Oh. May I *really*, Addie?

ADDIE. Better ask Mama.

ALEXANDRA. May I, Mama?

REGINA (*nods, smiles*). In Mr. Marshall's honor.

ALEXANDRA (*smiles*). Mr. Marshall, this will be the first taste of port I've ever had.

(ADDIE *serves* LEO.)

MARSHALL. No one ever had their first taste of a better port. (*He lifts his glass in a toast; she lifts hers; they both drink*) Well, I suppose it is all true, Mrs. Giddens.

REGINA. What is true?

MARSHALL. That you Southerners occupy a unique position in America. You live better than the rest of us, you eat better, you drink better. I wonder you find time, or want to find time, to do business.

BEN. A great many Southerners don't.

MARSHALL. Do all of you live here together?

REGINA. Here with me? (*Laughs*) Oh, no. My brother Ben lives next door. My brother Oscar and his family live in the next square.

BEN. But we are a very close family. We've always wanted it that way.

MARSHALL. That is very pleasant. Keeping your family together to share each other's lives. My family moves around too much. My children seem never to come home. Away at school in the winter; in the summer, Europe with their mother—

REGINA (*eagerly*). Oh, yes. Even down here we read about Mrs. Marshall in the society pages.

MARSHALL. I dare say. She moves about a great deal. And all of you are part of the same business? Hubbard Sons?

BEN (*motions to* OSCAR). Oscar and me. (*Motions to* REGINA) My sister's good husband is a banker.

MARSHALL (*looks at* REGINA, *surprised*). Oh.

REGINA. I am so sorry that my husband isn't here to meet you. He's been very ill. He is at Johns Hopkins. But he will be home soon. We think he is getting better now.

LEO. I work for Uncle Horace. (REGINA *looks at him*) I mean I work for Uncle Horace at his bank. I keep an eye on things while he's away.

REGINA (*smiles*). Really, Leo?

BEN (*looks at* LEO, *then to* MARSHALL). Modesty in the young is as excellent as it is rare. (*Looks at* LEO *again.*)

OSCAR (*to* LEO). Your uncle means that a young man should speak more modestly.

LEO (*hastily, taking a step to* BEN). Oh, I didn't mean, sir—

MARSHALL. Oh, Mrs. Hubbard. Where's that Wagner autograph you promised to let me see? My train will be leaving soon and—

BIRDIE. The autograph? Oh. Well. Really, Mr. Marshall, I didn't mean to chatter so about it. Really I— (*Nervously, looking at* OSCAR) You must excuse me. I didn't get it because, well, because I had—I—I had a little headache and—

OSCAR. My wife is a miserable victim of headaches.

REGINA (*quickly*). Mr. Marshall said at supper that he would like you to play for him, Alexandra.

ALEXANDRA (*who has been looking at* BIRDIE). It's not I who play well, sir. It's my aunt. She plays just wonderfully. She's my teacher. (*Rises. Eagerly*) May we play a duet? May we, Mama?

BIRDIE (*taking* ALEXANDRA'S *hand*). Thank you, dear. But I have my headache now. I—

OSCAR (*sharply*). Don't be stubborn, Birdie. Mr. Marshall wants you to play.

MARSHALL. Indeed I do. If your headache isn't—

BIRDIE (*hesitates, then gets up, pleased*). But I'd like to, sir. Very much. (*She and* ALEXANDRA *go to the piano.*)

MARSHALL. It's very remarkable how you Southern aristocrats have kept together. Kept together and kept what belonged to you.

BEN. You misunderstand, sir. Southern aristocrats have *not* kept together and have *not* kept what belonged to them.

MARSHALL (*laughs, indicates room*). You don't call this keeping what belongs to you?

BEN. But we are not aristocrats. (*Points to* BIRDIE *at the piano*) Our brother's wife is the only one of us who belongs to the Southern aristocracy.

(BIRDIE *looks toward* BEN.)

MARSHALL (*smiles*). My information is that you people have been here, and solidly here, for a long time.

OSCAR. And so we have. Since our great-grandfather.

BEN (*smiles*). Who was *not* an aristocrat, like Birdie's.

MARSHALL (*a little sharply*). You make great distinctions.

BEN. Oh, they have been made for us. And maybe they are important distinctions. (*Leans forward, intimately*) Now you take Birdie's family. When my great-grandfather came here they were the highest-tone plantation owners in this state.

LEO (*steps to* MARSHALL. *Proudly*). My mother's grandfather was *governor* of the state before the war.

OSCAR. They owned the plantation, Lionnet. You may have heard of it, sir?

MARSHALL (*laughs*). No, I've never heard of anything but brick houses on a lake, and cotton mills.

BEN. Lionnet in its day was the best cotton land in the South. It still brings us in a fair crop. (*Sits back*) Ah, they were great days for those people—even when I can remember. They had the best of everything. (BIRDIE *turns to them*) Cloth from Paris, trips to Europe, horses you can't raise any more, niggers to lift their fingers—

BIRDIE (*suddenly*). We were good to our people. Everybody knew that. We were better to them than—

(MARSHALL *looks up at* BIRDIE.)

REGINA. Why, Birdie. You aren't playing.

BEN. But when the war comes these fine gentlemen ride off and leave the cotton, *and* the women, to rot.

BIRDIE. My father was killed in the war. He was a fine soldier, Mr. Marshall. A fine man.

REGINA. Oh, certainly, Birdie. A famous soldier.

BEN (*to* BIRDIE). But that isn't the tale I am telling Mr. Marshall. (*To* MARSHALL) Well, sir, the war ends. (BIRDIE *goes back to piano*) Lionnet is almost ruined, and the sons finish ruining it. And there were thousands like them. Why? (*Leans forward*) Because the Southern aristrocrat can adapt himself to nothing. Too high-tone to try.

MARSHALL. Sometimes it is difficult to learn new ways. (BIRDIE *and* ALEXANDRA *begin to play*. MARSHALL *leans forward, listening*.)

BEN. Perhaps, perhaps. (*He sees that* MARSHALL *is listening to the music. Irritated, he turns to* BIRDIE *and* ALEXANDRA *at the piano, then back to* MARSHALL) You're right, Mr. Marshall. It is difficult to learn new ways. But maybe that's why it's profitable. *Our* grandfather and *our* father learned the new ways and learned how to make them pay. (*Smiles nastily*) *They* were in trade. Hubbard Sons, Merchandise. Others, Birdie's family, for example, looked down on them. (*Settles back in chair*) To make a long story short, Lionnet now belongs to *us*. (BIRDIE *stops playing*) Twenty years ago we took over their land, their cotton, and their daughter. (BIRDIE *rises and stands stiffly by the piano*. MARSHALL, *who has been watching her, rises*.)

MARSHALL. May I bring you a glass of port, Mrs. Hubbard?

BIRDIE (*Softly*). No, thank you, sir. You are most polite.

REGINA (*Sharply, to* BEN). You are boring Mr. Marshall with these ancient family tales.

BEN. I hope not. I hope not. I am trying to make an important point— (*Bows to* MARSHALL) for our future business partner.

OSCAR (*to* MARSHALL). My brother always says that it's folks like us who have struggled and fought to bring to our land some of the prosperity of your land.

BEN. Some people call that patriotism.

REGINA (*laughs gaily*). I hope you don't find my brothers too obvious, Mr. Marshall. I'm afraid they mean that this is the time for the ladies to leave the gentlemen to talk business.

MARSHALL (*hastily*). Not at all. We settled everything this afternoon. (MARSHALL *looks at his watch*) I have only a few minutes before I must leave for the train. (*Smiles at her*) And I insist they be spent with you.

REGINA. *And* with another glass of port.

MARSHALL. Thank you.

BEN (*to* REGINA). My sister is right. (*To* MARSHALL) I am a plain man and I am trying to say a plain thing. A man ain't only in business for what he can get out of it. It's got to give him something here. (*Puts hand to his breast*) That's every bit as true for the nigger picking cotton for a silver quarter, as it is for you and me. (REGINA *gives* MARSHALL *a glass of port*) If it don't give him something here, then he don't pick the cotton right. Money isn't all. Not by three shots.

MARSHALL. Really? Well, I always thought it was a great deal.

REGINA. And so did I, Mr. Marshall.

MARSHALL (*leans forward. Pleasantly, but with meaning*). Now you don't have to convince me that you are the right people for the deal. I wouldn't be here if you hadn't convinced me six months ago. You want the mill here, and I want it here. It isn't my business to find out why you want it.

BEN. To bring the machine to the cotton, and not the cotton to the machine.

MARSHALL (*amused*). You have a turn for neat phrases, Hubbard. Well, however grand your reasons are, mine are simple: I want to make money and I believe I'll make it on you. (*As* BEN *starts to speak, he smiles*) Mind you, I have no objections to more high-minded reasons. They are mighty valuable in business. It's fine to have partners who so closely follow the teachings of Christ. (*Gets up*) And now I must leave for my train.

REGINA. I'm sorry you won't stay over with us, Mr. Marshall, but you'll come again. Any time you like.

BEN (*motions to* LEO, *indicating the bottle*). Fill them up, boy, fill them up. (LEO *moves around filling the glasses as* BEN *speaks*) Down here, sir, we have a strange custom. We drink the *last* drink for a toast. That's to prove that the Southerner is always still on his feet for the last drink. (*Picks up his glass*) It was Henry Frick, your Mr. Henry Frick, who said, "Railroads are the Rembrandts of investments." Well, *I* say, "Southern cotton mills *will be* the Rembrandts of investment." So I give you the firm of Hubbard Sons and Marshall, Cotton Mills, and to it a long and prosperous life. (*They all pick up their glasses.* MARSHALL *looks at them, amused. Then he, too, lifts his glass, smiles.*)

OSCAR. The children will drive you to the depot. Leo! Alexandra! You will drive Mr. Marshall down.

LEO (*eagerly, looks at* BEN *who nods*). Yes, sir. (*To* MARSHALL) Not often Uncle Ben lets *me* drive the horses. And a beautiful pair they are. (*Starts for hall*) Come on, Zan.

ALEXANDRA. May I drive tonight, Uncle Ben, please? I'd like to and—

BEN (*shakes his head, laughs*). In your evening clothes? Oh, no, my dear.

ALEXANDRA. But Leo always—(*Stops, exits quickly.*)

REGINA. I don't like to say good-bye to you, Mr. Marshall.

MARSHALL. Then we won't say good-bye. You have promised that you would come and let me show you Chicago. Do I have to make you promise again?

REGINA (*looks at him as he presses her hand*). I promise again.

MARSHALL (*touches her hand again, then moves to* BIRDIE). Good-bye, Mrs. Hubbard.

BIRDIE (*shyly, with sweetness and dignity*). Good-bye, sir.

MARSHALL (*as he passes* REGINA). Remember.

REGINA. I will.

OSCAR. We'll see you to the carriage. (MARSHALL *exits, followed by* BEN *and* OSCAR. *For a second* REGINA *and* BIRDIE *stand looking after them. Then* REGINA *throws up her arms, laughs happily.*)

REGINA. And there, Birdie, goes the man who has opened the door to our future.

BIRDIE (*surprised at the unaccustomed friendliness*) What?

REGINA (*turning to her*). *Our future.* Yours and mine, Ben's and Oscar's, the children— (*Looks at* BIRDIE's *puzzled face, laughs*) Our future! (*Gaily*) You were charming at supper, Birdie. Mr. Marshall certainly thought so.

BIRDIE (*pleased*). Why, Regina! Do you think he did?

REGINA. Can't you tell when you're being admired?

BIRDIE. Oscar said I bored Mr. Marshall. (*Then quietly*) But he admired *you*. He told me so.

REGINA. What did he say?

BIRDIE. He said to me, "I hope your sister-in-law will come to Chicago. Chicago will be at her feet." He said the ladies would bow to your manners and the gentlemen to your looks.

REGINA. Did he? He seems a lonely man. Imagine being lonely with all that money. I don't think he likes his wife.

BIRDIE. Not like his wife? What a thing to say.

REGINA. She's away a great deal. He said that several times. And once he made fun of her being so social and high-tone. But that fits in all right. (*Sits back, arms on back of sofa, stretches*) Her being social, I mean. She can introduce me. It won't take long with an introduction from her.

BIRDIE (*bewildered*). Introduce you? In Chicago? You mean you really might go? Oh, Regina, you can't leave here. What about Horace?

REGINA. Don't look so scared about everything, Birdie I'm going to live in Chicago. I've always wanted to. And now there'll be plenty of money to go with.

BIRDIE. But Horace won't be able to move around. You know what the doctor wrote.

REGINA. There'll be millions, Birdie, millions. You know what I've always said when people told me we were rich? I said I think you should either be a nigger or a millionaire. In between, like us, what for? (*Laughs. Looks at* BIRDIE) But I'm not going away tomorrow, Birdie. There's plenty of time to worry about Horace when he comes home. If he ever decides to come home.

BIRDIE. Will we be going to Chicago? I mean, Oscar and Leo and me?

REGINA. You? I shouldn't think so. (*Laughs*) Well, we must remember tonight. It's a very important night and we mustn't forget it. We shall plan all the things we'd like to have and then we'll really have them. Make a wish, Birdie, any wish. It's bound to come true now. (BEN *and* OSCAR *enter.*)

BIRDIE (*laughs*). Well. Well, I don't know. Maybe. (REGINA *turns to look at* BEN) Well, I guess I'd know right off what I wanted. (OSCAR *stands by the upper window, waves to the departing carriage.*)

REGINA (*looks up at* BEN, *smiles. He smiles back at her*). Well, you did it.

BEN. Looks like it might be we did.

REGINA (*springs up, laughs*). Looks like it! Don't pretend. You're like a cat who's been licking the cream. (*Crosses to wine bottle*) Now we must all have a drink to celebrate.

OSCAR. The children, Alexandra and Leo, make a very handsome couple, Regina. Marshall remarked himself what fine young folks they were. How well they looked together!

REGINA (*sharply*). Yes. You said that before, Oscar.

BEN. Yes, sir. It's beginning to look as if the deal's all set. I may not be a subtle man—but— (*Turns to them. After a second*) Now somebody ask me how I know the deal is set.

OSCAR. What do you mean, Ben?

BEN. You remember I told him that down here we drink the *last* drink for a toast?

OSCAR (*thoughtfully*). Yes. I never heard that before.

BEN. Nobody's ever heard it before. God forgives those who invent what they need. I already had his signature. But we've all done business with men whose word over a glass is better than a bond. Anyway it don't hurt to have both.

OSCAR (*turns to* REGINA). You understand what Ben means?

REGINA (*smiles*). Yes, Oscar. I understand. I understood immediately.

BEN (*looks at her admiringly*). Did you, Regina? Well, when he lifted his glass to drink, I closed my eyes and saw the bricks going into place.

REGINA. And *I* saw a lot more than that.

BEN. Slowly, slowly. As yet we have only our hopes.

REGINA. Birdie and I have just been planning what we want. I know what I want. What will you want, Ben?

BEN. Caution. Don't count the chickens. (*Leans back, laughs*) Well, God would allow us a little daydreaming. Good for the soul when you've worked hard enough to deserve it. (*Pauses*) I think I'll have a stable. For a long time I've had my good eyes on Carter's in Savannah. A rich man's pleasure, the sport of kings, why not the sport of Hubbards? Why not?

REGINA (*smiles*). Why not? What will you have, Oscar?

OSCAR. I don't know. (*Thoughtfully*) The pleasure of seeing the bricks grow will be enough for me.

BEN. Oh, of course. Our greatest pleasure will be to see the bricks grow. But we are all entitled to a little side indulgence.

OSCAR. Yes, I suppose so. Well, then, I think we might take a few trips here and there, eh, Birdie?

BIRDIE (*surprised at being consulted*). Yes, Oscar. I'd like that.

OSCAR. We might even make a regular trip to Jekyll Island. I've heard the Cornelly place is for sale. We might think about buying it. Make a nice change. Do you good, Birdie, a change of climate. Fine shooting on Jekyll, the best.

BIRDIE. I'd like—

OSCAR (*indulgently*). What would you like?

BIRDIE. Two things. Two things I'd like most.

REGINA. Two! I should like a thousand. You are modest, Birdie.

BIRDIE (*warmly, delighted with the unexpected interest*). I should like to have Lionnet back. I know you own it now, but I'd like to see it fixed up again, the way Mama and Papa had it. Every year it used to get a nice coat of paint—Papa was very particular about the paint —and the lawn was so smooth all the way down to the river, with the trims of zinnias and red-feather plush. And the figs and blue little plums and the scuppernongs — (*Smiles. Turns to* REGINA) The organ is still there and it wouldn't cost much to fix. We could have parties for Zan, the way Mama used to have for me.

BEN. That's a pretty picture, Birdie. Might be a most pleasant way to live. (*Dismissing* BIRDIE) What do you want, Regina?

BIRDIE (*very happily, not noticing that they are no longer listening to her*). I could have a cutting garden. Just where Mama's used to be. Oh, I do think we could be happier there. Papa used to say that *nobody* had ever lost their temper at Lionnet, and *nobody* ever would. Papa would never let anybody be nasty-spoken or mean. No, sir. He just didn't like it.

BEN. What do you want, Regina?

REGINA. I'm going to Chicago. And when I'm settled there and know the right people and the right things to buy— because I certainly don't now—I shall go to Paris and buy them. (*Laughs*) I'm going to leave you and Oscar to count the bricks.

BIRDIE. Oscar. Please let me have Lionnet back.

OSCAR (*to* REGINA). You are serious about moving to Chicago?

BEN. She is going to see the great world and leave us in the little one. Well, we'll come and visit you and meet all the great and be proud you are our sister.

REGINA (*gaily*). Certainly. And you won't even have to learn to be subtle, Ben. Stay as you are. You will be rich and the rich don't have to be subtle.

OSCAR. But what about Alexandra? She's seventeen. Old enough to be thinking about marrying.

BIRDIE. And, Oscar, I have one more wish. Just one more wish.

OSCAR (*turns*). What is it, Birdie? What are you saying?

BIRDIE. I want you to stop shooting. I mean, so much. I don't like to see animals and birds killed just for the killing. You only throw them away—

BEN (*to* REGINA). It'll take a great deal of money to live as you're planning, Regina.

REGINA. Certainly. But there'll be plenty of money. You have estimated the profits very high.

BEN. I have—

BIRDIE (OSCAR *is looking at her furiously*). And you never let anybody else shoot, and the niggers need it so much to keep from starving. It's wicked to shoot food just because you like to shoot, when poor people need it so—

BEN (*laughs*). I have estimated the profits very high—for myself.

REGINA. What did you say?

BIRDIE. I've always wanted to speak about it, Oscar.

OSCAR (*slowly, carefully*). What are you chattering about?

BIRDIE (*nervously*). I was talking about Lionnet and—and about your shooting—

OSCAR. You are exciting yourself.

REGINA (*to* BEN). I didn't hear you. There was so much talking.

OSCAR (*to* BIRDIE). You have been acting very childish, very excited, all evening.

BIRDIE. Regina asked me what I'd like.

REGINA. What did you say, Ben?

BIRDIE. Now that we'll be so rich everybody was saying what they would like, so *I* said what *I* would like, too.

BEN. I said— (*He is interrupted by* OSCAR.)

OSCAR (*to* BIRDIE). Very well. We've all heard you. That's enough now.

BEN. I am waiting. (*They stop*) I am waiting for you to finish. You and Birdie. Four conversations are three too many. (BIRDIE *slowly sits down.* BEN *smiles, to* REGINA) I said that I had, and I do, estimate the profits very high—for myself, and Oscar, of course.

REGINA (*slowly*). And what does that mean? (BEN *shrugs, looks toward* OSCAR.)

OSCAR (*looks at* BEN, *clears throat*). Well, Regina, it's like this. For forty-nine per cent Marshall will put up four hundred thousand dollars. For fifty-one per cent— (*Smiles archly*) a controlling interest, mind you, we will put up two hundred and twenty-five thousand dollars besides offering him certain benefits that our (*looks at* BEN) local position allows us to manage. Ben means that two hundred and twenty-five thousand dollars is a lot of money.

REGINA. I know the terms and I know it's a lot of money.

BEN (*nodding*). It is.

OSCAR. Ben means that we are ready with our two-thirds of the money. Your third, Horace's I mean, doesn't seem to be ready. (*Raises his hand as* REGINA *starts to speak*) Ben has written to Horace, I have written, and you have written. He answers. But he never mentions this business. Yet we have explained it to him in great detail, and told him the urgency. Still he never mentions it. Ben has been very patient, Regina. Naturally, you are our sister and we want you to benefit from anything we do.

REGINA. And in addition to your concern for me, you do not want control to go out of the family. (*To* BEN) That right, Ben?

BEN. That's cynical. (*Smiles*) Cynicism is an unpleasant way of saying the truth.

OSCAR. No need to be cynical. We'd have no trouble raising the third share, the share that you want to take.

REGINA. I am sure you could get the third share, the share you were saving for me. But that would give you a strange partner. And strange partners sometimes want a great deal. (*Smiles unpleasantly*) But perhaps it would be wise for you to find him.

OSCAR. Now, now. Nobody says we *want* to do that. We would like to have you in and you would like to come in.

REGINA. Yes. I certainly would.

BEN (*laughs, puts up his hand*). But we haven't heard from Horace.

REGINA. I've given my word that Horace will put up the money. That should be enough.

BEN. Oh, it was enough. I took your word. But I've got to have more than your word now. The contracts will be signed this week, and Marshall will want to see our money soon after. Regina, Horace has been in Baltimore for five months. I know that you've written him to come home, and that he hasn't come.

OSCAR. It's beginning to look as if he doesn't want to come home.

REGINA. Of course he wants to come home. You can't move around with heart trouble at any moment you choose. You know what doctors are like once they get their hands on a case like this—

OSCAR. They can't very well keep him from answering letters, can they? (REGINA *turns to* BEN) They couldn't keep him from arranging for the money if he wanted to—

REGINA. Has it occurred to you that Horace is also a good businessman?

BEN. Certainly. He is a shrewd trader. Always has been. The bank is proof of that.

REGINA. Then, possibly, he may be keeping silent because he doesn't think he is getting enough for his money. (*Looks at* OSCAR) Seventy-five thousand he has to put up. That's a lot of money, too.

OSCAR. Nonsense. He knows a good thing when he hears it. He knows that we can make *twice* the profit on cotton goods manufactured here than can be made in the North.

BEN. That isn't what Regina means. (*Smiles*) May I interpret you, Regina? (*To* OSCAR) Regina is saying that Horace wants *more* than a third of our share.

OSCAR. But he's only putting up a third of the money. You put up a third and you get a third. What else could he expect?

REGINA. Well, *I* don't know. I don't know about these things. It would seem that if you put up a third you should only get a third. But then again, there's no law about it, is there? I should think that if you knew your money was very badly needed, well, you just might say, I want more, I want a bigger share. You boys have done that. I've heard you say so.

BEN (*after a pause, laughs*). So you believe he has deliberately held out? For a larger share? (*Leaning forward*) Well, I don't believe it. But I do believe that's what *you* want. Am I right, Regina?

REGINA. Oh, I shouldn't like to be too definite. But I could say that I wouldn't like to persuade Horace unless he did get a larger share. I must look after his interests. It seems only natural—

OSCAR. And where would the larger share come from?

REGINA. I don't know. That's not my business. (*Giggles*) But perhaps it could come off your share, Oscar. (REGINA *and* BEN *laugh*.)

OSCAR (*rises and wheels furiously on both of them as they laugh*). What kind of talk is this?

BEN. I haven't said a thing.

OSCAR (*to* REGINA). *You* are talking very big tonight.

REGINA (*stops laughing*). Am I? Well, you should know me well enough to know that I wouldn't be asking for things I didn't think I could get.

OSCAR. Listen. I don't believe you can even get Horace to come home, much less get money from him or talk quite so big about what you want.

REGINA. Oh, I can get him home.

OSCAR. Then why haven't you?

REGINA. I thought I should fight his battles for him, before he came home. Horace is a very sick man. And even if *you* don't care how sick he is, I do.

BEN. Stop this foolish squabbling. How can you get him home?

REGINA. I will send Alexandra to Baltimore. She will ask him to come home. She will say that she wants him to come home, and that *I* want him to come home.

BIRDIE (*suddenly*). Well, of course she wants him here, but he's sick and maybe he's happy where he is.

REGINA (*ignores* BIRDIE, *to* BEN). You agree that he will come home if she asks him to, if she says that I miss him and want him—

BEN (*looks at her, smiles*). I admire you, Regina. And I
   agree. That's settled now and— (*Starts to rise.*)
REGINA (*quickly*). But before she brings him home, I want
   to know what he's going to get.
BEN. What do you want?
REGINA. Twice what you offered.
BEN. Well, you won't get it.
OSCAR (*to* REGINA). I think you've gone crazy.
REGINA. I don't want to fight, Ben—
BEN. I don't either. You won't get it. There isn't any chance
   of that. (*Roguishly*) You're holding us up, and that's not
   pretty, Regina, not pretty. (*Holds up his hand as he sees
   she is about to speak*) But we need you, and I don't
   want to fight. Here's what I'll do: I'll give Horace forty
   per cent, instead of the thirty-three and a third he really
   should get. I'll do that, provided he is home and his
   money is up within two weeks. How's that?
REGINA. All right.
OSCAR. I've asked before: where is this extra share coming
   from?
BEN (*pleasantly*). From you. From your share.
OSCAR (*furiously*). From me, is it? That's just fine and
   dandy. That's my reward. For thirty-five years I've
   worked my hands to the bone for you. For thirty-five
   years I've done all the things you didn't want to do.
   And this is what I—
BEN (*turns slowly to look at* OSCAR. OSCAR *breaks off*). My,
   my. I am being attacked tonight on all sides. First by
   my sister, then by my brother. And I ain't a man who
   likes being attacked. I can't believe that God wants the
   strong to parade their strength, but I don't mind doing
   it if it's got to be done. (*Leans back in his chair*) You
   ought to take these things better, Oscar. I've made you
   money in the past. I'm going to make you more money
   now. You'll be a very rich man. What's the difference to
   any of us if a little more goes here, a little less goes

there—it's all in the family. And it will stay in the family. I'll never marry. (ADDIE *enters, begins to gather the glasses from the table.* OSCAR *turns to* BEN) So my money will go to Alexandra and Leo. They may even marry some day and— (ADDIE *looks at* BEN.)

BIRDIE (*rising*). Marry—Zan and Leo—

OSCAR (*carefully*). That would make a great difference in my feelings. If they married.

BEN. Yes, that's what I mean. Of course it would make a difference.

OSCAR (*carefully*). Is that what *you* mean, Regina?

REGINA. Oh, it's too far away. We'll talk about it in a few years.

OSCAR. I want to talk about it now.

BEN (*nods*). Naturally.

REGINA. There's a lot of things to consider. They are first cousins, and—

OSCAR. That isn't unusual. Our grandmother and grandfather were first cousins.

REGINA (*giggles*). And look at us. (BEN *giggles.*)

OSCAR (*angrily*). You're both being very gay with my money.

BEN (*sighs*). These quarrels. I dislike them so. (*Leans forward to* REGINA) A marriage might be a very wise arrangement, for several reasons. And then, Oscar has given up something for you. You should try to manage something for him.

REGINA. I haven't said I was opposed to it. But Leo is a wild boy. There were those times when he took a little money from the bank and—

OSCAR. That's all past history—

REGINA. Oh, I know. And I know all young men are wild. I'm only mentioning it to show you that there are considerations—

BEN (*irritated because she does not understand that he is trying to keep* OSCAR *quiet*). All right, so there are. But please assure Oscar that you will think about it very seriously.

REGINA (*smiles, nods*). Very well. I assure Oscar that I will think about it seriously.

OSCAR (*sharply*). That is not an answer.

REGINA (*rises*). My, you're in a bad humor and you shall put me in one. I have said all that I am willing to say now. After all, Horace has to give his consent, too.

OSCAR. Horace will do what you tell him to.

REGINA. Yes, I think he will.

OSCAR. And I have your word that you will try to—

REGINA (*patiently*). Yes, Oscar. You have my word that I will think about it. Now do leave me alone. (*There is the sound of the front door being closed.*)

BIRDIE. I—Alexandra is only seventeen. She—

REGINA (*calling*). Alexandra? Are you back?

ALEXANDRA. Yes, Mama.

LEO (*comes into the room*). Mr. Marshall got off safe and sound. Weren't those fine clothes he had? You can always spot clothes made in a good place. Looks like maybe they were done in England. Lots of men in the North send all the way to England for their stuff.

BEN (*to* LEO). Were you careful driving the horses?

LEO. Oh, yes, sir. I was. (ALEXANDRA *has come in on* BEN'S *question, hears the answer, looks angrily at* LEO.)

ALEXANDRA. It's a lovely night. You should have come, Aunt Birdie.

REGINA. Were you gracious to Mr. Marshall?

ALEXANDRA. I think so, Mama. I liked him.

REGINA. Good. And now I have great news for you. You are going to Baltimore in the morning to bring your father home.

ALEXANDRA (*gasps, then delighted*). Me? Papa said I should come? That must mean— (*Turns to* ADDIE) Addie, he must be well. Think of it, he'll be back home again. We'll bring him home.

REGINA. You are going alone, Alexandra.

ADDIE (ALEXANDRA *has turned in surprise*). Going alone? Going by herself? A child that age! Mr. Horace ain't going to like Zan traipsing up there by herself.

REGINA (*sharply*). Go upstairs and lay out Alexandra's things.

ADDIE. He'd expect me to be along—

REGINA. I'll be up in a few minutes to tell you what to pack. (ADDIE *slowly begins to climb the steps. To* ALEXANDRA) I should think you'd like going alone. At your age it certainly would have delighted me. You're a strange girl, Alexandra. Addie has babied you so much.

ALEXANDRA. I only thought it would be more fun if Addie and I went together.

BIRDIE (*timidly*). Maybe I could go with her, Regina. I'd really like to.

REGINA. She is going alone. She is getting old enough to take some responsibilities.

OSCAR. She'd better learn now. She's almost old enough to get married. (*Jovially, to* LEO, *slapping him on shoulder*) Eh, son?

LEO. Huh?

OSCAR (*annoyed with* LEO *for not understanding*). Old enough to get married, you're thinking, eh?

LEO. Oh, yes, sir. (*Feebly*) Lots of girls get married at Zan's age. Look at Mary Prester and Johanna and—

REGINA. Well, she's not getting married tomorrow. But she is going to Baltimore tomorrow, so let's talk about that. (*To* ALEXANDRA) You'll be glad to have Papa home again.

ALEXANDRA. I wanted to go before, Mama. You remember that. But you said *you* couldn't go, and that *I* couldn't go alone.

REGINA. I've changed my mind. (*Too casually*) You're to tell Papa how much you missed him, and that he must come home now—for your sake. Tell him that you *need* him home.

ALEXANDRA. Need him home? I don't understand.

REGINA. There is nothing for you to understand. You are simply to say what I have told you.

BIRDIE (*rises*). He may be too sick. She couldn't do that—

ALEXANDRA. Yes. He may be too sick to travel. I couldn't make him think he had to come home for me, if he is too sick to—

REGINA (*looks at her, sharply, challengingly*). You *couldn't* do what I tell you to do, Alexandra?

ALEXANDRA (*quietly*). No. I couldn't. If I thought it would hurt him.

REGINA (*after a second's silence, smiles pleasantly*). But you are doing this for Papa's own good. (*Takes* ALEXANDRA's *hand*) You must let me be the judge of his condition. It's the best possible cure for him to come home and be taken care of here. He mustn't stay there any longer and listen to those alarmist doctors. You are doing this entirely for his sake. Tell your papa that I want him to come home, that I miss him very much.

ALEXANDRA (*slowly*). Yes, Mama.

REGINA (*to the others. Rises*). I must go and start getting Alexandra ready now. Why don't you all go home?

BEN (*rises*). I'll attend to the railroad ticket. One of the boys will bring it over. Good night, everybody. Have a nice trip, Alexandra. The food on the train is very good. The celery is so crisp. Have a good time and act like a little lady. (*Exits.*)

REGINA. Good night, Ben. Good night, Oscar— (*Playfully*) Don't be so glum, Oscar. It makes you look as if you had chronic indigestion.

BIRDIE. Good night, Regina.

REGINA. Good night, Birdie. (*Exits upstairs.*)

OSCAR (*starts for hall*). Come along.

LEO (*to* ALEXANDRA). Imagine your not wanting to go!

What a little fool you are. Wish it were me. What I
could do in a place like Baltimore!

ALEXANDRA (*angrily, looking away from him*). Mind your
business. I can guess the kind of things *you* could do.

LEO (*laughs*). Oh, no, you couldn't. (*He exits.*)

REGINA (*calling from the top of the stairs*). Come on, Alexandra.

BIRDIE (*quickly, softly*). Zan.

ALEXANDRA. I don't understand about my going, Aunt
Birdie. (*Shrugs*) But anyway, Papa will be home again.
(*Pats* BIRDIE'S *arm*) Don't worry about me. I can take
care of myself. Really I can.

BIRDIE (*shakes her head, softly*). That's not what I'm worried about. Zan—

ALEXANDRA (*comes close to her*). What's the matter?

BIRDIE. It's about Leo—

ALEXANDRA (*whispering*). He beat the horses. That's why
we were late getting back. We had to wait until they
cooled off. He always beats the horses as if—

BIRDIE (*whispering frantically, holding* ALEXANDRA'S
hands). He's my son. My own son. But you are
more to me—more to me than my own child. I love you
more than anybody else—

ALEXANDRA. Don't worry about the horses. I'm sorry I told
you.

BIRDIE (*her voice rising*). *I am not worrying about the
horses.* I am worrying about *you.* You are *not* going to
marry Leo. I am not going to let them do that to you—

ALEXANDRA. Marry? To Leo? (*Laughs*) I wouldn't marry,
Aunt Birdie. I've never even thought about it—

BIRDIE. But they have thought about it. (*Wildly*) Zan, I
couldn't stand to think about such a thing. You and—
(OSCAR *has come into the doorway on* ALEXANDRA'S
speech. He is standing quietly, listening.)

ALEXANDRA (*laughs*). But I'm not going to marry. And I'm
certainly not going to marry Leo.

BIRDIE. Don't you understand? They'll make you. They'll make you—

ALEXANDRA (*takes* BIRDIE's *hands, quietly, firmly*). That's foolish, Aunt Birdie. I'm grown now. Nobody can make me do anything.

BIRDIE. I just couldn't stand—

OSCAR (*sharply*). Birdie. (BIRDIE *looks up, draws quickly away from* ALEXANDRA. *She stands rigid, frightened. Quietly*) Birdie, get your hat and coat.

ADDIE (*calls from upstairs*). Come on, baby. Your mama's waiting for you, and she ain't nobody to keep waiting.

ALEXANDRA. All right. (*Then softly, embracing* BIRDIE) Good night, Aunt Birdie. (*As she passes* OSCAR) Good night, Uncle Oscar. (BIRDIE *begins to move slowly toward the door as* ALEXANDRA *climbs the stairs.* ALEXANDRA *is almost out of view when* BIRDIE *reaches* OSCAR *in the doorway. As* BIRDIE *quickly attempts to pass him, he slaps her hard, across the face.* BIRDIE *cries out, puts her hand to her face. On the cry,* ALEXANDRA *turns, begins to run down the stairs*) Aunt Birdie! What happened? What happened? I—

BIRDIE (*softly, without turning*). Nothing, darling. Nothing happened. (*Quickly, as if anxious to keep* ALEXANDRA *from coming close*) Now go to bed. (OSCAR *exits*) Nothing happened. I only—I only twisted my ankle. (*She goes out.* ALEXANDRA *stands on the stairs looking after her as if she were puzzled and frightened.*)

Curtain

ACT TWO

SCENE: *Same as Act One. A week later, morning.*

AT RISE: *The light comes from the open shutter of the right window; the other shutters are tightly closed.* ADDIE *is standing at the window, looking out. Near the dining room doors are brooms, mops, rags, etc. After a second,* OSCAR *comes into the entrance hall, looks in the room, shivers, decides not to take his hat and coat off, comes into the room. At the sound of the door,* ADDIE *turns.*

ADDIE (*without interest*). Oh, it's you, Mr. Oscar.

OSCAR. What is this? It's not night. What's the matter here? (*Shivers*) Fine thing at this time of the morning. Blinds all closed. (ADDIE *begins to open shutters*) Where's Miss Regina? It's cold in here.

ADDIE. Miss Regina ain't down yet.

OSCAR. She had any word?

ADDIE (*wearily*). No, sir.

OSCAR. Wouldn't you think a girl that age could get on a train at one place and have sense enough to get off at another?

ADDIE. Something must have happened. If Zan say she was coming last night, she's coming last night. Unless something happened. Sure fire disgrace to let a baby like that go all that way alone to bring home a sick man without—

OSCAR. You do a lot of judging around here, Addie, eh? Judging of your white folks, I mean.

ADDIE (*looks at him, sighs*). I'm tired. I been up all night watching for them.

REGINA (*speaking from the upstairs hall*). Who's down-stairs, Addie? (*She appears in a dressing gown, peers down from the landing.* ADDIE *picks up broom, dustpan and brush and exits*) Oh, it's you, Oscar. What are you doing here so early? I haven't been down yet. I'm not finished dressing.

OSCAR (*speaking up to her*). You had any word from them?

REGINA. No.

OSCAR. Then something certainly has happened. People don't just say they are arriving on Thursday night, and they haven't come by Friday morning.

REGINA. Oh, nothing has happened. Alexandra just hasn't got sense enough to send a message.

OSCAR. If nothing's happened, then why aren't they here?

REGINA. You asked me that ten times last night. My, you do fret so, Oscar. Anything might have happened. They may have missed connections in Atlanta, the train may have been delayed—oh, a hundred things could have kept them.

OSCAR. Where's Ben?

REGINA (*as she disappears upstairs*). Where should he be? At home, probably. Really, Oscar, I don't tuck him in his bed and I don't take him out of it. Have some coffee and don't worry so much.

OSCAR. Have some coffee? There isn't any coffee. (*Looks at his watch, shakes his head. After a second* CAL *enters with a large silver tray, coffee urn, small cups, news-paper*) Oh, there you are. Is everything in this fancy house always late?

CAL (*looks at him surprised*). You ain't out shooting this morning, Mr. Oscar?

OSCAR. First day I missed since I had my head cold. First day I missed in eight years.

CAL. Yes, sir. I bet you. Simon he say you had a mighty good day yesterday morning. That's what Simon say. (*Brings* OSCAR *coffee and newspaper.*)

OSCAR. Pretty good, pretty good.

CAL (*laughs, slyly*). Bet you got enough bobwhite and squirrel to give every nigger in town a Jesus-party. Most of 'em ain't had no meat since the cotton picking was over. Bet they'd give anything for a little piece of that meat—

OSCAR (*turns his head to look at* CAL). Cal, if I catch a nigger in this town going shooting, you know what's going to happen. (LEO *enters.*)

CAL (*hastily*). Yes, sir, Mr. Oscar. I didn't say nothing about nothing. It was Simon who told me and— Morning, Mr. Leo. You gentlemen having your breakfast with us here?

LEO. The boys in the bank don't know a thing. They haven't had any message. (CAL *waits for an answer, gets none, shrugs, moves to door, exits.*)

OSCAR (*peers at* LEO). What you doing here, son?

LEO. You told me to find out if the boys at the bank had any message from Uncle Horace or Zan—

OSCAR. I told you if they had a message to bring it here. I told you that if they didn't have a message to stay at the bank and do your work.

LEO. Oh, I guess I misunderstood.

OSCAR. You didn't misunderstand. You just were looking for any excuse to take an hour off. (LEO *pours a cup of coffee*) You got to stop that kind of thing. You got to start settling down. You going to be a married man one of these days.

LEO. Yes, sir.

OSCAR. You also got to stop with that woman in Mobile. (*As* LEO *is about to speak*) You're young and I haven't got no objections to outside women. That is, I haven't got no objections so long as they don't interfere with serious things. Outside women are all right in their place, but *now* isn't their place. You got to realize that.

LEO (*nods*). Yes, sir. I'll tell her. She'll act all right about it.

OSCAR. Also, you got to start working harder at the bank. You got to convince your Uncle Horace you going to make a fit husband for Alexandra.

LEO. What do you think has happened to them? Supposed to be here last night— (*Laughs*) Bet you Uncle Ben's mighty worried. Seventy-five thousand dollars worried.

OSCAR (*smiles happily*). Ought to be worried. Damn well ought to be. First he don't answer the letters, then he don't come home— (*Giggles.*)

LEO. What will happen if Uncle Horace don't come home or don't—

OSCAR. Or don't put up the money? Oh, we'll get it from outside. Easy enough.

LEO (*surprised*). But *you* don't want outsiders.

OSCAR. What do I care who gets my share? I been shaved already. Serve Ben right if he had to give away some of his.

LEO. Damn shame what they did to you.

OSCAR (*looking up the stairs*). Don't talk so loud. Don't you worry. When I die, you'll have as much as the rest. You might have yours *and* Alexandra's. I'm not so easily licked.

LEO. I wasn't thinking of myself, Papa—

OSCAR. Well, you should be, you should be. It's every man's duty to think of himself.

LEO. You think Uncle Horace don't want to go in on this?

OSCAR (*giggles*). That's my hunch. He hasn't showed any signs of loving it yet.

LEO (*laughs*). But he hasn't listened to Aunt Regina yet, either. Oh, he'll go along. It's too good a thing. Why wouldn't he want to? He's got plenty and plenty to invest with. He don't even have to sell anything. Eighty-eight thousand worth of Union Pacific bonds sitting right in his safe deposit box. All he's got to do is open the box.

OSCAR (*after a pause. Looks at his watch*). Mighty late breakfast in this fancy house. Yes, he's had those bonds for fifteen years. Bought them when they were low and just locked them up.

LEO. Yeah. Just has to open the box and take them out. That's all. Easy as easy can be. (*Laughs*) The things in that box! There's all those bonds, looking mighty fine. (OSCAR *slowly puts down his newspaper and turns to* LEO) Then right next to them is a baby shoe of Zan's and a cheap old cameo on a string, and, *and*—nobody'd believe this—a piece of an old violin. Not even a whole violin. Just a piece of an old thing, a piece of a violin.

OSCAR (*very softly, as if he were trying to control his voice*). A piece of a violin! What do you think of that!

LEO. Yes, sirree. A lot of other crazy things, too. A poem, I guess it is, signed with his mother's name, and two old schoolbooks with notes and— (LEO *catches* OSCAR's *look. His voice trails off. He turns his head away.*)

OSCAR (*very softly*). How do you know what's in the box, son?

LEO (*stops, draws back, frightened, realizing what he has said*). Oh, well. Well, er. Well, one of the boys, sir. It was one of the boys at the bank. He took old Manders' keys. It was Joe Horns. He just up and took Manders' keys and, and—well, took the box out. (*Quickly*) Then they all asked me if I wanted to see, too. So I looked a little, I guess, but then I made them close up the box quick and I told them never—

OSCAR (*looks at him*). Joe Horns, you say? He opened it?

LEO. Yes, sir, yes, he did. My word of honor. (*Very nervously looking away*) I suppose that don't excuse *me* for looking— (*Looking at* OSCAR) but I did make him close it up and put the keys back in Manders' drawer—

OSCAR (*leans forward, very softly*). Tell me the truth, Leo. I am not going to be angry with you. Did you open the box yourself?

LEO. *No, sir, I didn't.* I told you I didn't. No, I—

OSCAR (*irritated, patient*). I am *not* going to be angry with you. (*Watching* LEO *carefully*) Sometimes a young fellow deserves credit for looking round him to see what's going on. Sometimes that's a good sign in a fellow your age. (OSCAR *rises*) Many great men have made their fortune with their eyes. Did you open the box?

LEO (*very puzzled*). No. I—

OSCAR (*moves to* LEO). Did you open the box? It may have been—well, it may have been a good thing if you had.

LEO (*after a long pause*). I opened it.

OSCAR (*quickly*). Is that the truth? (LEO *nods*) Does anybody else know that you opened it? Come, Leo, don't be afraid of speaking the truth to me.

LEO. No. Nobody knew. Nobody was in the bank when I did it. But—

OSCAR. Did your Uncle Horace ever know you opened it?

LEO (*shakes his head*). He only looks in it once every six months when he cuts the coupons, and sometimes Manders even does that for him. Uncle Horace don't even have the keys. Manders keeps them for him. Imagine not looking at all that. You can bet if I had the bonds, I'd watch 'em like—

OSCAR. If you had them. (LEO *watches him*) *If* you had them. Then you could have a share in the mill, you and me. A fine, big share, too. (*Pauses, shrugs*) Well, a man can't be shot for wanting to see his son get on in the world, can he, boy?

LEO (*looks up, begins to understand*). No, he can't. Natural enough. (*Laughs*) But I haven't got the bonds and Uncle Horace has. And now he can just sit back and wait to be a millionaire.

OSCAR (*innocently*). You think your Uncle Horace likes

you well enough to lend you the bonds if he decides
not to use them himself?

LEO. Papa, it must be that you haven't had your breakfast!
(*Laughs loudly*) Lend me the bonds! My God—

OSCAR (*disappointed*). No, I suppose not. Just a fancy of
mine. A loan for three months, maybe four, easy enough
for us to pay it back then. Anyway, this is only April—
(*Slowly counting the months on his fingers*) and if he
doesn't look at them until Fall, he wouldn't even miss
them out of the box.

LEO. That's it. He wouldn't even miss them. Ah, well—

OSCAR. No, sir. Wouldn't even miss them. How could he
miss them if he never looks at them? (*Sighs as* LEO *stares
at him*) Well, here we are sitting around waiting for
him to come home and invest his money in something
he hasn't lifted his hand to get. But I can't help thinking he's acting strange. You laugh when I say he could
lend you the bonds if he's not going to use them himself. But would it hurt him?

LEO (*slowly looking at* OSCAR). No. No, it wouldn't.

OSCAR. People ought to help other people. But that's not
always the way it happens. (BEN *enters, hangs his coat
and hat in hall. Very carefully*) And so sometimes you
got to think of yourself. (*As* LEO *stares at him,* BEN *appears in the doorway*) Morning, Ben.

BEN (*coming in, carrying his newspaper*). Fine sunny
morning. Any news from the runaways?

REGINA (*on the staircase*). There's no news or you would
have heard it. Quite a convention so early in the morning, aren't you all? (*Goes to coffee urn.*)

OSCAR. You rising mighty late these days. Is that the way
they do things in Chicago society?

BEN (*looking at his paper*). Old Carter died up in Senateville. Eighty-one is a good time for us all, eh? What do
you think has really happened to Horace, Regina?

REGINA. Nothing.

BEN (*too casually*). You don't think maybe he never started from Baltimore and never intends to start?

REGINA (*irritated*). Of course they've started. Didn't I have a letter from Alexandra? What is so strange about people arriving late? He has that cousin in Savannah he's so fond of. He may have stopped to see him. They'll be along today some time, very flattered that you and Oscar are so worried about them.

BEN. I'm a natural worrier. Especially when I am getting ready to close a business deal and one of my partners remains silent *and* invisible.

REGINA (*laughs*). Oh, is that it? I thought you were worried about Horace's health.

OSCAR. Oh, that too. Who could help but worry? I'm worried. This is the first day I haven't shot since my head cold.

REGINA (*starts toward dining room*). Then you haven't had your breakfast. Come along. (OSCAR *and* LEO *follow her.*)

BEN. Regina. (*She turns at dining-room door*) That cousin of Horace's has been dead for years and, in any case, the train does not go through Savannah.

REGINA (*laughs, continues into dining room, seats herself*). Did he die? You're always remembering about people dying. (BEN *rises*) Now I intend to eat my breakfast in peace, and read my newspaper.

BEN (*goes toward dining room as he talks*). This is second breakfast for me. My first was bad. Celia ain't the cook she used to be. Too old to have taste any more. If she hadn't belonged to Mama, I'd send her off to the country.

(OSCAR *and* LEO *start to eat.* BEN *seats himself.*)

LEO. Uncle Horace will have some tales to tell, I bet. Baltimore is a lively town.

REGINA (*to* CAL). The grits isn't hot enough. Take it back.

CAL. Oh, yes'm. (*Calling into the kitchen as he exits*) Grits didn't hold the heat. Grits didn't hold the heat.

LEO. When I was at school three of the boys and myself took a train once and went over to Baltimore. It was so big we thought we were in Europe. I was just a kid then—

REGINA. I find it very pleasant (ADDIE *enters*) to have breakfast alone. I hate chattering before I've had something hot. (CAL *closes the dining-room doors*) Do be still, Leo.

(ADDIE *comes into the room, begins gathering up the cups, carries them to the large tray. Outside there are the sounds of voices. Quickly* ADDIE *runs into the hall. A few seconds later she appears again in the doorway, her arm around the shoulders of* HORACE GIDDENS, *supporting him.* HORACE *is a tall man of about forty-five. He has been good looking, but now his face is tired and ill. He walks stiffly, as if it were an enormous effort, and carefully, as if he were unsure of his balance.* ADDIE *takes off his overcoat and hangs it on the hall tree. She then helps him to a chair.*)

HORACE. How are you, Addie? How have you been?

ADDIE. I'm all right, Mr. Horace. I've just been worried about you.

(ALEXANDRA *enters. She is flushed and excited, her hat awry, her face dirty. Her arms are full of packages, but she comes quickly to* ADDIE.)

ALEXANDRA. Don't tell me how worried you were. We couldn't help it and there was no way to send a message.

ADDIE (*begins to take packages from* ALEXANDRA). Yes, sir, I was mighty worried.

ALEXANDRA. We had to stop in Mobile over night. Papa— (*Looks at him*) Papa didn't feel well. The trip was too much for him, and I made him stop and rest— (*As* ADDIE *takes the last package*) No, don't take that. That's father's medicine. I'll hold it. It mustn't break. Now, about the stuff outside. Papa must have his wheel chair. I'll get that and the valises—

ADDIE (*very happy, holding* ALEXANDRA'S *arms*). Since when you got to carry your own valises? Since when I ain't old enough to hold a bottle of medicine? (HORACE *coughs*) You feel all right, Mr. Horace?

HORACE (*nods*). Glad to be sitting down.

ALEXANDRA (*opening package of medicine*). He doesn't feel all right. (ADDIE *looks at her, then at* HORACE) He just says that. The trip was very hard on him, and now he must go right to bed.

ADDIE (*looking at him carefully*). Them fancy doctors, they give you help?

HORACE. They did their best.

ALEXANDRA (*has become conscious of the voices in the dining room*). I bet Mama was worried. I better tell her we're here now. (*She starts for door.*)

HORACE. Zan. (*She stops*) Not for a minute, dear.

ALEXANDRA. Oh, Papa, you feel bad again. I knew you did. Do you want your medicine?

HORACE. No, I don't feel that way. I'm just tired, darling. Let me rest a little.

ALEXANDRA. Yes, but Mama will be mad if I don't tell her we're here.

ADDIE. They're all in there eating breakfast.

ALEXANDRA. Oh, are they all here? Why do they *always* have to be here? I was hoping Papa wouldn't have to see anybody, that it would be nice for him and quiet.

ADDIE. Then let your papa rest for a minute.

HORACE. Addie, I bet your coffee's as good as ever. They don't have such good coffee up north. (*Looks at the urn*) Is it as good, Addie? (ADDIE *starts for coffee urn.*)

ALEXANDRA. No. Dr. Reeves said not much coffee. Just now and then. I'm the nurse now, Addie.

ADDIE. You'd be a better one if you didn't look so dirty.

Now go and take a bath. Change your linens, get out a fresh dress and give your hair a good brushing—go on—

ALEXANDRA. Will you be all right, Papa?

ADDIE. Go on.

ALEXANDRA (*on stairs, talks as she goes up*). The pills Papa must take once every four hours. And the bottle only when—only if he feels very bad. Now don't move until I come back and don't talk much and remember about his medicine, Addie—

ADDIE. Ring for Belle and have her help you and then I'll make you a fresh breakfast.

ALEXANDRA (*as she disappears*). How's Aunt Birdie? Is she here?

ADDIE. It ain't right for you to have coffee? It will hurt you?

HORACE (*slowly*). Nothing can make much difference now. Get me a cup, Addie. (*She looks at him, crosses to urn, pours a cup*) Funny. They can't make coffee up north. (ADDIE *brings him a cup*) They don't like red pepper, either. (*He takes the cup and gulps it greedily*) God, that's good. You remember how I used to drink it? Ten, twelve cups a day. So strong it had to stain the cup. (*Then slowly*) Addie, before I see anybody else, I want to know why Zan came to fetch me home. She's tried to tell me, but she doesn't seem to know herself.

ADDIE (*turns away*). I don't know. All I know is big things are going on. Everybody going to be high-tone rich. Big rich. You too. All because smoke's going to start out of a building that aint' even up yet.

HORACE. I've heard about it.

ADDIE And, er— (*Hesitates—steps to him*) And—well, Zan, she going to marry Mr. Leo in a little while.

HORACE (*looks at her, then very slowly*). What are you talking about?

ADDIE. That's right. That's the talk, God help us.

HORACE (*angrily*). *What's* the talk?

ADDIE. I'm telling you. There's going to be a wedding—
(*Angrily turns away*) Over my dead body there is.

HORACE (*after a second, quietly*). Go and tell them I'm home.

ADDIE (*hesitates*). Now you ain't to get excited. You're to be in your bed—

HORACE. Go on, Addie. Go and say I'm back. (ADDIE *opens dining-room doors. He rises with difficulty, stands stiff, as if he were in pain, facing the dining room.*)

ADDIE. Miss Regina. They're home. They got here—

REGINA. Horace! (REGINA *quickly, rises, runs into the room. Warmly*) Horace! You've finally arrived. (*As she kisses him, the others come forward, all talking together.*)

BEN (*in doorway, carrying a napkin*). Well, sir, you had us all mighty worried. (*He steps forward. They shake hands.* ADDIE *exits.*)

OSCAR. You're a sight for sore eyes.

HORACE. Hello, Ben.

(LEO *enters, eating a biscuit.*)

OSCAR. And how you feel? Tip-top, I bet, because that's the way you're looking.

HORACE (*coldly, irritated with* OSCAR's *lie*). Hello, Oscar. Hello, Leo, how are you?

LEO (*shaking hands*). I'm fine, sir. But a lot better now that you're back.

REGINA. Now sit down. What did happen to you and where's Alexandra? I am so excited about seeing you that I almost forgot about her.

HORACE. I didn't feel good, a little weak, I guess, and we stopped over night to rest. Zan's upstairs washing off the train dirt.

REGINA. Oh, I am so sorry the trip was hard on you. I didn't think that—

HORACE. Well, it's just as if I had never been away. All of you here—

BEN. Waiting to welcome you home.

(BIRDIE *bursts in. She is wearing a flannel kimono and her face is flushed and excited.*)

BIRDIE (*runs to him, kisses him*). Horace!

HORACE (*warmly pressing her arm*). I was just wondering where you were, Birdie.

BIRDIE (*excited*). Oh, I would have been here. I didn't know you were back until Simon said he saw the buggy. (*She draws back to look at him. Her face sobers*) Oh, you don't look well, Horace. No, you don't.

REGINA (*laughs*). Birdie, what a thing to say—

HORACE (*looking at* OSCAR). Oscar thinks I look very well.

OSCAR (*annoyed. Turns on* LEO). Don't stand there holding that biscuit in your hand.

LEO. Oh, well. I'll just finish my breakfast, Uncle Horace, and then I'll give you all the news about the bank— (*He exits into the dining room.*)

OSCAR. And what is that costume you have on?

BIRDIE (*looking at* HORACE). Now that you're home, you'll feel better. Plenty of good rest and we'll take such fine care of you. (*Stops*) But where is Zan? I missed her so much.

OSCAR. I asked you what is that strange costume you're parading around in?

BIRDIE (*nervously, backing toward stairs*). Me? Oh! It's my wrapper. I was so excited about Horace I just rushed out of the house—

OSCAR. Did you come across the square dressed that way? My dear Birdie, I—

HORACE (*to* REGINA, *wearily*). Yes, it's just like old times.

REGINA (*quickly to* OSCAR). Now, no fights. This is a holiday.

BIRDIE (*runs quickly up the stairs*). Zan! Zannie!

OSCAR. Birdie! (*She stops.*)

BIRDIE. Oh. Tell Zan I'll be back in a little while. (*Whispers*) Sorry, Oscar. (*Exits.*)

REGINA (*to* OSCAR *and* BEN). Why don't you go finish your breakfast and let Horace rest for a minute?

BEN (*crossing to dining room with* OSCAR). Never leave a meal unfinished. There are too many poor people who need the food. Mighty glad to see you home, Horace. Fine to have you back. Fine to have you back.

OSCAR (*to* LEO *as* BEN *closes dining-room doors*). Your mother has gone crazy. Running around the streets like a woman—

(*The moment* REGINA *and* HORACE *are alone, they become awkward and self-conscious.*)

REGINA (*laughs awkwardly*). Well. Here we are. It's been a long time. (HORACE *smiles*) Five months. You know, Horace, I wanted to come and be with you in the hospital, but I didn't know where my duty was. Here, or with you. But you know how much I *wanted* to come.

HORACE. That's kind of you, Regina. There was no need to come.

REGINA. Oh, but there was. Five months lying there all by yourself, no kinfolks, no friends. Don't try to tell me you didn't have a bad time of it.

HORACE. I didn't have a bad time. (*As she shakes her head, he becomes insistent*) No, I didn't, Regina. Oh, at first when I—when I heard the news about myself—but after I got used to that, I liked it there.

REGINA. You *liked* it? (*Coldly*) Isn't that strange. You liked it so well you didn't want to come home?

HORACE. That's not the way to put it. (*Then, kindly, as he sees her turn her head away*) But there I was and I got kind of used to it, kind of to like lying there and thinking. (*Smiles*) I never had much time to think before. And time's become valuable to me.

REGINA. It sounds almost like a holiday.

HORACE (*laughs*). It was, sort of. The first holiday I've had since I was a little kid.

REGINA. And here I was thinking you were in pain and—

HORACE (*quietly*). I was in pain.

REGINA. And instead you were having a holiday! A holiday of thinking. Couldn't you have done that here?

HORACE. I wanted to do it before I came here. I was thinking about us.

REGINA. About us? About you and me? Thinking about you and me after all these years. (*Unpleasantly*) You shall tell me everything you thought—some day.

HORACE (*there is silence for a minute*). Regina. (*She turns to him*) Why did you send Zan to Baltimore?

REGINA. Why? Because I wanted you home. You can't make anything suspicious out of that, can you?

HORACE. I didn't mean to make anything suspicious about it. (*Hesitantly, taking her hand*) Zan said you wanted me to come home. I was so pleased at that and touched it made me feel good.

REGINA (*taking away her hand, turns*). Touched that I should want you home?

HORACE (*sighs*). I'm saying all the wrong things as usual. Let's try to get along better. There isn't so much more time. Regina, what's all this crazy talk I've been hearing about Zan and Leo? Zan and Leo marrying?

REGINA (*turning to him, sharply*). Who gossips so much around here?

HORACE (*shocked*). Regina!

REGINA (*annoyed, anxious to quiet him*). It's some foolishness that Oscar thought up. I'll explain later. I have no intention of allowing any such arrangement. It was simply a way of keeping Oscar quiet in all this business I've been writing you about—

HORACE (*carefully*). What has Zan to do with any business of Oscar's? Whatever it is, you had better put it out of Oscar's head immediately. You know what I think of Leo.

REGINA. But there's no need to talk about it now.

HORACE. There is no need to talk about it ever. Not as

long as I live. (HORACE *stops, slowly turns to look at her*) As long as I live. I've been in a hospital for five months. Yet since I've been here you have not once asked me about—about my health. (*Then gently*) Well, I suppose they've written you. I can't live very long.

REGINA (*coldly*). I've never understood why people have to talk about this kind of thing.

HORACE (*there is a silence. Then he looks up at her, his face cold*). You misunderstand. I don't intend to gossip about my sickness. I thought it was only fair to tell you. I was not asking for your sympathy.

REGINA (*sharply, turns to him*). What do the doctors think caused your bad heart?

HORACE. What do you mean?

REGINA. They didn't think it possible, did they, that your fancy women may have—

HORACE (*smiles unpleasantly*). Caused my heart to be bad? I don't think that's the best scientific theory. You don't catch heart trouble in bed.

REGINA (*angrily*). I didn't think you did. I only thought you might catch a bad conscience—in bed, as you say.

HORACE. I didn't tell them about my bad conscience. Or about my fancy women. Nor did I tell them that my wife has not wanted me in bed with her for— (*Sharply*) How long is it, Regina? (REGINA *turns to him*) Ten years? Did you bring me home for this, to make me feel guilty again? That means you want something. But you'll not make me feel guilty any more. My "thinking" has made a difference.

REGINA. I see that it has. (*She looks toward dining-room door. Then comes to him, her manner warm and friendly*) It's foolish for us to fight this way. I didn't mean to be unpleasant. I was stupid.

HORACE (*wearily*). God knows I didn't either. I came home wanting so much not to fight, and then all of a sudden there we were. I got hurt and—

REGINA (*hastily*). It's all my fault. I didn't ask about—about your illness because I didn't want to remind you of it. Anyway I never believe doctors when they talk about— (*Brightly*) when they talk like that.

HORACE (*not looking at her*). Well, we'll try our best with each other. (*He rises.*)

REGINA (*quickly*). I'll try. Honestly, I will. Horace, Horace, I know you're tired but, but—couldn't you stay down here a few minutes longer? I want Ben to tell you something.

HORACE. Tomorrow.

REGINA. I'd like to now. It's very important to me. It's very important to all of us. (*Gaily, as she moves toward dining room*) Important to your beloved daughter. She'll be a very great heiress—

HORACE. Will she? That's nice.

REGINA (*opens doors*). Ben, are you finished breakfast?

HORACE. Is this the mill business I've had so many letters about?

REGINA (*to* BEN). Horace would like to talk to you now.

HORACE. Horace would not like to talk to you now. I am very tired, Regina—

REGINA (*comes to him*). Please. You've said we'll try our best with each other. I'll try. Really, I will. Please do this for me now. You will see what I've done while you've been away. How I watched your interests. (*Laughs gaily*) And I've done very well too. But things can't be delayed any longer. Everything must be settled this week— (HORACE *sits down.* BEN *enters.* OSCAR *has stayed in the dining room, his head turned to watch them.* LEO *is pretending to read the newspaper*) Now you must tell Horace all about it. Only be quick because he is very tired and must go to bed. (HORACE *is looking up at her. His face hardens as she speaks*) But I think your news will be better for him than all the medicine in the world.

BEN (*looking at* HORACE). It could wait. Horace may not feel like talking today.

REGINA. What an old faker you are! You know it can't wait. You know it must be finished this week. You've been just as anxious for Horace to get here as I've been.

BEN (*very jovial*). I suppose I have been. And why not? Horace has done Hubbard Sons many a good turn. Why shouldn't I be anxious to help him now?

REGINA (*laughs*). Help him! Help, him when you need him, that's what you mean.

BEN. What a woman you married, Horace. (*Laughs awkwardly when* HORACE *does not answer*) Well, then I'll make it quick. You know what I've been telling you for years. How I've always said that every one of us little Southern businessmen had great things— (*Extends his arm*)—right beyond our finger tips. It's been my dream: my dream to make those fingers grow longer. I'm a lucky man, Horace, a lucky man. To dream and to live to get what you've dreamed of. That's *my* idea of a lucky man. (*Looks at his fingers as his arm drops slowly*) For thirty years I've cried bring the cotton mills to the cotton. (HORACE *opens medicine bottle*) Well, finally I got up nerve to go to Marshall Company in Chicago.

HORACE. I know all this. (*He takes the medicine.* REGINA *rises, steps to him.*)

BEN. Can I get you something?

HORACE. Some water, please.

REGINA (*turns quickly*). Oh, I'm sorry. Let me. (*Brings him a glass of water. He drinks as they wait in silence*) You feel all right now?

HORACE. Yes. You wrote me. I know all that.

(OSCAR *enters from dining room.*)

REGINA (*triumphantly*). But you don't know that in the last few days Ben has agreed to give us—you, I mean— a much larger share.

HORACE. Really? That's very generous of him.

BEN (*laughs*). It wasn't so generous of me. It was smart of Regina.

REGINA (*as if she were signaling* HORACE). I explained to Ben that perhaps you hadn't answered his letters because you didn't think he was offering you enough, and that the time was getting short and you could guess how much he needed you—

HORACE (*smiles at her, nods*). And I could guess that he wants to keep control in the family.

REGINA (*to* BEN, *triumphantly*). Exactly. (*To* HORACE) So I did a little bargaining for you and convinced my brothers they weren't the only Hubbards who had a business sense.

HORACE. Did you have to convince them of that? How little people know about each other! (*Laughs*) But you'll know better about Regina next time, eh, Ben? (BEN, REGINA, HORACE *laugh together.* OSCAR's *face is angry*) Now let's see. We're getting a bigger share. (*Looking at* OSCAR) Who's getting less?

BEN. Oscar.

HORACE. Well, Oscar, you've grown very unselfish. What's happened to you?

(LEO *enters from dining room.*)

BEN (*quickly, before* OSCAR *can answer*). Oscar doesn't mind. Not worth fighting about now, eh, Oscar?

OSCAR (*angrily*). I'll get mine in the end. You can be sure of that. I've got my son's future to think about.

HORACE (*sharply*). Leo? Oh, I see. (*Puts his head back, laughs.* REGINA *looks at him nervously*) I am beginning to see. Everybody will get theirs.

BEN. I knew you'd see it. Seventy-five thousand, and that seventy-five thousand will make you a million.

REGINA (*steps to table, leaning forward*). It will, Horace, it will.

HORACE. I believe you. (*After a second*) Now I can understand Oscar's self-sacrifice, but what did you have to promise Marshall Company besides the money you're putting up?

BEN. They wouldn't take promises. They wanted guarantees.

HORACE. Of what?

BEN (*nods*). Water power. Free and plenty of it.

HORACE. You got them that, of course.

BEN. Cheap. You'd think the Governor of a great state would make his price a little higher. From pride, you know. (HORACE *smiles.* BEN *smiles*) Cheap wages. "What do you mean by cheap wages?" I say to Marshall. "Less than Massachusetts," he says to me, "and that averages eight a week." "Eight a week! By God," I tell him, "*I'd* work for eight a week myself." Why, there ain't a mountain white or a town nigger but wouldn't give his right arm for three silver dollars every week, eh, Horace?

HORACE. Sure. And they'll take less than that when you get around to playing them off against each other. You can save a little money that way, Ben. (*Angrily*) And make them hate each other just a little more than they do now.

REGINA. What's all this about?

BEN (*laughs*). There'll be no trouble from anybody, white or black. Marshall said that to me. "What about strikes? That's all we've had in Massachusetts for the last three years." I say to him, "What's a strike? I never heard of one. Come South, Marshall. We got good folks and we don't stand for any fancy fooling."

HORACE. You're right. (*Slowly*) Well, it looks like you made a good deal for yourselves, and for Marshall, too. (*To* BEN) Your father used to say he made the thousands and you boys would make the millions. I think he was right. (*Rises.*)

REGINA (*they are all looking at* HORACE. *She laughs nervously*). Millions for *us*, too.

HORACE. Us? You and me? I don't think so. We've got enough money, Regina. We'll just sit by and watch the boys grow rich. (*They watch* HORACE *tensely as he begins to move toward the staircase. He passes* LEO, *looks at him for a second*) How's everything at the bank, Leo?

LEO. Fine, sir. Everything is fine.

HORACE. How are all the ladies in Mobile? (HORACE *turns to* REGINA, *sharply*) Whatever made you think I'd let Zan marry—

REGINA. Do you mean that you are turning this down? Is it possible that's what you mean?

BEN. No, that's not what he means. Turning down a fortune. Horace is tired. He'd rather talk about it tomorrow—

REGINA. We can't keep putting it off this way. Oscar must be in Chicago by the end of the week with the money and contracts.

OSCAR (*giggles, pleased*). Yes, sir. Got to be there end of the week. No sense going without the money.

REGINA (*tensely*). I've waited long enough for your answer. I'm not going to wait any longer.

HORACE (*very deliberately*). I'm very tired now, Regina.

BEN (*hastily*). Now, Horace probably has his reasons. Things he'd like explained. Tomorrow will do. I can—

REGINA (*turns to* BEN, *sharply*). I want to know his reasons now! (*Turns back to* HORACE.)

HORACE (*as he climbs the steps*). I don't know them all myself. Let's leave it at that.

REGINA. We shall not leave it at that! We have waited for you here like children. Waited for you to come home.

HORACE. So that you could invest my money. So that is why you wanted me home? Well, I had hoped— (*Quietly*) If you are disappointed, Regina, I'm sorry. But I must do what I think best. We'll talk about it another day.

REGINA. We'll talk about it now. Just you and me.

HORACE (*looks down at her. His voice is tense*). Please, Regina, it's been a hard trip. I don't feel well. Please leave me alone now.

REGINA (*quietly*). I want to talk to you, Horace. I'm coming up. (*He looks at her for a minute, then moves on again out of sight. She begins to climb the stairs.*)

BEN (*softly. REGINA turns to him as he speaks*). Sometimes it is better to wait for the sun to rise again. (*She does not answer*) And sometimes, as our mother used to tell you, (REGINA *starts up stairs*) it's unwise for a good-looking woman to frown. (BEN *rises, moves toward stairs*) Softness and a smile do more to the heart of men — (*She disappears.* BEN *stands looking up the stairs. There is a long silence. Then, suddenly,* OSCAR *giggles.*)

OSCAR. Let us hope she'll change his mind. Let us hope. (*After a second* BEN *crosses to table, picks up his newspaper.* OSCAR *looks at* BEN. *The silence makes* LEO *uncomfortable.*)

LEO. The paper says twenty-seven cases of yellow fever in New Orleans. Guess the flood-waters caused it. (*Nobody pays attention*) Thought they were building the levees high enough. Like the niggers always say: a man born of woman can't build nothing high enough for the Mississippi. (*Gets no answer. Gives an embarrassed laugh.*)

(*Upstairs there is the sound of voices. The voices are not loud, but* BEN, OSCAR, LEO *become conscious of them.* LEO *crosses to landing, looks up, listens.*)

OSCAR (*pointing up*). Now just suppose she don't change his mind? Just suppose he keeps on refusing?

BEN (*without conviction*). He's tired. It was a mistake to talk to him today. He's a sick man, but he isn't a crazy one.

OSCAR (*giggles*). But just suppose he is crazy. What then?

BEN (*puts down his paper, peers at* OSCAR). Then we'll go

outside for the money. There's plenty who would give it.

OSCAR. And plenty who will want a lot for what they give. The ones who are rich enough to give will be smart enough to want. That means we'd be working for them, don't it, Ben?

BEN. You don't have to tell me the things I told you six months ago.

OSCAR. Oh, you're right not to worry. She'll change his mind. She always has. (*There is a silence. Suddenly* REGINA's *voice becomes louder and sharper. All of them begin to listen now. Slowly* BEN *rises, goes to listen by the staircase.* OSCAR, *watching him, smiles. As they listen* REGINA's *voice becomes very loud.* HORACE'S *voice is no longer heard*) Maybe. But I don't believe it. I never did believe he was going in with us.

BEN (*turning on him*). What the hell do you expect me to do?

OSCAR (*mildly*). Nothing. You done your almighty best. Nobody could blame you if the whole thing just dripped away right through our fingers. You can't do a thing. But there may be something I could do for us. (OSCAR *rises*) Or, I might better say, Leo could do for us. (BEN *stops, turns, looks at* OSCAR. LEO *is staring at* OSCAR) Ain't that true, son? Ain't it true you might be able to help your own kinfolks?

LEO (*nervously taking a step to him*). Papa, I—

BEN (*slowly*). How would he help us, Oscar?

OSCAR. Leo's got a friend. Leo's friend owns eighty-eight thousand dollars in Union Pacific bonds. (BEN *turns to look at* LEO) Leo's friend don't look at the bonds much —not for five or six months at a time.

BEN (*after a pause*). Union Pacific. Uh, huh. Let me understand. Leo's friend would—would lend him these bonds and he—

OSCAR (*nods*). Would be kind enough to lend them to us.

BEN. Leo.

LEO (*excited, comes to him*). Yes, sir?

BEN. When would your friend be wanting the bonds back?

LEO (*very nervous*). I don't know. I—well, I—

OSCAR (*sharply. Steps to him*). You told me he won't look at them until Fall—

LEO. Oh, that's right. But I—not till Fall. Uncle Horace never—

BEN (*sharply*). Be still.

OSCAR (*smiles at* LEO). Your uncle doesn't wish to know your friend's name.

LEO (*starts to laugh*). That's a good one. Not know his name—

OSCAR. Shut up, Leo! (LEO *turns away slowly, moves to table.* BEN *turns to* OSCAR) He won't look at them again until September. That gives us five months. Leo will return the bonds in three months. And we'll have no trouble raising the money once the mills are going up. Will Marshall accept bonds?

(BEN *stops to listen to sudden sharp voices from above. The voices are now very angry and very loud.*)

BEN (*smiling*). Why not? Why not? (*Laughs*) Good. We are lucky. We'll take the loan from Leo's friend—I think he will make a safer partner than our sister. (*Nods toward stairs. Turns to* LEO) How soon can you get them?

LEO. Today. Right now. They're in the safe-deposit box and—

BEN (*sharply*). I don't want to know where they are.

OSCAR (*laughs*). We will keep it secret from you. (*Pats* BEN's *arm.*)

BEN (*smiles*). Good. Draw a check for our part. You can take the night train for Chicago. Well, Oscar (*Holds out his hand*), good luck to us.

OSCAR. Leo will be taken care of?

LEO. I'm entitled to Uncle Horace's share. I'd enjoy being a partner—

BEN (*turns to stare at him*). You would? You can go to hell, you little— (*Starts toward* LEO.)

OSCAR (*nervously*). Now, now. He didn't mean that. I only want to be sure he'll get something out of all this.

BEN. Of course. We'll take care of him. We won't have any trouble about that. I'll see you at the store.

OSCAR (*nods*). That's settled then. Come on, son. (*Starts for door.*)

LEO (*puts out his hand*) I was only going to say what a great day this was for me and— (BEN *ignores his hand.*)

BEN. Go on.

(LEO *looks at him, turns, follows* OSCAR *out.* BEN *stands where he is, thinking. Again the voices upstairs can be heard.* REGINA's *voice is high and furious.* BEN *looks up, smiles, winces at the noise.*)

ALEXANDRA (*upstairs*). Mama—Mama—don't . . . (*The noise of running footsteps is heard and* ALEXANDRA *comes running down the steps, speaking as she comes*) Uncle Ben! Uncle Ben! Please go up. Please make Mama stop. Uncle Ben, he's sick, he's so sick. How can Mama talk to him like that—please, make her stop. She'll—

BEN. Alexandra, you have a tender heart.

ALEXANDRA (*crying*). Go on up, Uncle Ben, please—

(*Suddenly the voices stop. A second later there is the sound of a door being slammed.*)

BEN. Now you see. Everything is over. Don't worry. (*He starts for the door*) Alexandra, I want you to tell your mother how sorry I am that I had to leave. And don't worry so, my dear. Married folk frequently raise their voices, unfortunately. (*He starts to put on his hat and coat as* REGINA *appears on the stairs.*)

ALEXANDRA (*furiously*). How can you treat Papa like this? He's sick. He's very sick. Don't you know that? I won't let you.

REGINA. Mind your business, Alexandra. (*To* BEN. *Her*

voice is cold and calm) How much longer can you wait for the money?

BEN (*putting on his coat*). He has refused? My, that's too bad.

REGINA. He will change his mind. I'll find a way to make him. What's the longest you can wait now?

BEN. I could wait until next week. But I can't wait until next week. (*He giggles, pleased at the joke*) I could but I can't. Could and can't. Well, I must go now. I'm very late—

REGINA (*coming downstairs toward him*). You're not going. I want to talk to you.

BEN. I was about to give Alexandra a message for you. I wanted to tell you that Oscar is going to Chicago tonight, so we can't be here for our usual Friday supper.

REGINA (*tensely*). Oscar is going to Chi— (*Softly*) What do you mean?

BEN. Just that. Everything is settled. He's going on to deliver to Marshall—

REGINA (*taking a step to him*). I demand to know what— You are lying. You are trying to scare me. *You haven't got the money.* How could you have it? You can't have— (BEN *laughs*) You will wait until I—

(HORACE *comes into view on the landing.*)

BEN. You are getting out of hand. Since when do I take orders from you?

REGINA. Wait, you— (BEN *stops*) How *can* he go to Chicago? Did a ghost arrive with the money? (BEN *starts for the hall*) I don't believe you. Come back here. (REGINA *starts after him*) Come back here, you— (*The door slams. She stops in the doorway, staring, her fists clenched. After a pause she turns slowly.*)

HORACE (*very quietly*). It's a great day when you and Ben cross swords. I've been waiting for it for years.

ALEXANDRA. Papa, Papa, please go back! You will—

HORACE. And so they don't need you, and so you will not have your millions, after all.

REGINA (*turns slowly*). You hate to see anybody live now, don't you? You hate to think that I'm going to be alive and have what I want.

HORACE. I should have known you'd think that was the reason.

REGINA. Because you're going to die and you know you're going to die.

ALEXANDRA (*shrilly*). Mama! Don't— Don't listen, Papa. Just don't listen. Go away—

HORACE. Not to keep you from getting what you want. Not even partly that. (*Holding to the rail*) I'm sick of you, sick of this house, sick of my life here. I'm sick of your brothers and their dirty tricks to make a dime. There must be better ways of getting rich than cheating niggers on a pound of bacon. Why should I give you the money? (*Very angrily*) To pound the bones of this town to make dividends for you to spend? You wreck the town, you and your brothers, *you* wreck the town and live on it. Not me. Maybe it's easy for the dying to be honest. But it's not my fault I'm dying. (ADDIE *enters, stands at door quietly*) I'll do no more harm now. I've done enough. I'll die my own way. And I'll do it without making the world any worse. I leave that to you.

REGINA (*looks up at him slowly, calmly*). I hope you die. I hope you die soon. (*Smiles*) I'll be waiting for you to die.

ALEXANDRA (*shrieking*). Papa! Don't— Don't listen— Don't—

ADDIE. Come here, Zan. Come out of this room.

(ALEXANDRA *runs quickly to* ADDIE, *who holds her.* HORACE *turns slowly and starts upstairs.*)

Curtain

ACT THREE

SCENE: *Same as Act One. Two weeks later. It is late afternoon and it is raining.*

AT RISE: HORACE *is sitting near the window in a wheel chair. On the table next to him is a safe-deposit box, and a small bottle of medicine.* BIRDIE *and* ALEXANDRA *are playing the piano. On a chair is a large sewing basket.*

BIRDIE (*counting for* ALEXANDRA). One and two and three and four. One and two and three and four. (*Nods— turns to* HORACE) We once played together, Horace. Remember?

HORACE (*has been looking out of the window*). What, Birdie?

BIRDIE. We played together. You and me.

ALEXANDRA. *Papa* used to play?

BIRDIE. Indeed he did. (ADDIE *appears at the door in a large kitchen apron. She is wiping her hands on a towel*) He played the fiddle and very well, too.

ALEXANDRA (*turns to smile at* HORACE). I never knew—

ADDIE. Where's your mama?

ALEXANDRA. Gone to Miss Safronia's to fit her dresses.

(ADDIE *nods, starts to exit.*)

HORACE. Addie.

ADDIE. Yes, Mr. Horace.

HORACE (*speaks as if he had made a sudden decision*). Tell Cal to get on his things. I want him to go an errand.

(ADDIE *nods, exits.* HORACE *moves nervously in his chair, looks out of the window.*)

220

ALEXANDRA (*who has been watching him*). It's too bad
it's been raining all day, Papa. But you can go out in
the yard tomorrow. Don't be restless.

HORACE. I'm not restless, darling.

BIRDIE. I remember so well the time we played together,
your papa and me. It was the first time Oscar brought
me here to supper. I had never seen all the Hubbards
together before, and you know what a ninny I am and
how shy. (*Turns to look at* HORACE) You said you could
play the fiddle and you'd be much obliged if I'd play
with you. I was obliged to *you*, all right, all right.
(*Laughs when he does not answer her*) Horace, you
haven't heard a word I've said.

HORACE. Birdie, when did Oscar get back from Chicago?

BIRDIE. Yesterday. Hasn't he been here yet?

ALEXANDRA (*stops playing*). No. Neither has Uncle Ben
since—since that day.

BIRDIE. Oh, I didn't know it was *that* bad. Oscar never
tells me anything—

HORACE (*smiles, nods*). The Hubbards have had their
great quarrel. I knew it would come some day.
(*Laughs*) It came.

ALEXANDRA. It came. It certainly came all right.

BIRDIE (*amazed*). But Oscar was in such a good humor
when he got home, I didn't—

HORACE. Yes, I can understand that.

(ADDIE *enters carrying a large tray with glasses, a carafe
of elderberry wine and a plate of cookies, which she
puts on the table.*)

ALEXANDRA. Addie! A party! What for?

ADDIE. Nothing for. I had the fresh butter, so I made the
cakes, and a little elderberry does the stomach good in
the rain.

BIRDIE. Isn't this nice! A party just for us. Let's play party
music, Zan.

(ALEXANDRA *begins to play a gay piece.*)

ADDIE (*to* HORACE, *wheeling his chair to center*). Come over here, Mr. Horace, and don't be thinking so much. A glass of elderberry will do more good.

(ALEXANDRA *reaches for a cake*. BIRDIE *pours herself a glass of wine*.)

ALEXANDRA. Good cakes, Addie. It's nice here. Just us. Be nice if it could always be this way.

BIRDIE (*nods happily*). Quiet and restful.

ADDIE. Well, it won't be that way long. Little while now, even sitting here, you'll hear the red bricks going into place. The next day the smoke'll be pushing out the chimneys and by church time that Sunday every human born of woman will be living on chicken. That's how Mr. Ben's been telling the story.

HORACE (*looks at her*). They believe it that way?

ADDIE. Believe it? They use to believing what Mr. Ben orders. There ain't been so much talk around here since Sherman's army didn't come near.

HORACE (*softly*). They are fools.

ADDIE (*nods, sits down with the sewing basket*). You ain't born in the South unless you're a fool.

BIRDIE (*has drunk another glass of wine*). But we didn't play together after that night. Oscar said he didn't like me to play on the piano. (*Turns to* ALEXANDRA) You know what he said that night?

ALEXANDRA. Who?

BIRDIE. Oscar. He said that music made him nervous. He said he just sat and waited for the next note. (ALEXANDRA *laughs*) He wasn't poking fun. He meant it. Ah, well— (*She finishes her glass, shakes her head.* HORACE *looks at her, smiles*) Your papa don't like to admit it, but he's been mighty kind to me all these years. (*Running the back of her hand along his sleeve*) Often he'd step in when somebody said something and once— (*She stops, turns away, her face still*) Once he stopped Oscar from— (*She stops, turns. Quickly*) I'm sorry I said that. Why, here I am so happy and yet I think about bad things. (*Laughs nervously*) That's not right, now, is it? (*She pours a drink.* CAL *appears in the door. He has on an old coat and is carrying a torn umbrella.*)

ALEXANDRA. Have a cake, Cal.

CAL (*comes in, takes a cake*). Yes'm. You want me, Mr. Horace?

HORACE. What time is it, Cal?

CAL. 'Bout ten minutes before it's five.

HORACE. All right. Now you walk yourself down to the bank.

CAL. It'll be closed. Nobody'll be there but Mr. Manders, Mr. Joe Horns, Mr. Leo—

HORACE. Go in the back way. They'll be at the table, going over the day's business. (*Points to the deposit box*) See that box?

CAL (*nods*). Yes, sir.

HORACE. You tell Mr. Manders that Mr. Horace says he's much obliged to him for bringing the box, it arrived all right.

CAL (*bewildered*). He know you got the box. He bring it himself Wednesday. I opened the door to him and he say, "Hello, Cal, coming on to summer weather."

HORACE. You say just what I tell you. Understand?

(BIRDIE *pours another drink, stands at table.*)

CAL. No, sir. I ain't going to say I understand. I'm going down and tell a man he give you something he already know he give you, and you say "understand."

HORACE. Now, Cal.

CAL. Yes, sir. I just going to say you obliged for the box coming all right. I ain't going to understand it, but I'm going to say it.

HORACE. And tell him I want him to come over here after supper, and to bring Mr. Sol Fowler with him.

CAL (*nods*). He's to come after supper and bring Mr. Sol Fowler, your attorney-*at*-law, with him.

HORACE (*smiles*). That's right. Just walk right in the back room and say your piece. (*Slowly*) In front of everybody.

CAL. Yes, sir. (*Mumbles to himself as he exits.*)

ALEXANDRA (*who has been watching* HORACE). Is anything the matter, Papa?

HORACE. Oh, no. Nothing.

ADDIE. Miss Birdie, that elderberry going to give you a headache spell.

BIRDIE (*beginning to be drunk. Gaily*). Oh, I don't think so. I don't think it will.

ALEXANDRA (*as* HORACE *puts his hand to his throat*). Do you want your medicine, Papa?

HORACE. No, no. I'm all right, darling.

BIRDIE. Mama used to give me elderberry wine when I was a little girl. For hiccoughs. (*Laughs*) You know, I don't think people get hiccoughs any more. Isn't that funny? (BIRDIE *laughs.* HORACE *and* ALEXANDRA *laugh*) I used to get hiccoughs just when I shouldn't have.

ADDIE (*nods*). And nobody gets growing pains no more. That is funny. Just as if there was some style in what you get. One year an ailment's stylish and the next year it ain't.

BIRDIE (*turns*). I remember. It was my first big party, at Lionnet I mean, and I was so excited, and there I was with hiccoughs and Mama laughing. (*Softly. Looking at carafe*) Mama always laughed. (*Picks up carafe*) A big party, a lovely dress from Mr. Worth in Paris, France, and hiccoughs. (*Pours drink*) My brother pounding me on the back and Mama with the elderberry bottle, laughing at me. Everybody was on their way to come, and I was such a ninny, hiccoughing away. (*Drinks*) You know, that was the first day I ever saw Oscar Hubbard. The Ballongs were selling their horses and he was going there to buy. He passed and

lifted his hat—we could see him from the window—
and my brother, to tease Mama, said maybe we should
have invited the Hubbards to the party. He said Mama
didn't like them because they kept a store, and he said
that was old-fashioned of her. (*Her face lights up*) And
then, and *then*, I saw Mama angry for the first time in
my life. She said that wasn't the reason. She said she
was old-fashioned, but not that way. She said she was
old-fashioned enough not to like people who killed
animals they couldn't use, and who made their money
charging awful interest to poor, ignorant niggers and
cheating them on what they bought. She was very
angry, Mama was. I had never seen her face like that.
And then suddenly she laughed and said, "Look, I've
frightened Birdie out of the hiccoughs." (*Her head
drops. Then softly*) And so she had. They were all gone.
(*Moves to sofa, sits.*)

ADDIE. Yeah, they got mighty well off cheating niggers.
Well, there are people who eat the earth and eat all
the people on it like in the Bible with the locusts. Then
there are people who stand around and watch them eat
it. (*Softly*) Sometimes I think it ain't right to stand and
watch them do it.

BIRDIE (*thoughtfully*). Like I say, if we could only go
back to Lionnet. Everybody'd be better there. They'd
be good and kind. I like people to be kind. (*Pours
drink*) Don't you, Horace; don't you like people to be
kind?

HORACE. Yes, Birdie.

BIRDIE (*very drunk now*). Yes, that was the first day I
ever saw Oscar. Who would have thought— (*Quickly*)
You all want to know something? Well, I don't like Leo.
My very own son, and I don't like him. (*Laughs, gaily*)
My, I guess I even like Oscar more.

ALEXANDRA. Why did you marry Uncle Oscar?

ADDIE (*sharply*). That's no question for you to be asking.

HORACE (*sharply*). Why not? She's heard enough around here to ask anything.

ALEXANDRA. Aunt Birdie, why did you marry Uncle Oscar?

BIRDIE. I don't know. I thought I liked him. He was kind to me and I thought it was because he liked me too. But that wasn't the reason— (*Wheels on* ALEXANDRA) Ask why *he* married *me*. I can tell you that: he's told it to me often enough.

ADDIE (*leaning forward*). Miss Birdie, don't—

BIRDIE (*speaking very rapidly, tensely*). My family was good and the cotton on Lionnet's fields was better. Ben Hubbard wanted the cotton and (*Rises*) Oscar Hubbard married it for him. He was kind to me, then. He used to smile at me. He hasn't smiled at me since. Everybody knew that's what he married me for. (ADDIE *rises*) Everybody but me. Stupid, stupid me.

ALEXANDRA (*to* HORACE, *holding his hand, softly*). I see. (*Hesitates*) Papa, I mean—when you feel better couldn't we go away? I mean, by ourselves. Couldn't we find a way to go—

HORACE. Yes, I know what you mean. We'll try to find a way. I promise you, darling.

ADDIE (*moves to* BIRDIE). Rest a bit, Miss Birdie. You get talking like this you'll get a headache and—

BIRDIE (*sharply, turning to her*). I've never had a headache in my life. (*Begins to cry hysterically*) You know it as well as I do. (*Turns to* ALEXANDRA) I never had a headache, Zan. That's a lie they tell for me. I drink. All by myself, in my own room, by myself, I drink. Then, when they want to hide it, they say, "Birdie's got a headache again"—

ALEXANDRA (*comes to her quickly*). Aunt Birdie.

BIRDIE (*turning away*). Even you won't like me now. You won't like me any more.

ALEXANDRA. I love you. I'll always love you.

BIRDIE (*furiously*). Well, don't. Don't love me. Because in twenty years you'll just be like me. They'll do all the same things to you. (*Begins to laugh hysterically*) You know what? In twenty-two years I haven't had a whole day of happiness. Oh, a little, like today with you all. But never a single, whole day. I say to myself, if only I had one more *whole* day, then— (*The laugh stops*) And that's the way you'll be. And you'll trail after them, just like me, hoping they won't be so mean that day or say something to make you feel so bad—only you'll be worse off because you haven't got my Mama to remember— (*Turns away, her head drops. She stands quietly, swaying a little, holding to the sofa.* ALEXANDRA *leans down, puts her cheek on* BIRDIE's *arm.*)

ALEXANDRA (*to* BIRDIE). I guess we were all trying to make a happy day. You know, we sit around and try to pretend nothing's happened. We try to pretend we are not here. We make believe we are just by ourselves, some place else, and it doesn't seem to work. (*Kisses* BIRDIE's *hand*) Come now, Aunt Birdie, I'll walk you home. You and me. (*She takes* BIRDIE's *arm. They move slowly out.*)

BIRDIE (*softly as they exit*). You and me.

ADDIE (*after a minute*). Well. First time I ever heard Miss Birdie say a word. (HORACE *looks at her*) Maybe it's good for her. I'm just sorry Zan had to hear it. (HORACE *moves his head as if he were uncomfortable*) You feel bad, don't you? (*He shrugs.*)

HORACE. So you didn't want Zan to hear? It would be nice to let her stay innocent, like Birdie at her age. Let her listen now. Let her see everything. How else is she going to know that she's got to get away? I'm trying to show her that. I'm trying, but I've only got a little time left. She can even hate me when I'm dead, if she'll only learn to hate and fear this.

ADDIE. Mr. Horace—

HORACE. Pretty soon there'll be nobody to help her but you.

ADDIE (*crossing to him*). What can I do?

HORACE. Take her away.

ADDIE. How can I do that? Do you think they'd let me just go away with her?

HORACE. I'll fix it so they can't stop you when you're ready to go. You'll go, Addie?

ADDIE (*after a second, softly*). Yes, sir. I promise. (*He touches her arm, nods.*)

HORACE (*quietly*). I'm going to have Sol Fowler make me a new will. They'll make trouble, but you make Zan stand firm and Fowler'll do the rest. Addie, I'd like to leave you something for yourself. I always wanted to.

ADDIE (*laughs*). Don't you do that, Mr. Horace. A nigger woman in a white man's will! I'd never get it nohow.

HORACE. I know. But upstairs in the armoire drawer there's seventeen hundred dollar bills. It's money left from my trip. It's in an envelope with your name. It's for you.

ADDIE. Seventeen hundred dollar bills! My God, Mr. Horace, I won't know how to count up that high. (*Shyly*) It's mighty kind and good of you. I don't know what to say for thanks—

CAL (*appears in doorway*). I'm back. (*No answer*) I'm back.

ADDIE. So we see.

HORACE. Well?

CAL. Nothing. I just went down and spoke my piece. Just like you told me. I say, "Mr. Horace he thank you mightily for the safe box arriving in good shape and he say you come right after supper to his house and bring Mr. Attorney-at-law Sol Fowler with you." Then I wipe my hands on my coat. Every time I ever told a lie in my whole life, I wipe my hands right after. Can't help doing it. Well, while I'm wiping my hands, Mr. Leo jump up and say to me, "What box? What you talking about?"

HORACE (*smiles*). Did he?

CAL. And Mr. Leo say he got to leave a little early cause he got something to do. And then Mr. Manders say Mr. Leo should sit right down and finish up his work and stop acting like somebody made him Mr. President. So he sit down. Now, just like I told you, Mr. Manders was mighty surprised with the message because he knows right well he brought the box— (*Points to box, sighs*) But he took it all right. Some men take everything easy and some do not.

HORACE (*puts his head back, laughs*). Mr. Leo was telling the truth; he *has* got something to do. I hope Manders don't keep him too long. (*Outside there is the sound of voices.* CAL *exits.* ADDIE *crosses quickly to* HORACE, *puts basket on table, begins to wheel his chair toward the stairs. Sharply*) No. Leave me where I am.

ADDIE. But that's Miss Regina coming back.

HORACE (*nods, looking at door*). Go away, Addie.

ADDIE (*hesitates*). Mr. Horace. Don't talk no more today. You don't feel well and it won't do no good—

HORACE (*as he hears footsteps in the hall*). Go on. (*She looks at him for a second, then picks up her sewing from table and exits as* REGINA *comes in from hall.* HORACE'S *chair is now so placed that he is in front of the table with the medicine.* REGINA *stands in the hall, shakes umbrella, stands it in the corner, takes off her cloak and throws it over the banister. She stares at* HORACE.)

REGINA (*as she takes off her gloves*). We had agreed that you were to stay in your part of this house and I in mine. This room is *my* part of the house. Please don't come down here again.

HORACE. I won't.

REGINA (*crosses toward bell-cord*). I'll get Cal to take you upstairs.

HORACE (*smiles*). Before you do I want to tell you that after all, we have invested our money in Hubbard Sons and Marshall, Cotton Manufacturers.

REGINA (*stops, turns, stares at him*). What are you talking about? You haven't seen Ben— When did you change your mind?

HORACE. I didn't change my mind. *I* didn't invest the money. (*Smiles*) It was invested for me.

REGINA (*angrily*). What—?

HORACE. I had eighty-eight thousand dollars' worth of Union Pacific bonds in that safe-deposit box. They are not there now. Go and look. (*As she stares at him, he points to the box*) Go and look, Regina. (*She crosses quickly to the box, opens it*) Those bonds are as negotiable as money.

REGINA (*turns back to him*). What kind of joke are you playing now? Is this for my benefit?

HORACE. I don't look in that box very often, but three days ago, on Wednesday it was, because I had made a decision—

REGINA. I want to know what you are talking about.

HORACE (*sharply*). Don't interrupt me again. Because I had made a decision, I sent for the box. The bonds were gone. Eighty-eight thousand dollars gone. (*He smiles at her.*)

REGINA (*after a moment's silence, quietly*). Do you think I'm crazy enough to believe what you're saying?

HORACE (*shrugs*). Believe anything you like.

REGINA (*stares at him, slowly*). Where did they go to?

HORACE. They are in Chicago. With Mr. Marshall, I should guess.

REGINA. What did they do? Walk to Chicago? Have you really gone crazy?

HORACE. Leo took the bonds.

REGINA (*turns sharply then speaks softly, without conviction*). I don't believe it.

HORACE (*leans forward*). I wasn't there but I can guess what happened. This fine gentleman, to whom you were willing to marry your daughter, took the keys and opened the box. You remember that the day of the fight Oscar went to Chicago? Well, he went with my bonds that his son Leo had stolen for him. (*Pleasantly*) And for Ben, of course, too.

REGINA (*slowly, nods*). When did you find out the bonds were gone?

HORACE. Wednesday night.

REGINA. I thought that's what you said. Why have you waited three days to do anything? (*Suddenly laughs*) This *will* make a fine story.

HORACE (*nods*). Couldn't it?

REGINA (*still laughing*). A fine story to hold over their heads. How could they be such fools? (*Turns to him.*)

HORACE. But I'm not going to hold it over their heads.

REGINA (*the laugh stops*). What?

HORACE (*turns his chair to face her*). I'm going to let them keep the bonds—as a loan from you. An eighty-eight-thousand-dollar loan; they should be grateful to you. They will be, I think.

REGINA (*slowly, smiles*). I see. You are punishing me. But I won't let you punish me. If you won't do anything, I will. Now. (*She starts for door.*)

HORACE. You won't do anything. Because you can't. (RE-GINA *stops*) It won't do you any good to make trouble because I shall simply say that I lent them the bonds.

REGINA (*slowly*). You would do that?

HORACE. Yes. For once in your life I am tying your hands. There is nothing for you to do. (*There is silence. Then she sits down.*)

REGINA. I see. You are going to lend them the bonds and let them keep all the profit they make on them, and there is nothing I can do about it. Is that right?

HORACE. Yes.

REGINA (*softly*). Why did you say that I was making this gift?

HORACE. I was coming to that. I am going to make a new will, Regina, leaving you eighty-eight thousand dollars in Union Pacific bonds. The rest will go to Zan. It's true that your brothers have borrowed your share for a little while. After my death I advise you to talk to Ben and Oscar. They won't admit anything and Ben, I think, will be smart enough to see that he's safe. Because I knew about the theft and said nothing. Nor will I say anything as long as I live. Is that clear to you?

REGINA (*nods, softly, without looking at him*). You will not say anything as long as you live.

HORACE. That's right. And by that time they will probably have replaced your bonds, and then they'll belong to you and nobody but us will ever know what happened. (*Stops, smiles*) They'll be around any minute to see what I am going to do. I took good care to see that word reached Leo. They'll be mighty relieved to know I'm going to do nothing and Ben will think it all a capital joke on you. And that will be the end of that. There's nothing you can do to them, nothing you can do to me.

REGINA. You hate me very much.

HORACE. No.

REGINA. Oh, I think you do. (*Puts her head back, sighs*) Well, we haven't been very good together. Anyway, I don't hate you either. I have only contempt for you. I've always had.

HORACE. From the very first?

REGINA. I think so.

HORACE. I was in love with *you*. But why did *you* marry *me*?

REGINA. I was lonely when I was young.

HORACE. *You* were lonely?

REGINA. Not the way people usually mean. Lonely for all

the things I wasn't going to get. Everybody in this house was so busy and there was so little place for what I wanted. I wanted the world. Then, and then— (*Smiles*) Papa died and left the money to Ben and Oscar.

HORACE. And you married me?

REGINA. Yes, I thought— But I was wrong. You were a small-town clerk then. You haven't changed.

HORACE (*nods, smiles*). And that wasn't what you wanted.

REGINA. No. No, it wasn't what I wanted. (*Pauses, leans back, pleasantly*) It took me a little while to find out I had made a mistake. As for you—I don't know. It was almost as if I couldn't stand the kind of man you were— (*Smiles, softly*) I used to lie there at night, praying you wouldn't come near—

HORACE. Really? It was as bad as that?

REGINA (*nods*). Remember when I went to Doctor Sloan and I told you he said there was something the matter with me and that you shouldn't touch me any more?

HORACE. I remember.

REGINA. But you believed it. I couldn't understand that. I couldn't understand that anybody could be such a soft fool. That was when I began to despise you.

HORACE (*puts his hand to his throat, looks at the bottle of medicine on table*). Why didn't you leave me?

REGINA. I told you I married you for something. It turned out it was only for this. (*Carefully*) This wasn't what I wanted, but it was something. I never thought about it much but if I had (HORACE *puts his hand to his throat*) I'd have known that you would die before I would. But I couldn't have known that you would get heart trouble so early and so bad. I'm lucky, Horace. I've always been lucky. (HORACE *turns slowly to the medicine*) I'll be lucky again. (HORACE *looks at her. Then he puts his hand to his throat. Because he cannot reach the bottle he moves the chair closer. He reaches for the medicine, takes out the cork, picks up the spoon. The bottle slips and smashes on the table. He draws in his breath, gasps.)*

HORACE. Please. Tell Addie— The other bottle is upstairs. (REGINA *has not moved. She does not move now. He stares at her. Then, suddenly as if he understood, he raises his voice. It is a panic-stricken whisper, too small to be heard outside the room*) Addie! Addie! Come— *(Stops as he hears the softness of his voice. He makes a sudden, furious spring from the chair to the stairs, taking the first few steps as if he were a desperate runner. On the fourth step he slips, gasps, grasps the rail, makes a great effort to reach the landing. When he reaches the landing, he is on his knees. His knees give way, he falls on the landing, out of view.* REGINA *has not turned during his climb up the stairs. Now she waits a second. Then she goes below the landing, speaks up.)*

REGINA. Horace. Horace. *(When there is no answer, she turns, calls)* Addie! Cal! Come in here. *(She starts up the steps.* ADDIE *and* CAL *appear. Both run toward the stairs)* He's had an attack. Come up here. *(They run up the steps quickly.)*

CAL. My God. Mr. Horace—

(They cannot be seen now.)

REGINA *(her voice comes from the head of the stairs)*. Be still, Cal. Bring him in here.

(Before the footsteps and the voices have completely died away, ALEXANDRA *appears in the hall door, in her raincloak and hood. She comes into the room, begins to unfasten the cloak, suddenly looks around, sees the empty wheel chair, stares, begins to move swiftly as if to look in the dining room. At the same moment* ADDIE *runs down the stairs.* ALEXANDRA *turns and stares up at* ADDIE.*)*

ALEXANDRA. Addie! What?

ADDIE *(takes* ALEXANDRA *by the shoulders)*. I'm going for

the doctor. Go upstairs. (ALEXANDRA *looks at her, then quickly breaks away and runs up the steps.* ADDIE *exits. The stage is empty for a minute. Then the front door bell begins to ring. When there is no answer, it rings again. A second later* LEO *appears in the hall, talking as he comes in.*)

LEO (*very nervous*). Hello. (*Irritably*) Never saw any use ringing a bell when a door was open. If you are going to ring a bell, then somebody should answer it. (*Gets in the room, looks around, puzzled, listens, hears no sound*) Aunt Regina. (*He moves around restlessly*) Addie. (*Waits*) Where the hell— (*Crosses to the bell cord, rings it impatiently, waits, gets no answer, calls*) Cal! Cal! (CAL *appears on the stair landing.*)

CAL (*his voice is soft, shaken*). Mr. Leo. Miss Regina says you stop that screaming noise.

LEO (*angrily*). Where is everybody?

CAL. Mr. Horace he got an attack. He's bad. Miss Regina says you stop that noise.

LEO. Uncle Horace— What— What happened? (CAL *starts down the stairs, shakes his head, begins to move swiftly off.* LEO *looks around wildly*) But when— You seen Mr. Oscar or Mr. Ben? (CAL *shakes his head. Moves on.* LEO *grabs him by the arm*) Answer me, will you?

CAL. No, I ain't seen 'em. I ain't got time to answer you. I got to get things. (CAL *runs off.*)

LEO. But what's the matter with him? When did this happen— (*Calling after* CAL) You'd think Papa'd be some place where you could find him. I been chasing him all afternoon.

(OSCAR *and* BEN *come quickly into the room.*)

LEO. Papa, I've been looking all over town for you and Uncle Ben—

BEN. Where is he?

OSCAR. Addie just told us it was a sudden attack, and—

BEN (*to* LEO). Where is he? When did it happen?

LEO. Upstairs. Will you listen to me, please? I been looking for you for—

OSCAR (*to* BEN). You think we should go up? (BEN, *looking up the steps, shakes his head.*)

BEN. I don't know. I don't know.

OSCAR (*shakes his head*). But he was all right—

LEO (*yelling*). *Will you listen to me?*

OSCAR (*sharply*). What is the matter with you?

LEO. I been trying to tell you. I been trying to find you for an hour—

OSCAR. Tell me what?

LEO. Uncle Horace knows about the bonds. He knows about them. He's had the box since Wednesday—

BEN (*sharply*). Stop shouting! What the hell are you talking about?

LEO (*furiously*). I'm telling you he knows about the bonds. Ain't that clear enough—

OSCAR (*grabbing* LEO's *arm*). You God-damn fool! Stop screaming!

BEN. Now what happened? Talk quietly.

LEO. You heard me. Uncle Horace knows about the bonds. He's known since Wednesday.

BEN (*after a second*). How do you know that?

LEO. Because Cal comes down to Manders and says the box came O.K. and—

OSCAR (*trembling*). That might not mean a thing—

LEO (*angrily*). No? It might not, huh? Then he says Manders should come here tonight and bring Sol Fowler with him. I guess that don't mean a thing either.

OSCAR (*to* BEN). Ben— What— Do you think he's seen the—

BEN (*motions to the box*). There's the box. (*Both* OSCAR *and* LEO *turn sharply.* LEO *makes a leap to the box*) You ass. Put it down. What are you going to do with it, eat it?

LEO. I'm going to— (*Starts.*)

BEN (*furiously*). Put it down. Don't touch it again. Now sit down and shut up for a minute.

OSCAR. Since Wednesday. (*To* LEO) You said he had it since Wednesday. Why didn't he say something— (*To* BEN) I don't understand—

LEO (*taking a step*). I can put it back. I can put it back before anybody knows.

BEN (*who is standing at the table, softly*). He's had it since Wednesday. Yet he hasn't said a word to us.

OSCAR. *Why? Why?*

LEO. What's the difference why? He was getting ready to say plenty. He was going to say it to Fowler tonight—

OSCAR (*angrily*). Be still. (*Turns to* BEN, *looks at him, waits.*)

BEN (*after a minute*). I don't believe that.

LEO (*wildly*). *You* don't believe it? What do I care what *you* believe? I do the dirty work and then—

BEN (*turning his head sharply to* LEO). I'm remembering that. I'm remembering that, Leo.

OSCAR. What do you mean?

LEO. You—

BEN (*to* OSCAR). If you don't shut that little fool up, I'll show you what I mean. For some reason he knows, but he don't say a word.

OSCAR. Maybe he didn't know that *we*—

BEN (*quickly*). That *Leo*— He's no fool. Does Manders know the bonds are missing?

LEO. How could I tell? I was half crazy. I don't think so. Because Manders seemed kind of puzzled and—

OSCAR. But we got to find out— (*He breaks off as* CAL *comes into the room carrying a kettle of hot water.*)

BEN. How is he, Cal?

CAL. I don't know, Mr. Ben. He was bad. (*Going toward stairs.*)

OSCAR. But when did it happen?

CAL (*shrugs*). He wasn't feeling bad early. (ADDIE *comes in quickly from the hall*) Then there he is next thing on the landing, fallen over, his eyes tight—

ADDIE (*to* CAL). Dr. Sloan's over at the Ballongs. Hitch the buggy and go get him. (*She takes the kettle and cloths from him, pushes him, runs up the stairs*) Go on. (*She disappears.* CAL *exits.*)

BEN. Never seen Sloan anywhere when you need him.

OSCAR (*softly*). Sounds bad.

LEO. He would have told *her* about it. Aunt Regina. He would have told his own wife—

BEN (*turning to* LEO). Yes, he might have told her. But they weren't on such pretty terms and maybe he didn't. Maybe he didn't. (*Goes quickly to* LEO) Now, listen to me. If she doesn't know, it may work out all right. If she does know, you're to say he lent you the bonds.

LEO. Lent them to me! Who's going to believe that?

BEN. Nobody.

OSCAR (*to* LEO). Don't you understand? It can't do no harm to say it—

LEO. Why should I say he lent them to me? Why not to you? (*Carefully*) Why not to Uncle Ben?

BEN (*smiles*). Just because he didn't lend them to me. Remember that.

LEO. But all he has to do is say he didn't lend them to me—

BEN (*furiously*). But for some reason, he doesn't seem to be talking, does he?

(*There are footsteps above. They all stand looking at the stairs.* REGINA *begins to come slowly down.*)

BEN. What happened?

REGINA. He's had a bad attack.

OSCAR. Too bad. I'm sorry we weren't here when—when Horace needed us.

BEN. When *you* needed us.

REGINA (*looks at him*). Yes.

BEN. How is he? Can we—can we go up?

REGINA (*shakes her head*). He's not conscious.

OSCAR (*pacing around*). It's that—it's that bad? Wouldn't you think Sloan could be found quickly, just once, just once?

REGINA. I don't think there is much for him to do.

BEN. Oh, don't talk like that. He's come through attacks before. He will now.

(REGINA *sits down. After a second she speaks softly.*)

REGINA. Well. We haven't seen each other since the day of our fight.

BEN (*tenderly*). That was nothing. Why, you and Oscar and I used to fight when we were kids.

OSCAR (*hurriedly*). Don't you think we should go up? Is there anything we can do for Horace—

BEN. You don't feel well. Ah—

REGINA (*without looking at them*). No, I don't. (*Slight pause*) Horace told me about the bonds this afternoon. (*There is an immediate shocked silence.*)

LEO. The bonds. What do you mean? What bonds? What—

BEN (*looks at him furiously. Then to* REGINA). The Union Pacific bonds? *Horace's* Union Pacific bonds?

REGINA. Yes.

OSCAR (*steps to her, very nervously*). Well. Well what— what about them? What—what could he say?

REGINA. He said that Leo had stolen the bonds and given them to you.

OSCAR (*aghast, very loudly*). That's ridiculous, Regina, absolutely—

LEO. I don't know what you're talking about. What would I— Why—

REGINA (*wearily to* BEN). Isn't it enough that he stole them from me? Do I have to listen to this in the bargain?

OSCAR. You are talking—

LEO. I didn't steal anything. I don't know why—

REGINA (*to* BEN). Would you ask them to stop that, please? (*There is silence for a minute.* BEN *glowers at* OSCAR *and* LEO.)

BEN. Aren't we starting at the wrong end, Regina? What did Horace tell you?

REGINA (*smiles at him*). He told me that Leo had stolen the bonds.

LEO. I didn't steal—

REGINA. Please. Let me finish. Then he told me that he was going to pretend that he had lent them to you (LEO *turns sharply to* REGINA, *then looks at* OSCAR, *then looks back at* REGINA) as a present from me—to my brothers. He said there was nothing I could do about it. He said the rest of his money would go to Alexandra. That is all. (*There is a silence.* OSCAR *coughs,* LEO *smiles slyly.*)

LEO (*taking a step to her*). I told you he had lent them— I could have told you—

REGINA (*ignores him, smiles sadly at* BEN). So I'm very badly off, you see. (*Carefully*) But Horace said there was nothing I could do about it as long as he was alive to say he had lent you the bonds.

BEN. You shouldn't feel that way. It can all be explained, all be adjusted. It isn't as bad—

REGINA. So you, at least, are willing to admit that the bonds were stolen?

BEN (OSCAR *laughs nervously*). I admit no such thing. It's possible that Horace made up that part of the story to tease you— (*Looks at her*) Or perhaps to punish you. Punish you.

REGINA (*sadly*). It's not a pleasant story. I feel bad, Ben, naturally. I hadn't thought—

BEN. Now you shall have the bonds safely back. That was the understanding, wasn't it, Oscar?

OSCAR. Yes.

REGINA. I'm glad to know that. (*Smiles*) Ah, I had greater hopes—

BEN. Don't talk that way. That's foolish. (*Looks at his watch*) I think we ought to drive out for Sloan ourselves. If we can't find him we'll go over to Senateville for Doctor Morris. And don't think I'm dismissing this other business. I'm not. We'll have it all out on a more appropriate day.

REGINA (*looks up, quietly*). I don't think you had better go yet. I think you had better stay and sit down.

BEN. We'll be back with Sloan.

REGINA. Cal has gone for him. I don't want you to go.

BEN. Now don't worry and—

REGINA. You will come back in this room and sit down. I have something more to say.

BEN (*turns, comes toward her*). Since when do I take orders from you?

REGINA (*smiles*). You don't—yet. (*Sharply*) Come back, Oscar. You too, Leo.

OSCAR (*sure of himself, laughs*). My dear Regina—

BEN (*softly, pats her hand*). Horace has already clipped your wings and very wittily. Do I have to clip them, too? (*Smiles at her*) You'd get farther with a smile, Regina. I'm a soft man for a woman's smile.

REGINA. I'm smiling, Ben. I'm smiling because you are quite safe while Horace lives. But I don't think Horace will live. And if he doesn't live I shall want seventy-five per cent in exchange for the bonds.

BEN (*steps back, whistles, laughs*). Greedy! What a greedy girl you are! You want so much of everything.

REGINA. Yes. And if I don't get what I want I am going to put all three of you in jail.

OSCAR (*furiously*). You're mighty crazy. Having just admitted—

BEN. And on what evidence would you put Oscar and Leo in jail?

REGINA (*laughs, gaily*). Oscar, listen to him. He's getting ready to swear that it was you and Leo! What do you say to that? (OSCAR *turns furiously toward* BEN) Oh, don't be angry, Oscar. I'm going to see that he goes in with you.

BEN. Try anything you like, Regina. (*Sharply*) And now we can stop all this and say good-bye to you. (ALEXANDRA *comes slowly down the steps*) It's his money and he's obviously willing to let us borrow it. (*More pleasantly*) Learn to make threats when you can carry them through. For how many years have I told you a good-looking woman gets more by being soft and appealing? Mama used to tell you that. (*Looks at his watch*) Where the hell is Sloan? (*To* OSCAR) Take the buggy and— (*As* BEN *turns to* OSCAR, *he sees* ALEXANDRA. *She walks stiffly. She goes slowly to the lower window, her head bent. They all turn to look at her.*)

OSCAR (*after a second, moving toward her*). What? Alexandra— (*She does not answer. After a second,* ADDIE *comes slowly down the stairs, moving as if she were very tired. At foot of steps, she looks at* ALEXANDRA, *then turns and slowly crosses to door and exits.* REGINA *rises.* BEN *looks nervously at* ALEXANDRA, *at* REGINA.)

OSCAR (*as* ADDIE *passes him, irritably to* ALEXANDRA). Well, what is— (*Turns into room—sees* ADDIE *at foot of steps*) —what's? (BEN *puts up a hand, shakes his head*) My God, I didn't know—who *could* have known—I didn't know he was that sick. Well, well—I— (REGINA *stands quietly, her back to them.*)

BEN (*softly, sincerely*). Seems like yesterday when he first came here.

OSCAR (*sincerely, nervously*). Yes, that's true. (*Turns to* BEN) The whole town loved him and respected him.

ALEXANDRA (*turns*). Did you love him, Uncle Oscar?

OSCAR. Certainly, I— What a strange thing to ask! I—

ALEXANDRA. Did you love him, Uncle Ben?

BEN (*simply*). He had—

ALEXANDRA (*suddenly starts to laugh very loudly*). And you, Mama, did you love him, too?

REGINA. I know what you feel, Alexandra, but please try to control yourself.

ALEXANDRA (*still laughing*). I'm trying, Mama. I'm trying very hard.

BEN. Grief makes some people laugh and some people cry. It's better to cry, Alexandra.

ALEXANDRA (*the laugh has stopped. Tensely moves toward* REGINA). What was Papa doing on the staircase?

(BEN *turns to look at* ALEXANDRA.)

REGINA. Please go and lie down, my dear. We all need time to get over shocks like this. (ALEXANDRA *does not move.* REGINA's *voice becomes softer, more insistent*) Please go, Alexandra.

ALEXANDRA. No, Mama. I'll wait. I've got to talk to you.

REGINA. Later. Go and rest now.

ALEXANDRA (*quietly*). I'll wait, Mama. I've plenty of time.

REGINA (*hesitates, stares, makes a half shrug, turns back to* BEN). As I was saying. Tomorrow morning I am going up to Judge Simmes. I shall tell him about Leo.

BEN (*motioning toward* ALEXANDRA). Not in front of the child, Regina. I—

REGINA (*turns to him. Sharply*). I didn't ask her to stay. Tomorrow morning I go to Judge Simmes—

OSCAR. And what proof? What proof of all this—

REGINA (*turns sharply*). None. I won't need any. The bonds are missing and they are with Marshall. That will be enough. If it isn't, I'll add what's necessary.

BEN. I'm sure of that.

REGINA (*turns to* BEN). You can be quite sure.

OSCAR. We'll deny—

REGINA. Deny your heads off. You couldn't find a jury that wouldn't weep for a woman whose brothers steal from her. And you couldn't find twelve men in this state you haven't cheated and who hate you for it.

OSCAR. What kind of talk is this? You couldn't do any-thing like that! We're your own brothers. (*Points up-stairs*) How can you talk that way when upstairs not five minutes ago—

REGINA (*slowly*). There are people who can't go back, who must finish what they start. I am one of those people, Oscar. (*After a slight pause*) Where was I? (*Smiles at* BEN) Well, they'll convict you. But I won't care much if they don't. (*Leans forward, pleasantly*) Because by that time you'll be ruined. I shall also tell my story to Mr. Marshall, who likes me, I think, and who will not want to be involved in your scandal. A respectable firm like Marshall and Company. The deal would be off in an hour. (*Turns to them angrily*) And you know it. Now I don't want to hear any more from any of you. *You'll do no more bargaining in this house.* I'll take my seventy-five per cent and we'll forget the story forever. That's one way of doing it, and the way I prefer. You know me well enough to know that I don't mind taking the other way.

BEN (*after a second, slowly*). None of us has ever known you well enough, Regina.

REGINA. You're getting old, Ben. Your tricks aren't as smart as they used to be. (*There is no answer. She waits, then smiles*) All right. I take it that's settled and I get what I asked for.

OSCAR (*furiously to* BEN). Are you going to let her do this—

BEN (*turns to look at him, slowly*). You have a suggestion?

REGINA (*puts her arms above her head, stretches, laughs*). No, he hasn't. All right. Now, Leo, I have forgotten that you ever saw the bonds. (*Archly, to* BEN *and* OSCAR) And as long as you boys both behave yourselves, I've forgotten that we ever talked about them. You can draw up the necessary papers tomorrow. (BEN *laughs.* LEO *stares at him, starts for door. Exits.* OSCAR *moves toward door angrily.* REGINA *looks at* BEN, *nods, laughs with him. For a second,* OSCAR *stands in the door, looking back at them. Then he exits.*)

REGINA. You're a good loser, Ben. I like that.

BEN (*he picks up his coat, then turns to her*). Well, I say to myself, what's the good? You and I aren't like Oscar. We're not sour people. I think that comes from a good digestion. Then, too, one loses today and wins tomorrow. I say to myself, years of planning and I get what I want. Then I don't get it. But I'm not discouraged. The century's turning, the world is open. Open for people like you and me. Ready for us, waiting for us. After all this is just the beginning. There are hundreds of Hubbards sitting in rooms like this throughout the country. All their names aren't Hubbard, but they are all Hubbards and they will own this country some day. We'll get along.

REGINA (*smiles*). I think so.

BEN. Then, too, I say to myself, things may change. (*Looks at* ALEXANDRA) I agree with Alexandra. What is a man in a wheel chair doing on a staircase? I ask myself that.

REGINA (*looks up at him*). And what do you answer?

BEN. I have no answer. But maybe some day I will. Maybe never, but maybe some day. (*Smiles. Pats her arm*) When I do, I'll let you know. (*Goes toward hall.*)

REGINA. When you do, write me. I will be in Chicago. (*Gaily*) Ah, Ben, if Papa had only left me his money.

BEN. I'll see you tomorrow.

REGINA. Oh, yes. Certainly. You'll be sort of working for me now.

BEN (*as he passes* ALEXANDRA, *smiles*). Alexandra, you're turning out to be a right interesting girl. (*Looks at* REGINA) Well, good night all. (*He exits.*)

REGINA (*Sits quietly for a second, stretches, turns to look at* ALEXANDRA). What do you want to talk to me about, Alexandra?

ALEXANDRA (*slowly*). I've changed my mind. I don't want to talk. There's nothing to talk about now.

REGINA. You're acting very strange. Not like yourself. You've had a bad shock today. I know that. And you loved Papa, but you must have expected this to come some day. You knew how sick he was.

ALEXANDRA. I knew. We all knew.

REGINA. It will be good for you to get away from here. Good for me, too. Time heals most wounds, Alexandra. You're young, you shall have all the things I wanted. I'll make the world for you the way I wanted it to be for me. (*Uncomfortably*) Don't sit there staring. You've been around Birdie so much you're getting just like her.

ALEXANDRA (*nods*). Funny. That's what Aunt Birdie said today.

REGINA (*nods*). Be good for you to get away from all this. (ADDIE *enters.*)

ADDIE. Cal is back, Miss Regina. He says Dr. Sloan will be coming in a few minutes.

REGINA. We'll go in a few weeks. A few weeks! That means two or three Saturdays, two or three Sundays. (*Sighs*) Well, I'm very tired. I shall go to bed. I don't want any supper. Put the lights out and lock up. (ADDIE *moves to the piano lamp, turns it out*) You go to your room, Alexandra. Addie will bring you something hot. You look very tired. (*Rises. To* ADDIE) Call me when Dr. Sloan gets here. I don't want to see anybody else. I don't want any condolence calls tonight. The whole town will be over.

ALEXANDRA. Mama, I'm not coming with you. I'm not going to Chicago.

REGINA (*turns to her*). You're very upset, Alexandra.

ALEXANDRA (*quietly*). I mean what I say. With all my heart.

REGINA. We'll talk about it tomorrow. The morning will make a difference.

ALEXANDRA. It won't make any difference. And there isn't anything to talk about. I am going away from you. Because I want to. Because I know Papa would want me to.

REGINA (*puzzled, careful, polite*). You *know* your papa wanted you to go away from me?

ALEXANDRA. Yes.

REGINA (*softly*). And if I say no?

ALEXANDRA (*looks at her*). Say it Mama, say it. And see what happens.

REGINA (*softly, after a pause*). And if I make you stay?

ALEXANDRA. That would be foolish. It wouldn't work in the end.

REGINA. You're very serious about it, aren't you? (*Crosses to stairs*) Well, you'll change your mind in a few days.

ALEXANDRA. You only change your mind when you want to. And I won't want to.

REGINA (*going up the steps*). Alexandra, I've come to the end of my rope. Somewhere there has to be what I want, too. Life goes too fast. Do what you want; think what you want; go where you want. I'd like to keep you with me, but I won't make you stay. Too many people used to make me do too many things. No, I won't make you stay.

ALEXANDRA. You couldn't, Mama, because I want to leave here. As I've never wanted anything in my life before. Because now I understand what Papa was trying to tell me. (*Pause*) All in one day: Addie said there were people who ate the earth and other people who stood around and watched them do it. And just now Uncle Ben said the same thing. Really, he said the same thing. (*Tensely*) Well, tell him for me, Mama, I'm not going to stand around and watch you do it. Tell him I'll be fighting as hard as he'll be fighting (*Rises*) some place where people don't just stand around and watch.

REGINA. Well, you have spirit, after all. I used to think

you were all sugar water. We don't have to be bad friends. I don't want us to be bad friends, Alexandra. (*Starts, stops, turns to* ALEXANDRA) Would you like to come and talk to me, Alexandra? Would you—would you like to sleep in my room tonight?

ALEXANDRA (*takes a step toward her*) Are you afraid, Mama? (REGINA *does not answer. She moves slowly out of sight.* ADDIE *comes to* ALEXANDRA, *presses her arm.*)

The Curtain Falls

WATCH ON THE RHINE

FOR

HERMAN SHUMLIN

THANKS AND AFFECTION

Watch on the Rhine was first produced at the Martin Beck Theatre, New York City, on April 1, 1941, with the following cast:

(In the order of their appearance)

ANISE	EDA HEINEMANN
JOSEPH	FRANK WILSON
FANNY FARRELLY	LUCILE WATSON
DAVID FARRELLY	JOHN LODGE
MARTHE DE BRANCOVIS	HELEN TRENHOLME
TECK DE BRANCOVIS	GEORGE COULOURIS
SARA MÜLLER	MADY CHRISTIANS
JOSHUA MÜLLER	PETER FERNANDEZ
BODO MÜLLER	ERIC ROBERTS
BABETTE MÜLLER	ANNE BLYTH
KURT MÜLLER	PAUL LUKAS

Produced and staged by HERMAN SHUMLIN

Setting designed by JO MIELZINER

Costumes designed by HELENE PONS

SCENE

The scene of the play is the living room of the Farrelly country house, about twenty miles from Washington. The time is late spring, 1940.

ACT ONE

Early on a Wednesday morning.

ACT TWO

Ten days later.

ACT THREE

A half hour later.

ACT ONE

SCENE: *The living room of the Farrelly house, about twenty miles from Washington, D. C., on a warm spring morning.*

Center stage are large French doors leading to an elevated open terrace. On the terrace are chairs, tables, a large table for dining. Some of this furniture we can see; most of it is on the left side of the terrace, beyond our sight. Left stage is an arched entrance, leading to the oval reception hall. We can see the main staircase as it goes off to the back of the hall. Right stage is a door leading to a library. The Farrelly house was built in the early nineteenth century. It has space, simplicity, style. The living room is large. Up stage right is a piano; down stage left, a couch; down stage right, a couch and chairs; up stage a few smaller chairs. Four or five generations have furnished this room and they have all been people of taste. There are no styles, no periods; the room has never been refurnished. Each careless aristocrat has thrown into the room what he or she liked as a child, what he or she brought home when grown up. Therefore the furniture is of many periods: the desk is English, the couch is Victorian, some of the pictures are modern, some of the ornaments French. The room has too many things in it: vases, clocks, miniatures, boxes, china animals. On the right wall is a large portrait of a big kind-faced man in an evening suit of 1900. On another wall is a large, very ugly landscape. The room is crowded. But it is cool and clean and its fabrics and woods are in soft colors.

AT RISE: ANISE, *a thin Frenchwoman of about sixty, in a dark housekeeper's dress, is standing at a table sorting mail. She takes the mail from a small basket, holds each letter to the light, reads each postal card, then places them in piles. On the terrace,* JOSEPH, *a tall, middle-aged Negro butler, wheels a breakfast wagon. As he appears,* FANNY FARRELLY *comes in from the hall. She is a handsome woman of about sixty-three. She has on a fancy, good-looking dressing-gown.*

Left and right are the audience's left and right.

FANNY (*stops to watch* ANISE. *Sees* JOSEPH *moving about on terrace. Calls*). Joseph! (*To* ANISE) Morning.

ANISE (*continues examining mail*). Good morning, Madame.

JOSEPH (*comes to terrace door*). Yes'm?

FANNY. Everybody down?

JOSEPH. No'm. Nobody. I'll get your tea. (*He returns to breakfast wagon on terrace.*)

FANNY. Mr. David isn't down yet? But he knows he is to meet the train.

JOSEPH (*comes in from the terrace with the cup of tea*). He's got plenty of time, Miss Fanny. The train ain't in till noon.

FANNY. Breakfast is at nine o'clock in this house and will be until the day after I die. Ring the bell.

JOSEPH. It ain't nine yet, Miss Fanny. It's eight-thirty.

FANNY. Well, put the clocks up to nine and ring the bell.

JOSEPH. Mr. David told me not to ring it any more. He says it's got too mean a ring, that bell. It disturbs folks.

FANNY. That's what it was put there for. I like to disturb folks.

JOSEPH. Yes'm.

FANNY. You slept well, Anise. You were asleep before I could dismantle myself.

ANISE. I woke several times during the night.

FANNY. Did you? Then you were careful not to stop snor-
ing. We must finally get around to rearranging your
room. (ANISE *hands her three or four letters*) Even
when you don't snore, it irritates me. (FANNY *opens a
letter, begins to read it. After a minute*) What time is it?

ANISE. It is about eight-thirty. Joseph just told you.

FANNY. I didn't hear him. I'm nervous. Naturally. My mail
looks dull. (*Reading the letter*) Jenny always tell you a
piece of gossip three times, as if it grew fresher with the
telling. Did you put flowers in their rooms?

ANISE. Certainly.

FANNY. David ought to get to the station by eleven-thirty.

ANISE (*patiently*). The train does not draw in until ten
minutes past noon.

FANNY. But it might come in early. It's been known.

ANISE. Never. Not in the Union Station in Washington,
the District of Columbia.

FANNY (*irritably*). But it might. It might. Don't argue
with me about everything. What time is it?

ANISE. It's now twenty-seven minutes before nine. It will
be impossible to continue telling you the time every
three minutes from now until Miss Sara arrives. I think
you are having a nervous breakdown. Compose yourself.

FANNY. It's been twenty years. Any mother would be nervous. If your daughter were coming home and you hadn't
seen her, and a husband, *and* grandchildren—

ANISE. I do not say that it is wrong to be nervous. I, too,
am nervous. I say only that you are.

FANNY. Very well. I heard you. *I* say that I am. (*She goes
back to reading her letter. Looks up*) Jenny's still in
California. She's lost her lavallière again. Birdie Chase's
daughter is still faire l'amouring with that actor. Taw-
dry, Jenny says it is. An actor. Fashions in sin change.
In my day, it was Englishmen. I don't understand infi-
delity. If you love a man, then why? If you don't love
him, then why stay with him? (*Without turning, she*

points over her head to Joshua Farrelly's portrait)
Thank God, I was in love. I thought about Joshua last
night. Three grandchildren. He would have liked that.
I hope I will. (*Points to other letters*) Anything in
anybody else's mail?

ANISE. Advertisements for Mr. David and legal things. For
our Count and Countess, there is nothing but what
seems an invitation to a lower-class embassy tea and
letters asking for bills to get paid.

FANNY. That's every morning. (*Thoughtfully*) In the six
weeks the Balkan nobility have been with us, they
seem to have run up a great many bills.

ANISE. Yes. *I* told you that. Then there was a night-letter
for Mr. David.

(*A very loud, very unpleasant bell begins to ring.*)

FANNY (*through the noise*). Really? From whom?

ANISE. From her. I took it on the telephone, and—

(*Bell drowns out her voice.*)

FANNY. Who is "her"? (*Bell becomes very loud*) Go tell
him to stop that noise—

ANISE (*goes toward terrace, calling*). Joseph! Stop that
bell. Miss Fanny says to stop it.

JOSEPH (*calls*). Miss Fanny said to start it.

FANNY (*shouts out to him*). I didn't tell you to hang yourself with it.

JOSEPH (*appears on terrace*). I ain't hung. Your breakfast
is ready. (*Disappears.*)

FANNY (*to* ANISE). Who is "her"?

ANISE. That Carter woman from Lansing, Michigan.

FANNY. Oh, my. Is she back in Washington again? What
did the telegram say?

ANISE. It said the long sickness of her dear Papa had termi-
nated in full recovery.

FANNY. That's too bad.

ANISE. She was returning, and would Mr. David come for
dinner a week from Thursday? "Love," it said, "to you

and your charming mother." (*To* FANNY) That's you. I think Miss Carter from Lansing, Michigan, was unwise in attending the illness of her Papa.

FANNY. I hope so. Why?

ANISE (*shrugs*). There is much winking of the eyes going on between our Countess and Mr. David.

FANNY (*eagerly*). I know that. Anything new happen?

ANISE (*too innocently*). Happen? I don't know what you mean?

FANNY. You know damn well what I mean.

ANISE. *That?* Oh, no, I don't think that.

JOSEPH (*appears in the door*). The sausage cakes is shrinking.

FANNY (*rises. To* ANISE). I want everybody down here immediately. Is the car ready? (ANISE *nods*) Did you order a good dinner? (*Shrieks*) David! Oh.

(DAVID FARRELLY, *a pleasant-looking man of thirty-nine, comes in from the entrance hall, almost bumps into* FANNY.)

DAVID. Good morning, everybody.

ANISE (*to* FANNY). Everything is excellent. You have been asking the same questions for a week. You have made the kitchen very nervous.

DAVID (*to* JOSEPH). Why did you ring that air-raid alarm again?

JOSEPH. Ain't me, Mr. David. I don't like no noise. Miss Fanny told me.

FANNY. Good morning, David.

DAVID (*to* JOSEPH). Tell Fred to leave the car. I'll drive to the station.

JOSEPH (*nods*). Yes, sir. (*Exits.*)

DAVID (*to* FANNY, *half amused, half annoyed, as he begins to read his mail*). Mama, I think we'll fix up the chicken-house for you as a playroom. We'll hang the room with bells and you can go into your second childhood in the proper privacy.

FANNY. I find it very interesting. You sleep soundly, you rise at your usual hour—although your sister, whom you haven't seen in years, is waiting at the station—

DAVID. She is not waiting at the station. (*Laughs*) The train does not come in until ten minutes past twelve.

FANNY (*airily*). It's almost that now.

ANISE (*turns to look at her*). Really, Miss Fanny, contain yourself. It is twenty minutes before nine.

DAVID. And I have *not* slept soundly. And I've been up since six o'clock.

FANNY. The Balkans aren't down yet. Where are they?

DAVID. I don't know.

ANISE. There's nothing in your mail, Mr. David. Only the usual advertisements.

DAVID. And for me, that is all that is ever likely to come— here.

ANISE (*haughtily, as she starts toward hall*). I cannot, of course, speak for Miss Fanny. *I* have never opened a letter in my life.

DAVID. I know. You don't have to. For you they fly open.

FANNY (*giggles*). It's true. You're a snooper, Anise. (ANISE *exits.* FANNY *talks as* ANISE *moves out*) I rather admire it. It shows an interest in life. (*She looks up at Joshua's portrait*) You know, I've been lying awake most of the night wondering what Papa would have thought about Sara. He'd have been very pleased, wouldn't he? I always find myself wondering what Joshua would have felt.

DAVID. Yes. But maybe it would be just as well if you didn't expect me to be wondering about it, too. I wasn't married to him, Mama. He was just my father.

FANNY. My. You got up on the wrong side of the bed. (*She moves past him. Points to the mail which he is still opening*) The bills are for our noble guests. Interesting, how many there are every morning. How much longer are they going to be with us?

DAVID (*without looking at her*). I don't know.

FANNY. It's been six weeks. Now that Sara and her family are coming, even this house might be a little crowded— (*He looks up at her. Quickly*) Yes. I know I invited them. I felt sorry for Marthe, and Teck rather amused me. He plays good cribbage, and he tells good jokes. But that's not enough for a lifetime guest. If you've been urging her to stay, I wish you'd stop it. They haven't any money; all right, lend them some—

DAVID. I have been urging them to stay?

FANNY. I'm not so old I don't recognize flirting when I see it.

DAVID. But you're old enough not to be silly.

FANNY. I'm not silly. I'm charming.

(MARTHE DE BRANCOVIS, *an attractive woman of thirty-one or thirty-two, enters.*)

MARTHE. Good morning, Fanny. Morning, David.

FANNY. Good morning, Marthe.

DAVID (*warmly*). Good morning.

MARTHE. Fanny, darling, couldn't you persuade yourself to let me have a tray in bed and some cotton for my ears?

DAVID. Certainly not. My father ate breakfast at nine; and whatever my father did . . .

FANNY (*carefully, to* DAVID). There was a night-letter for you from that Carter woman in Lansing, Michigan. She is returning and you are to come to dinner next Thursday. (*As she exits on terrace*) C-A-R-T-E-R. (*Pronounces it carefully*) Lansing, Michigan.

DAVID (*laughs*). I know how to spell Carter, but thank you. (FANNY *exits.* DAVID *looks up at* MARTHE) Do you understand my mother?

MARTHE. Sometimes.

DAVID. Miss Carter was done for your benefit.

MARTHE (*smiles*). That means she has guessed that I would be jealous. And she has guessed right.

DAVID (*looks at her*). Jealous?

MARTHE. I know I've no right to be, but I am. And Fanny knows it.

DAVID (*carelessly*). Don't pay any attention to Mama. She has a sure instinct for the women I like, and she begins to hammer away early. Marthe— (*Goes to decanter on side-table*) I'm going to have a drink. I haven't had a drink before breakfast since the day I took my bar examination. (*Pours himself a drink, gulps it down*) What's it going to be like to stand on a station platform and see your sister after all these years? I'm afraid, I guess.

MARTHE. Why?

DAVID. I don't know. Afraid she won't like me— (*Shrugs*) We were very fond of each other, but it's been a long time.

MARTHE. I remember Sara. Mama brought me one day when your father was stationed in Paris. I was about six and Sara about fifteen and you were—

DAVID. You were a pretty little girl.

MARTHE. Do you really remember me? You never told me before.

FANNY (*yelling from the terrace*). David! Come to breakfast.

DAVID (*as if he had not been listening*). You know, I've never met Sara's husband. Mama did. I think the first day Sara met him, in Munich. Mama didn't like the marriage much in those days—and Sara didn't care, and Mama didn't like Sara not caring. Mama cut up about it, bad.

MARTHE. Why?

DAVID. Probably because they didn't let her arrange it. Why does Mama ever act badly? She doesn't remember ten minutes later.

MARTHE. Wasn't Mr. Müller poor?

DAVID. Oh, Mama wouldn't have minded that. If they'd

only come home and let her fix their lives for them—
(*Smiles*) But Sara didn't want it that way.

MARTHE. You'll have a house full of refugees—us and—

DAVID. Are you and Teck refugees? I'm not sure I know
what you're refugees from.

MARTHE. From Europe.

DAVID. From what Europe?

MARTHE (*smiles, shrugs*). I don't know. I don't know myself, really. Just Europe. (*Quickly, comes to him*) Sara
will like you. I like you. (*Laughs*) That doesn't make
sense, does it?

(*On her speech,* TECK DE BRANCOVIS *appears in the hall.
He is a good-looking man of about forty-five. She stops
quickly.*)

TECK (*to* MARTHE *and* DAVID). Good morning.

(*The bell gives an enormous ring.*)

DAVID (*goes to terrace*). Good morning, Teck. For years
I've been thinking they were coming for Mama with a
net. I'm giving up hope. I may try catching her myself. (*Disappears, calling*) Mama! Stop that noise.

TECK. I wonder if science has a name for women who enjoy
noise? (*Goes to table, picks up his mail*) Many mis-
taken people, Marthe, seem to have given you many
charge accounts.

MARTHE. The Countess de Brancovis. That still does it. It
would be nice to be able to pay bills again—

TECK. Do not act as if I refused to pay them. I did not
sleep well last night. I was worried. We have eighty-
seven dollars in American Express checks. (*Pleasantly,
looking at her*) That's all we have, Marthe.

MARTHE (*shrugs*). Maybe something will turn up. It's due.

TECK (*carefully*). David? (*Then, as she turns to look at
him*) The other relatives will arrive this morning?

MARTHE. Yes.

TECK (*points to porch*). I think Madame Fanny and Mr

David may grow weary of accents and charity guests. Or is the husband of the sister a rich one?

MARTHE. No. He's poor. He had to leave Germany in '33.

TECK. A Jew?

MARTHE. No. I don't think so.

TECK. Why did he have to leave Germany?

MARTHE (*still reading*). Oh, I don't know, Teck. He's an anti-Nazi.

TECK. A political?

MARTHE. No, I don't think so. He was an engineer. I don't know. I don't know much about him.

TECK. Did you sleep well?

MARTHE. Yes. Why not?

TECK. Money does not worry you?

MARTHE. It worries me very much. But I just lie still now and hope. I'm glad to be here. (*Shrugs*) Maybe something good will happen. We've come to the end of a road. That's been true for a long time. Things will have to go one way or the other. Maybe they'll go well, for a change.

TECK. I have not come to the end of any road.

MARTHE (*looks at him*). No? I admire you.

TECK. I'm going into Washington tonight. Phili has a poker game every Wednesday evening. He has arranged for me to join it.

MARTHE (*after a pause*). Have you been seeing Phili?

TECK. Once or twice. Why not? Phili and I are old friends. He may be useful. I do not want to stay in this country forever.

MARTHE. You can't leave them alone. Your favorite dream, isn't it, Teck? That they will let you play with them again? I don't think they will, and I don't think you should be seeing Phili, or that you should be seen at the Embassy.

TECK (*smiles*). You have political convictions now?

MARTHE. I don't know what I have. I've never liked Nazis,

as you know, and you should have had enough of them. They seem to have had enough of you, God knows. It would be just as well to admit they are smarter than you are and let them alone.

TECK (*looking at her carefully, after a minute*). That is interesting.

MARTHE. What is interesting?

TECK. I think you are trying to say something to me. What is it?

MARTHE. That you ought not to be at the Embassy, and that it's insane to play cards in a game with Von Seitz with eighty-seven dollars in your pocket. I don't think he'd like your not being able to pay up. Suppose you lose?

TECK. I shall try not to lose.

MARTHE. But if you do lose and can't pay, it will be all over Washington in an hour. (*Points to terrace*) They'll find out about it, and we'll be out of here when they do.

TECK. I think I want to be out of here. I find that I do not like the picture of you and our host.

MARTHE (*carefully*). There is no picture, as you put it, to like or dislike.

TECK. Not yet? I am glad to hear that. (*Comes toward her slowly*) Marthe, you understand that I am not really a fool? You understand that it is unwise to calculate me that way?

MARTHE (*slowly, as if it were an effort*). Yes, I understand that. And I understand that I am getting tired. Just plain tired. The whole thing's too much for me. I've always meant to ask you, since you played on so many sides, why we didn't come out any better. I've always wanted to ask you what happened. (*Sharply*) I'm tired, see? And I just want to sit down. Just to sit down in a chair and stay.

TECK (*carefully*). Here?

MARTHE. I don't know. Any place—

TECK. You have thus arranged it with David?

MARTHE. I've arranged nothing.

TECK. But you are trying, eh? (*He comes close to her*) I think not. I would not like that. Do not make any arrangements, Marthe. I may not allow you to carry them through. (*Smiles*) Come to breakfast now. (*He passes her, disappears on the terrace. She stands still and thoughtful. Then she, too, moves to the terrace, disappears.* JOSEPH *appears on the terrace, carrying a tray toward the unseen breakfast table. The stage is empty. After a minute, there are sounds of footsteps in the hall.* SARA MÜLLER *appears in the doorway, comes toward the middle of the room as if expecting to find somebody, stops, looks around, begins to smile. Behind her in the doorway, are three children; behind them,* KURT MÜLLER. *They stand waiting, watching* SARA. SARA *is forty-one or forty-two, a good-looking woman, with a well-bred, serious face. She is very badly dressed. Her dress is too long, her shoes were bought a long time ago and have no relation to the dress, and the belt of her dress has become untied and is hanging down. She looks clean and dowdy. As she looks around the room, her face is gay and surprised. Smiling, without turning, absently, she motions to the children and* KURT. *Slowly, the children come in.* BODO MÜLLER, *a boy of nine, comes first. He is carrying coats. Behind him, carrying two cheap valises, is* JOSHUA MÜLLER, *a boy of fourteen. Behind him is* BABETTE MÜLLER, *a pretty little girl of twelve. They are dressed for a much colder climate. They come forward, look at their mother, then move to a couch. Behind them is* KURT MÜLLER, *a large, powerful, German-looking man of about forty-seven. He is carrying a shabby valise and a brief-case. He stands watching* SARA. JOSHUA *puts down the valises, goes to his father, takes the valise from* KURT, *puts it neatly near his, and*

. *puts the brief-case near* KURT. BABETTE *goes to* SARA, *takes a package from her, places it near the valise. Then she turns to* BODO, *takes the coats he is carrying, puts them neatly on top of the valises. After a second,* KURT *sits down. As he does so, we see that his movements are slow and careful, as if they are made with effort.*)

BABETTE (*points to a couch near which they are standing She has a slight accent*). Is it allowed?

KURT (*smiles. He has an accent*). Yes. It is allowed. (BABETTE *and* BODO *sit stiffly on the couch.*)

JOSHUA (*nervously. He has a slight accent*). But we did not sound the bell—

SARA (*idly, as she wanders around the room, her face excited*). The door isn't locked. It never was. Never since I can remember.

BODO (*softly, puzzled*). The entrance of the home is never locked. So.

KURT (*looks at him*). You find it curious to believe there are people who live and do not need to watch, eh, Bodo?

BODO. Yes, Papa.

KURT (*smiles*). You and I.

JOSHUA (*smiles*). It is strange. But it must be good, I think.

KURT. Yes.

SARA. Sit back. Be comfortable. I—I wonder where Mama and David— (*Delighted, sees portrait of Joshua Farrelly, points to it*) And that was my Papa. That was the famous Joshua Farrelly. (*They all look up at it. She wanders around the room*) My goodness, isn't it a fine room? I'd almost forgotten— (*Picks up a picture from the table*) And this was my grandmother. (*Very nervously*) Shall I go and say we're here? They'd be having breakfast, I think. Always on the side terrace in nice weather. I don't know. Maybe— (*Picks up another picture*) "To Joshua and Fanny Farrelly. With admiration. Alfonso, May 7, 1910." I had an ermine boa and a pink coat. I was angry because it was too warm in Madrid to wear it.

BODO. Alfons von Spanien? Der hat immer Bilder von sich verschenkt. Ein schlectes Zeichen für einen Mann.

JOSHUA. Mama told you it is good manners to speak the language of the country you visit. Therefore, speak in English.

BODO. I said he seemed always to give his photograph. I said that is a bad flag on a man. Grow fat on the poor people and give pictures of the face. (JOSHUA *sits down.*)

SARA. I remember a big party and cakes and a glass of champagne for me. I was ten, I guess— (*Suddenly laughs*) That was when Mama said the first time a king got shot at, he was a romantic, but the fifth time he was a comedian. And when my father gave his lecture in Madrid, he repeated it—right in Madrid. It was a great scandal. You know, Alfonso was always getting shot at or bombed.

BODO (*shrugs*). Certainement.

JOSHUA. Certainement? As-tu perdu la tête?

BABETTE. Speak in English, please.

KURT (*without turning*). You are a terrorist, Bodo?

BODO (*slowly*). No.

JOSHUA. Then since when has it become *natural* to shoot upon people?

BODO. Do not give me lessons. It is neither right nor natural to shoot upon people. I know that.

SARA (*looks at* BABETTE, *thoughtfully*). An ermine boa. A boa is a scarf. I should like to have one for you, Babbie. Once, in Prague, I saw a pretty one. I wanted to buy it for you. But we had to pay our rent. (*Laughs*) But I almost bought it.

BABETTE. Yes, Mama. Thank you. Tie your sash, Mama.

SARA (*thoughtfully*). Almost twenty years.

BODO. You were born here, Mama?

SARA. Upstairs. And I lived here until I went to live with your father. (*Looks out beyond terrace*) Your Uncle David and I used to have a garden, behind the terrace. I wonder if it's still there. I like a garden. I've always hoped we'd have a house some day and settle down— (*Stops, nervously, turns to stare at* KURT, *who is looking at her*) I am talking so foolish. Sentimental. At my age. Gardens and ermine boas. I haven't wanted anything—

KURT (*comes toward her, takes her hand*). Sara. Stop it. This is a fine room. A fine place to be. Everything is so pleasant and full of comfort. This will be a good piano on which to play again. And it is all so clean. I like that. Now, you shall not be a baby. You must enjoy your house, and not be afraid that you hurt me with it. Yes?

BABETTE. Papa, tie Mama's sash, please.

SARA (*shyly smiles at him as he leans down to tie the belt*). Yes, of course. It's strange, that's all. We've never been in a place like this together—

KURT. That does not mean, and should not mean, that we do not remember how to enjoy what comes our way. We are on a holiday.

JOSHUA. A holiday? But for how long? And what plans afterward?

KURT (*quietly*). We will have plans when the hour arrives to make them. (ANISE *appears from the hall. She starts into the room, stops, bewildered. The* MÜLLERS *have not seen her. Then, as* SARA *turns,* ANISE *speaks. As she speaks, the children rise.*)

ANISE. What? What?

SARA (*softly*). Anise. It's me. It's Sara.

ANISE (*coming forward slowly*). What? (*Then as she approaches* SARA, *she begins to run toward her*) Miss Sara! Miss Sara! (*They reach each other, both laugh happily.* SARA *kisses* ANISE) I would have known you. Yes, I would. I would have known— (*Excited, bewildered,*

nervous, she looks toward KURT) How do you do, sir?
How do you do? (*Turns toward the children*) How do
you do?

JOSHUA. Thank you, Miss Anise. We are in good health.

SARA (*very happily*). You look the same. I think you look
the same. Just the way I've always remembered. (*To the
others*) This is the Anise I have told you about. She was
here before I was born.

ANISE. But how— Did you just come in? What a way to
come home! And after all the plans we've made! But you
were to come on the twelve o'clock train, and Mr. David
was to meet you—

BABETTE. The twelve o'clock train was most expensive.
We could not have come with that train. We liked the
train we came on. It was most luxurious.

ANISE (*very nervously, very rattled*). But Madame Fanny
will have a fit. I will call her— She will not be able to
contain herself. She—

SARA (*softly*). I wanted a few minutes. I'm nervous about
coming home, I guess.

BODO (*conversationally*). You are French, Madame Anise?

ANISE. Yes, I am from the Bas Rhin. (*She looks past* SARA,
and bobs her head idiotically at KURT) Sara's husband.
That is nice. That is nice.

BODO. Yes. Your accent is from the North. That is fine country. We were in hiding there once. (BABETTE *quickly
pokes him.*)

ANISE. Hiding? You— (*Turns nervously to* KURT) But here
we stand and talk. You have not had your breakfast, sir!

BABETTE (*simply, eagerly*). It would be nice to have breakfast.

ANISE. Yes, of course— I will go and order it.

SARA (*to the children*). What would you like for breakfast?

BABETTE (*surprised*). What would we like? Why, Mama,

we will have anything that can be spared. If eggs are not too rare or too expensive—

ANISE (*amazed*). Rare? Why— Oh, I—I must call Miss Fanny now. It is of a necessity. (*Excited, rushing toward terrace, calling*) Miss Fanny. Miss Fanny. (*Back to* SARA) Have you forgotten your Mama's nature? She cannot bear not knowing things. Miss Fanny! What a way to come home! After twenty years and nobody at the station—

FANNY'S VOICE. Don't yell at me. What is the matter with you?

ANISE (*excitedly, as* FANNY *draws near*). She's here. They're here. Miss Sara. She's here, I tell you. (*FANNY comes up to her, stares at her, then looks slowly around until she sees* SARA.)

SARA (*softly*). Hello, Mama.

FANNY (*after a long pause, softly, coming toward her*). Sara. Sara, darling. You're here. You're really here. (*She reaches her, takes her arms, stares at her, smiles*) Welcome. Welcome. Welcome to your house. (*Slowly*) You're not young, Sara.

SARA (*smiles*). No, Mama. I'm forty-one.

FANNY (*softly*). Forty-one. Of course. (*Presses her arms again*) Oh, Sara, I'm— (*Then quickly*) You look more like Papa now. That's good. The years have helped you. (*Turns to look at* KURT) Welcome to this house, sir.

KURT (*warmly*). Thank you, Madame.

FANNY (*turns to look at* SARA *again, nervously pats her arm. Nods, turns again to stare at* KURT. *She is nervous and chatty*). You are a good-looking man, for a German. I didn't remember you that way. I like a good-looking man. I always have.

KURT (*smiles*). I like a good-looking woman. I always have.

FANNY. Good. That's the way it should be.

BODO (*to* SARA). Ist das Grossmama?

FANNY (*looks down*). Yes. I am your grandmother. Also,
I speak German, so do not talk about me. I speak languages very well. But there is no longer anybody to
speak with. Anise has half forgotten her French, which
was always bad; and I have nobody with whom to
speak my Italian or German or—Sara, it's very good
to have you home. I'm chattering away, I—

JOSHUA. Now you have us, Madame. We speak ignorantly,
but fluently, in German, French, Italian, Spanish—

KURT. And boastfully in English.

BODO. There is never a need for boasting. If we are to fight
for the good of all men, it is to be accepted that we must
be among the most advanced.

ANISE. My God.

FANNY (*to* SARA). Are these your *children?* Or are they
dressed up midgets?

SARA (*laughs*). These are my children, Mama. This, Babette. (BABETTE *bows*) This, Joshua. (JOSHUA *bows*) This
is Bodo. (BODO *bows.*)

FANNY. Joshua was named for Papa. You wrote me. (*Indicates picture of Joshua Farrelly*) You bear a great
name, young man.

JOSHUA (*smiles, indicates his father*). My name is Müller.

FANNY (*looks at him, laughs*). Yes. You look a little like
your grandfather. (*To* BABETTE) And so do you. You
are a nice-looking girl. (*To* BODO) You look like nobody.

BODO (*proudly*). I am not beautiful.

FANNY (*laughs*). Well, Sara, well. Three children. You
have done well. (*To* KURT) You, too, sir, of course. Are
you quite recovered? Sara wrote that you were in Spain
and—

BODO. Did Mama write that Papa was a great hero? He was
brave, he was calm, he was expert, he was resourceful,
he was—

KURT (*laughs*). My biographer. And as unprejudiced as most of them.

SARA. Where is David? I am so anxious— Has he changed much? Does he . . .

FANNY (*to* ANISE). Don't stand there. Go and get him right away. Go get David. (*As* ANISE *exits*) He's out having breakfast with the titled folk. Do you remember Marthe Randolph? I mean, do you remember Hortie Randolph, her mother, who was my friend? Can you follow what I'm saying? I'm not speaking well today.

SARA (*laughs*). Of course I remember Marthe and Hortie. You and she used to scream at each other.

FANNY. Well, Martha, her daughter, married Teck de Brancovis. *Count* de Brancovis. He was fancy when she married him. Not so fancy now, I suspect. Although still chic and tired. You know what I mean, the way they are in Europe. Well, they're here.

SARA. What's David like now? I—

FANNY. Like? Like? I don't know. He's a lawyer. You know that. Papa's firm. He's never married. You know that, too—

SARA. Why hasn't he married?

FANNY. Really, I don't know. I don't think he likes his own taste. Which is very discriminating of him. He's had a lot of girls, of course, one more ignorant and silly than the other— (*Goes toward terrace, begins to scream*) And where is he? David! David!

ANISE'S VOICE. He's coming, Miss Fanny. He's coming. Contain yourself. He was down at the garage getting ready to leave—

FANNY. I don't care where he is. Tell him to come.— David! (*Suddenly points to picture of Joshua*) That's my Joshua. Handsome, eh? We were very much in love. Hard to believe of people nowadays, isn't it?

SARA. Kurt and I love each other.

FANNY. Oh. You do? I daresay. But there are ways and ways of loving.

SARA. How dare you, Mama—

KURT (*laughs*). Ladies, ladies.

SARA (*giggles*). Why, I almost got mad then. You know, I don't think I've been mad since I last saw you.

BODO. My! You and Mama must not get angry. Anger is protest. And so you must direction it to the proper channels and then harness it for the good of other men. That is correct, Papa?

FANNY (*peers down at him*). If you grow up to talk like that, and stay as ugly as you are, you are going to have one of those successful careers on the lecture platform. (JOSHUA *and* BABETTE *laugh.*)

JOSHUA (*to* BODO). Ah. It is a great pleasure to hear Grandma talk with you.

BODO (*to* FANNY, *tenderly*). We will not like each other. (KURT *has wandered to the piano. Standing, he touches the keys in the first bars of a Mozart Rondo.*)

FANNY. You are wrong. I think we are rather alike; if that is so, let us at least remember to admire each other. (DAVID *comes running in from the entrance hall. At the door he stops, stares at* SARA.)

DAVID (*to* SARA). Sara. Darling—

SARA (*wheels, goes running toward him. She moves into his arms. He leans down, kisses her with great affection*). David. David.

DAVID (*softly*). It's been a long, long time. I got to thinking it would never happen. (*He leans down, kisses her hair. After a minute, he smiles, presses her arm.*)

SARA (*excited*). David, I'm excited. Isn't it strange? To be here, to see each other— But I am forgetting. This is my husband. These are my children. Babette, Joshua, Bodo. (*They all three advance, stand in line to shake hands.*)

BODO (*shaking hand*). How do you do, Uncle David?

DAVID. How do you do, Bodo? (DAVID *shakes hands with*

JOSHUA) Boys can shake hands. But so pretty a girl must be kissed. (*He kisses* BABETTE. *She smiles, very pleased, and crosses to the side of* SARA.)

BABETTE. Thank you. Fix your hairpin, Mama. (SARA *shoves back a falling hairpin.*)

DAVID (*crossing to* KURT). I'm happy to meet you, sir, and to have you here.

KURT. Thank you. Sara has told me so much from you. You have a devoted sister.

DAVID (*very pleased*). Have I? Still? That's mighty good to hear. (ANISE *comes in from the library.*)

ANISE. Your breakfast is coming. Shall I wash the children, Miss Sara?

JOSHUA (*amazed*). Wash us? Do people wash each other?

SARA. No, but the washing is a good idea. Go along now, and hurry. (*All three start for the hall*) And then we'll all have a fine, big breakfast again. (*The children exit.*)

FANNY. Again? Don't you usually have a good breakfast?

KURT (*smiles*). No, Madame. Only sometimes.

SARA (*laughs*). Oh, we do all right, usually. (*Very happily, very gaily*) Ah, it's good to be here. (*Puts her arm in* DAVID's) We were kids. Now we're all grown up! I've got children, you're a lawyer, and a fine one, I bet—

FANNY. The name of Farrelly on the door didn't, of course, hurt David's career.

DAVID (*smiles*). Sara, you might as well know Mama thinks of me only as a monument to Papa and a not very well-made monument at that. I am not the man Papa was.

SARA (*to* FANNY, *smiles*). How do you know he's not?

FANNY (*carefully*). I beg your pardon. That is the second time you have spoken disrespectfully of your father. (SARA *and* DAVID *laugh.* FANNY *turns to* KURT) I hope you will like me.

KURT. I hope so.

SARA (*pulls him to the couch, sits down with him*). Now I want to hear about you— (*Looks at him, laughs*) I'm awfully nervous about seeing you. Are you, about me?

DAVID. Yes. I certainly am.

SARA (*looks around*). I'm like an idiot. I want to see everything right away. The lake, and my old room—and I want to talk and ask questions . . .

KURT (*laughs*). More slow, Sara. It is most difficult to have twenty years in a few minutes.

SARA. Yes, I know, but— Oh, well. Kurt's right. We'll say it all slowly. It's just nice being back. Haven't I fine children?

DAVID. Very fine. You're lucky. I wish I had them.

FANNY. How could you have them? All the women you like are too draughty, if you know what I mean. I'm sure that girl from Lansing, Michigan, would be sterile. Which is as God in his wisdom would have it.

SARA. Oh. So you have a girl?

DAVID. I have no girl. This amuses Mama.

FANNY. He's very attractive to some women. (*To* KURT) Both my children are attractive, whatever else they're not. Don't you think so? (*Points to* DAVID) He's flirting with our Countess now, Sara. You will see for yourself.

DAVID (*sharply*). You are making nervous jokes this morning, Mama. And they're not very good ones.

FANNY (*gaily*). I tell the truth. If it turns out to be a joke, all the better.

SARA (*affectionately*). Ah, Mama hasn't changed. And that's good, too.

FANNY. Don't mind me, Sara. I, too, am nervous about seeing you. (*To* KURT) You'll like it here. You are an engineer?

KURT. Yes.

FANNY. Do you remember the day we met in München? The day Sara brought you to lunch? I thought you were rather a clod and that Sara would have a miserable life. I think I was wrong. (*To* DAVID) You see? I always admit when I'm wrong.

DAVID. You are a woman who is noble in all things, at all times.

FANNY. Oh, you're mad at me. (*To* KURT) As I say, you'll like it here. I've already made some plans. The new wing will be for you and Sara. The old turkey-house we'll fix up for the children. A nice, new bathroom, and we'll put in their own kitchen, and Anise will move in with them—

SARA. That's kind of you, Mama. But—but—we won't make any plans for a while— (*Very quietly*) A good, long vacation; God knows Kurt needs it—

FANNY. A vacation? You'll be staying here, of course. You don't have to worry about work—engineers can always get jobs, David says, and he's already begun to inquire—

KURT. I have not worked as an engineer since many years, Madame.

DAVID. Haven't you? I thought— Didn't you work for Dornier?

KURT. Yes. Before '33.

FANNY. But you have worked in other places. A great many other places, I should say. Every letter of Sara's seemed to have a new postmark.

KURT (*smiles*). We move most often.

DAVID. You gave up engineering?

KURT. I gave it up? (*Shrugs*) One could say it that way.

FANNY. What do you do?

SARA. Mama, we—

KURT. It is difficult to explain.

DAVID (*after a slight pause*). If you'd rather not.

FANNY. No, I—I'm trying to find out something. (*To* KURT) May I ask it, sir?

KURT. Let me help you, Madame. You wish to know whether not being an engineer buys adequate breakfasts for my family. It does not. I have no wish to make a mystery of what I have been doing; it is only that it is awkward to place neatly. (*Smiles, motions with his hand*) It sounds so big: it is so small. I am an Anti-Fascist. And that does not pay well.

FANNY. Do you mind questions?

SARA. Yes.

KURT (*sharply*). Sara. (*To* FANNY) Perhaps I shall not answer them. But I shall try.

FANNY. Are you a radical?

KURT. You would have to tell me what that word means to you, Madame.

FANNY (*after a slight pause*). That is just. Perhaps we all have private definitions. We all are Anti-Fascists, for example—

SARA. Yes. But Kurt works at it.

FANNY. What kind of work?

KURT. Any kind. Anywhere.

FANNY (*sharply*). I will stop asking questions.

SARA (*very sharply*). That would be sensible, Mama.

DAVID. Darling, don't be angry. We've been worried about you, naturally. We knew so little, except that you were having a bad time.

SARA. I didn't have a bad time. We never—

KURT. Do not lie for me, Sara.

SARA. I'm not lying. I didn't have a bad time, the way they mean. I—

FANNY (*slowly*). You had a bad time just trying to live, didn't you? That's obvious, Sara, and foolish to pretend it isn't. Why wouldn't you take money from us? What kind of nonsense—

SARA (*slowly*). We've lived the way we wanted to live. I don't know the language of rooms like this any more. And I don't want to learn it again.

KURT. Do not bristle about it.

SARA. I'm not bristling. (*To* FANNY) I married because I fell in love. You can understand that.

FANNY (*slowly*). Yes.

SARA. For almost twelve years, Kurt went to work every

morning and came home every night, and we lived
modestly, and happily— (*Sharply*) As happily as
people could in a starved Germany that was going to
pieces—

KURT. Sara, please. You are angry. I do not like it that way.
I will try to find a way to tell you with quickness. Yes.
(SARA *turns, looks at him, starts to speak, stops*) I was
born in a town called Fürth. (*Pauses. Looks up, smiles*)
There is a holiday in my town. We call it Kirchweih.
It was a gay holiday with games and music and a hot
white sausage to eat with the wine. I grow up, I move
away—to school, to work—but always I come back for
Kirchweih. It is for me, the great day of the year.
(*Slowly*) But after the war, that day begins to change.
The sausage is made from bad stuff, the peasants come
in without shoes, the children are too sick— (*Carefully*) It is bad for my people, those years, but always
I have hope. In the festival of August, 1931, more than
a year before the storm, I give up that hope. On that
day, I see twenty-seven men murdered in a Nazi street
fight. I cannot stay by now and watch. My time has
come to move. I say with Luther, "Here I stand. I can
do nothing else. God help me. Amen."

SARA. It doesn't pay well to fight for what we believe in.
But I wanted it the way Kurt wanted it. (*Shrugs*) They
don't like us in Europe; I guess they never did. So Kurt
brought us home. You've always said you wanted us.
If you don't, I will understand.

DAVID. Darling, of course we want you—

FANNY (*rises*). I am old. And made of dry cork. And bad-
mannered. Please forgive me.

SARA (*goes quickly to* FANNY). Shut up, Mama. We're all
acting like fools. I'm glad to be home. That's all I know.
So damned glad.

DAVID. And we're damned glad to have you. Come on. Let's
walk to the lake. We've made it bigger and planted the

island with blackberries— (*She smiles and goes to him.
Together they move out the hall entrance.*)

FANNY (*after a silence*). They've always liked each other.
We're going to have Zwetschgen-Knoedel for dinner.
You like them?

KURT. Indeed.

FANNY. I hope you like decent food.

KURT. I do.

FANNY. That's a good sign in a man.

MARTHE (*coming in from the terrace. Stops in the doorway*). Oh, I'm sorry, Fanny. We were waiting. I didn't
want to interrupt the family reunion. I—

FANNY. This is my son-in-law, Herr Müller. The Countess
de Brancovis.

KURT AND MARTHE (*together*). How do you do?

MARTHE. And how is Sara, Herr Müller? I haven't seen her
since I was a little girl. She probably doesn't remember
me at all. (TECK *comes in from the hall. She turns*) This
is my husband, Herr Müller.

KURT. How do you do?

TECK. How do you do, sir? (KURT *bows. They shake hands*)
Would it be impertinent for one European to make
welcome another?

KURT (*smiles*). I do not think so. It would be friendly.

BODO (*appears at the hall door*). Papa— (*Sees* TECK *and*
MARTHE, *bows*) Oh, good morning. Miss Anise says you
are the Count and Countess. Once before we met a
Count and Countess. They had a small room bordering
on ours in Copenhagen. They were more older than you,
and more poor. We shared with them our newspaper.

MARTHE (*laughs*). It wasn't us, but it might have been.
What's your name?

TECK (*laughs*). We hope you will be as kind to us.

BODO. My name is Bodo. It's a strange name. No? (*To*
KURT) Papa, this is the house of great wonders. Each has

his bed, each has his bathroom. The arrangement of it,
that is splendorous.

FANNY (*laughs*). You are a fancy talker, Bodo.

KURT. Oh, yes. In many languages.

BODO (*to* FANNY). Please to correct me when I am wrong.
Papa, the plumbing is such as you have never seen.
Each implement is placed on the floor, and all are simul-
taneous in the same room. You will therefore see that
being placed most solidly on the floor allows of no rats,
rodents or crawlers, and is most sanitary. (*To the
others*) Papa will be most interested. He likes to know
how each thing of everything is put together. And he is
so fond of being clean—

KURT (*laughs. To* FANNY). I am a hero to my children. It
bores everybody but me.

TECK. It is most interesting, Herr Müller. I thought I had
a good ear for the accents of your country. But yours is
most difficult to place. It is Bayrisch? Or is it—

BODO. That's because Papa has worked in so many—

KURT (*quickly*). German accents are the most difficult to
identify. I, myself, when I try, am usually incorrect. It
would be particularly difficult with me because I speak
other languages. Yours would be Roumanian?

MARTHE (*laughs*). My God, is it that bad?

KURT (*smiles*). I am showing off. I know the Count de
Brancovis is Roumanian.

TECK (*heartily*). So? We have met before? I thought so,
but I cannot remember—

KURT. No, sir. We have not met before. I read your name
in the newspapers.

TECK (*to* KURT). Strange. I was sure I had met you. I was
in the Paris Legation for many years, and I thought perhaps—

KURT. Oh, no. If it is possible to believe, I am the exile who
is not famous. (*To* FANNY) I have been thinking with

pleasure, Madame Fanny, of breakfast on your porch. (*He points to the picture of Joshua Farrelly*) Your husband once wrote: "I am getting older now and Europe seems far away. Fanny and I will have an early breakfast on the porch and then I shall drive the bays into Washington." (*Remembering*) And then he goes on: "Henry Adams tells me he has been reading Karl Marx. I shall have to tell him my father made me read Marx many years ago and that, since he proposes to exhibit himself to impress me, will spoil Henry's Sunday."

FANNY (*laughs, delighted. Takes* KURT's *arm*). And so it did. I had forgotten that. I am pleased with you. I shall come and serve your food myself. I had forgotten Joshua ever wrote it. (*They start out of the terrace doors together, followed by* BODO.)

KURT (*as they disappear*). I try to impress you. I learned it last night. (FANNY *laughs. They disappear.*)

TECK (*smiles*). He is a clever man. A quotation from Joshua Farrelly is a sure road to Fanny's heart. Where did you say Herr Müller was from?

MARTHE. Germany.

TECK. I know that. (*Goes to a valise. He leans over, stares at it, looks at the labels, pushes the lock. The lock opens; he closes it. Then he turns and, as he speaks, picks up the brief-case*) What part of Germany?

MARTHE. I don't know. And I never knew you were an expert on accents.

TECK. I never knew it either. Are you driving into Washington with David this morning?

MARTHE. I was going to. But he may not be going to the office, now that Sara's here. I was to have lunch with Sally Tyne. (TECK *puts down the brief-case*) What are you doing?

TECK. Wondering why luggage is unlocked and a shabby brief-case is so carefully locked.

MARTHE. You're very curious about Mr. Müller.

TECK. Yes. And I do not know why. Something far away
. . . I am curious about a daughter of the Farrellys' who
marries a German who has bullet scars on his face and
broken bones in his hands.

MARTHE (*sharply*). Has he? There are many of them now,
I guess.

TECK. So there are. But this one is in this house. (*He goes
to the bell cord, pulls it. She watches him nervously.*)

MARTHE. Is it—is he any business of yours?

TECK. What is my business? Anything might be my business now.

MARTHE. Yes—unfortunately. You might inquire from your
friend Von Seitz. They always know their nationals.

TECK. (*pleasantly, ignoring the sharpness with which she
has spoken*). Oh, yes, I will do that, of course. But I do
not like to ask questions without knowing the value of
the answers.

MARTHE. Teck. This man is a little German Sara married
years ago. I remember Mama talking about it. He was
nothing then and he isn't now. They've had a tough
enough time already without—

TECK. Have you— Have you been sleeping with David?

MARTHE (*stops, stares at him, then simply*). No. I have
not been. And that hasn't been your business for a good
many years now.

TECK. You like him?

MARTHE (*nervously*). What's this for, Teck?

TECK. Answer me, please.

MARTHE. I— (*She stops.*)

TECK. Yes? Answer me.

MARTHE. I do like him.

TECK. What does he feel about you?

MARTHE. I don't know.

TECK. But you are trying to find out. You have made plans
with him?

MARTHE. Of course not. I—

TECK. But you will try to make him have plans. I have rec-
ognized it. Well, we have been together a long— (JO-
SEPH *enters.* TECK *stops*) Joseph, Miss Fanny wishes you
to take the baggage upstairs.

JOSEPH. Yes, sir. I was going to. (*He begins to pick up the
baggage.* MARTHE *has turned sharply and is staring at*
TECK. *Then she rises, watches* JOSEPH *pick up the baggage, turns again to look at* TECK.)

TECK. As I was saying. It is perhaps best that we had this
talk.

MARTHE (*she stops, waits for* JOSEPH *to move off. He exits,
carrying the valises*). Why did you do that? Why did
you tell Joseph that Fanny wanted him to take the baggage upstairs?

TECK. Obviously it is more comfortable to look at baggage
behind closed doors.

MARTHE (*very sharply*). What kind of silliness is this now?
Leave these people alone— (*As he starts to exit*) I won't
let you—

TECK. What? (*As he moves again, she comes after him.*)

MARTHE. I said I won't let you. You are not—

TECK. How many times have you seen me angry? (MARTHE
looks up, startled) You will not wish to see another. Run
along now and have lunch with something you call Sally
Tyne. But do not make plans with David. You will not
be able to carry them out. You will go with me, when I
am ready to go. You understand. (*He exits during his
speech. The last words come as he goes through the
door, and as the curtain falls.*)

ACT TWO

SCENE: *The same as Act One, about ten days later. During the act it will begin to grow dark; but the evening is warm and the terrace doors are open.*

AT RISE: SARA *is sitting on the couch, crocheting.* FANNY *and* TECK *are sitting at a small table playing cribbage.* BODO *is sitting near them, at a large table, working on a heating pad. The cord is torn from the bag, the bag is ripped open.* ANISE *sits next to him, anxiously watching him. Outside on the terrace,* JOSHUA *is going through baseball motions, coached by* JOSEPH. *From time to time they move out of sight, reappear, move off again.*

FANNY (*playing a card*). One.

BODO (*after a minute, to* TECK). The arrangement of this heating pad grows more complex.

TECK (*smiles, moves on the cribbage board*). And the more wires you remove, the more complex it will grow.

BODO (*points to bag*). Man has learned to make man comfortable. Yet all cannot have the comforts. (*To* ANISE) How much did this cost you?

ANISE. It cost me ten dollars. And you have made a ruin of it.

BODO. That is not yet completely true. (*To* FANNY) Did I not install for you a twenty-five-cent button-push for your radio?

TECK (*playing a card*). Two and two. (*Moves pegs on the cribbage board.*)

FANNY. Yes, you're quite an installer.

BODO (*to* TECK). As I was wishing to tell you, Count de

283

Brancovis, comfort and plenty exist. Yet all cannot have them it. Why?

TECK. I do not know. It has worried many men. Why?

ANISE (*to* BODO). Yes, why?

BODO (*takes a deep breath, raises his finger as if about to lecture*). Why? (*Considers a moment, then deflates himself*) I am not as yet sure.

ANISE. I thought not.

FANNY (*turns to look at* JOSHUA *and* JOSEPH *on the terrace*). Would you mind doing that dancing some place else?

JOSEPH (*looking in.*) Yes'm. That ain't dancing. I'm teaching Josh baseball.

FANNY. Then maybe he'd teach you how to clean the silver.

JOSEPH. I'm a good silver-cleaner, Miss Fanny.

FANNY. But you're getting out of practice.

JOSEPH (*after a moment's thought*). Yes'm. I see what you mean. (*He exits.*)

FANNY (*playing a card*). Three.

JOSHUA. It is my fault. I'm crazy about baseball.

BODO. Baseball players are among the most exploited people in this country. I read about it.

FANNY. You never should have learned to read.

BODO. Their exploited condition is foundationed on the fact that—

JOSHUA (*bored*). All right, all right. I still like baseball.

SARA. Founded, Bodo, not foundationed.

JOSHUA. He does it always. He likes long words. In all languages.

TECK. How many languages do you children speak?

BODO. Oh, we do not really know any very well, except German and English. We speak bad French and—

SARA. And bad Danish and bad Czech.

TECK. You seem to have stayed close to the borders of Germany. Did Herr Müller have hopes, as so many did, that National Socialism would be overthrown on every tomorrow?

SARA. We have not given up that hope. Have you, Count de Brancovis?

TECK. I never had it.

JOSHUA (*pleasantly*). Then it must be most difficult for you to sleep.

TECK. I beg your pardon?

SARA. Schweig doch, Joshua!

FANNY (*to* TECK). Sara told Joshua to shut up. (*Playing a card*) Twelve.

TECK. I have offended you, Mrs. Müller. I am most sorry.

SARA (*pleasantly*). No, sir, you haven't offended me. I just don't like polite political conversations any more.

TECK (*nods*). All of us, in Europe, had too many of them.

SARA. Yes. Too much talk. By this time all of us must know where we are and what we have to do. It's an indulgence to sit in a room and discuss your beliefs as if they were a juicy piece of gossip.

FANNY. You know, Sara, I find it very pleasant that Kurt, considering his history, doesn't make platform speeches. He hasn't tried to convince anybody of anything.

SARA (*smiles*). Why should he, Mama? You are quite old enough to have your own convictions—or Papa's.

FANNY (*turns to look at her*). I am proud to have Papa's convictions.

SARA. Of course. But it might be well to have a few new ones, now and then.

FANNY (*peers over at her*). Are you criticizing me?

SARA (*smiles*). Certainly not.

BABETTE (*comes running in from the right entrance door. She has on an apron and she is carrying a plate. She goes to* FANNY). Eat it while it's hot, Grandma.

(FANNY *peers down, takes the fork, begins to eat.* ANISE *and* BODO *both rise, move to* FANNY, *inspect the plate.*)

FANNY (*to them*). Go away.

ANISE. It is a potato pancake.

FANNY. And the first good one I've eaten in many, many years. I love a good potato pancake.

BODO. I likewise.

BABETTE. I am making a great number for dinner. Move away, Bodo.

TECK (*playing a card*). Fifteen and two.

ANSIE (*who has followed* BODO *back to the table, leans over to look at the heating pad*). You've ruined it! I shall sue you.

JOSHUA. I told you not to let him touch it.

SARA (*laughs*). I remember you were always saying that, Anise—that you were going to sue. That's very French. I was sick once in Paris, and Babbie stayed up for a whole night and day and finished a dress I was making for a woman in the Rue Jacob. I told her to tell the woman she'd done it—I thought perhaps the woman would give her a candy or something—and anyway, I was very proud of her work. But no. The woman admitted the dress was well done, but said she was going to sue because I hadn't done it myself. Fancy that.

FANNY (*slowly*). You sewed for a living?

SARA. Not a very good one. But Babbie and I made a little something now and then. Didn't we, darling?

FANNY (*sharply*). Really, Sara, were these—these things necessary? Why couldn't you have written?

SARA (*laughs*). You've asked me that a hundred times in the last week.

JOSHUA (*gently*). I think it is only that Grandma feels sorry for us. Grandma has not seen much of the world.

FANNY. Don't you start giving me lectures, Joshua. I'm fond of you. And of you, Babbie. (*To* ANISE) Are there two desserts for dinner? And are they sweet?

ANISE. Yes.

FANNY (*turns to* BODO). I wish I were fond of you.

BODO. You are. (*Happily*) You are very fond of me.

FANNY (*playing a card*). Twenty-five.

BABETTE. This is for you, Grandma. I'm making a bed-jacket. It is nice lace. Papa brought it to me from Spain and I mean for you to have it.

FANNY (*kisses* BABETTE). Thank you, darling. A sequence and three. A pair and five. (*To* TECK, *as they finish the cribbage game*) There. That's two dollars off. I owe you eight-fifty.

TECK. Let us carry it until tomorrow. You shall give it to me as a going-away token.

FANNY (*too pleased*). You're going away?

TECK (*laughs*). Ah, Madame Fanny. Do not sound *that* happy.

FANNY. Did I? That's rude of me. When are you going?

TECK. In a few days, I think. (*Turns to look at* SARA) We're too many refugees, eh, Mrs. Müller?

SARA (*pleasantly*). Perhaps.

TECK. Will you be leaving, also?

SARA. I beg your pardon?

TECK. I thought perhaps you, too, would be moving on. Herr Müller does not give me the feeling of a man who settles down. Men who have done his work, seldom leave it. Not for a quiet country house.

(*All three children look up.*)

SARA (*very quietly*). What work do you think my husband has done, Count de Brancovis?

TECK. Engineering?

SARA (*slowly*). Yes. Engineering.

FANNY (*very deliberately to* TECK). I don't know what you're saying. They shall certainly not be leaving—ever. Is that understood, Sara?

SARA. Well, Mama—

FANNY. There are no wells about it. You've come home to see me die and you will wait until I'm ready.

SARA (*laughs*). Really, Mama, that isn't the reason I came home.

FANNY. It's a good enough reason. I shall do a fine death. I intend to be a great deal of trouble to everybody.

ANISE. I daresay.

FANNY. I shall take to my bed early and stay for years. In great pain.

ANISE. I am sure of it. You will duplicate the disgrace of the birth of Miss Sara.

SARA (*laughs*). Was I born in disgrace?

ANISE. It was not your fault. But it was disgusting. Three weeks before you were to come—all was excellent, of course, in so healthy a woman as Madame Fanny—a great dinner was given here and, most unexpectedly, attended by a beautiful lady from England.

FANNY. Do be still. You are dull and fanciful—

ANISE. Mr. Joshua made the great error of waltzing the beauty for two dances, Madame Fanny being unfitted for the waltz and under no circumstances being the most graceful of dancers.

FANNY (*her voice rising*). Are you crazy? I danced magnificently.

ANISE. It is well you thought so. A minute did not elapse between the second of the waltzes and a scream from Madame Fanny. She was in labor. Two hundred people, and if we had left her alone, she would have remained in the ballroom—

FANNY. How you invent! How you invent!

ANISE. Do not call to me that I am a liar. For three weeks you are in the utmost agony—

FANNY. And so I was. I remember it to this day—

ANISE (*to* SARA, *angrily*). Not a pain. Not a single pain. She would lie up there in state, stealing candy from herself. Then, when your Papa would rest himself for a minute at the dinner or with a book, a scream would dismantle the house—it was revolting. (*Spitefully to* FANNY) And now the years have passed I may dis-

close to you that Mr. Joshua knew you were going
through the play-acting—

FANNY (*rises*). He did not. You are a malicious—

ANISE. Once he said to me, "Anise, it is well that I am in
love. This is of a great strain and her great-uncle Fred-
die was not right in the head, neither."

FANNY (*screaming*). You will leave this house— You are
a liar, a woman of—

SARA. Mama, sit down.

ANISE. I will certainly leave this house. I will—

SARA (*sharply*). Both of you. Sit down. And be still.

ANISE. She has intimated that I lie—

FANNY (*screaming*). Intimated! Is that what I was doing—
(ANISE *begins to leave the room*) All right. I beg your
pardon. I apologize.

(ANISE *turns.*)

SARA. Both of you. You are acting like children.

BODO. Really, Mama. You insult us.

ANISE. I accept your apology. Seat yourself.

(*They both sit down.*)

FANNY (*after a silence*). I am unloved.

BABETTE. I love you, Grandma.

FANNY. Do you, Babbie?

JOSHUA. And I.

FANNY (*nods, very pleased. To* BODO). And you?

BODO. *I* loved you the primary second I saw you.

FANNY. You are a charlatan.

ANISE. As for me, I am fond of all the living creatures. It is
true that the children cause me greater work, which in
turn more greatly inconveniences the feet. However, I
do not complain. I believe in children.

FANNY. Rather like believing in the weather, isn't it?
(DAVID *and* KURT *come in from the terrace. Both are in
work clothes, their sleeves rolled up*) Where have you
been?

DAVID. Oh, we've been helping Mr. Chabeuf spray the fruit trees.

ANISE. Mr. Chabeuf says that Herr Müller has the makings of a good farmer. From a Frenchman that is a large thing to say.

KURT (*who has looked around the room, looked at* TECK, *strolled over to* BODO). Mr. Chabeuf and I have an excellent time exchanging misinformation. My father was a farmer. I have a wide knowledge of farmer's misinformation.

FANNY. This is good farm land. Perhaps, in time—

DAVID (*laughs*). Mama would give you the place, Kurt, if you guaranteed that your great-grandchildren would die here.

KURT (*smiles*). I would like to so guarantee.

TECK. A farmer. That is very interesting. Abandon your ideals, Herr Müller?

KURT. Ideals? (*Carefully*) Sara, heisst das auf deutsch "Ideale"?

SARA. Yes.

KURT. Is that what I have now? I do not like the word. It gives to me the picture of a small, pale man at a seaside resort. (*To* BODO) What are you doing?

BODO. Preparing an elderly electric pad for Miss Anise. I am confused.

KURT (*wanders toward the piano*). So it seems.

BODO. Something has gone wrong with the principle on which I have been working. It is probably that I will ask your assistance.

KURT (*bows to him*). Thank you. Whenever you are ready. (*Begins to pick out notes with one hand.*)

FANNY. We shall have a little concert tomorrow evening. In honor of Babbie's birthday. (*To* KURT) Kurt, you and I will play "The Clock Symphony." Then Joshua and I will play the duet we've learned, and Babbie will sing. And I shall finish with a Chopin Nocturne.

DAVID (*laughs*). I thought you'd be the last on the program.

TECK. Where is Marthe?

FANNY. She'll be back soon. She went into town to do an errand for me. (*To* DAVID) Did you buy presents for everybody?

DAVID. I did.

SARA (*smiles, to* BABETTE). We always did that here. If somebody had a birthday, we all got presents. Nice, isn't it?

DAVID (*to* ANISE). I shall buy you an electric pad. You will need it.

ANISE. Indeed.

FANNY. Did you buy me a good present?

DAVID. Pretty good. (*Pats* BABETTE's *head*) The best present goes to Babbie; it's *her* birthday.

FANNY. Jewelry?

DAVID. No, not jewelry.

FANNY. Oh. Not jewelry.

DAVID. Why?

FANNY (*too casually*). I just asked you.

TECK (*gets up*). It was a natural mistake, David. You see, Mrs. Mellie Sewell told your mother that she had seen you and Marthe in Barstow's. And your mother said you were probably buying her a present, or one for Babbie.

DAVID (*too sharply*). Yes.

TECK (*laughs*). Yes what?

DAVID (*slowly*). Just yes.

FANNY (*too hurriedly*). Mellie gets everything wrong. She's very anxious to meet Marthe because she used to know Francie Cabot, her aunt. Marthe's aunt, I mean, not Mellie's.

SARA (*too hurriedly*). She really came to inspect Kurt and me. But I saw her first. (*She looks anxiously at* DAVID, *who has turned his back on the room and is facing the terrace*) You were lucky to be out, David.

DAVID. Oh, she calls every Saturday afternoon, to bring Mama all the Washington gossip of the preceding week. She gets it all wrong, you understand, but that doesn't make any difference to either Mama or her. Mama then augments it, wits it up, Papa used to say—

FANNY. Certainly. I sharpen it a little. Mellie has no sense of humor.

DAVID. So Mama sharpens it a little, and delivers it to-morrow afternoon to old lady Marcy down the road. Old lady Marcy hasn't heard a word in ten years, so she unsharpens it again, and changes the names. By Wednesday afternoon—

TECK (*smiles*). By Wednesday afternoon it will not be you who were in Barstow's, and it will be a large diamond pin with four sapphires delivered to Gaby Deslys.

DAVID (*turns, looks at him*). Exactly.

FANNY (*very nervously*). Francie Cabot, Marthe's aunt, you understand— (*To* KURT) Did you ever know Paul von Seitz, a German?

KURT. I have heard of him.

FANNY (*speaking very rapidly*). Certainly. He was your Ambassador to somewhere, I've forgotten. Well, Francie Cabot married him. I could have. Any American, not crippled, whose father had money— He was crazy about me. I was better-looking than Francie. Well, years later when he was your Ambassador—my father was, too, as you probably know—not your Ambassador, of course, ours—but I am talking about Von Seitz.

DAVID (*laughs to* KURT). You can understand how it goes. Old lady Marcy is not entirely to blame.

FANNY. Somebody asked me if I didn't regret not marrying him. I said, "Madame, je le regrette tous les jours et j'en suis heureuse chaque soir." (FANNY *turns to* DAVID) That means I regret it every day and am happy about it every night. You understand what I meant, by *night?* Styles in wit change so.

DAVID. I understood it, Mama.

JOSHUA. We, too, Grandma.

BABETTE (*approvingly*). It was most witty.

BODO. I do not know that I understood. You will explain to me, Grandma?

SARA. Later.

FANNY (*turns to look at* TECK). You remember the old Paul von Seitz?

TECK (*nods*). He was stationed in Paris when I first was there.

FANNY. Of course. I always forget you were a diplomat.

TECK. It is just as well.

FANNY. There's something insane about a Roumanian diplomat. Pure insane. I knew another one, once. He wanted to marry me, too.

SARA (*laughs*). All of Europe.

FANNY. Not all. Some. Naturally. I was rich, I was witty, my family was of the best. I was handsome, unaf·fected—

DAVID. And noble and virtuous and kind and elegant and fashionable and simple—it's hard to remember everything you were. I've often thought it must have been boring for Papa to have owned such perfection.

FANNY (*shrieks*). What! Your father bored with me! Not for a second of our life—

DAVID (*laughs*). Oh God, when will I learn?

BODO. Do not shriek, Grandma. It is an unpleasant sound for the ear.

FANNY. Where was I? Oh, yes. What I started out to say was— (*She turns, speaks carefully to* TECK) Mellie Sewell told me, when you left the room, that she had heard from Louis Chandler's child's governess that you had won quite a bit of money in a poker game with Sam Chandler and some Germans at the Embassy. (KURT, *who has been playing the piano, stops playing very abruptly.* TECK *turns to look at him*) That's how

I thought of Von Seitz. His nephew Philip was in on the game.

DAVID (*looks at* TECK). It must have been a big game. Sam Chandler plays in big games.

TECK. Not big enough.

DAVID. Have you known Sam long?

TECK. For years. Every Embassy in Europe knew him.

DAVID (*sharply*). Sam and Nazis must make an unpleasant poker game.

(KURT *begins to play a new melody.*)

TECK (*who has not looked away from* KURT). I do not play poker to be amused.

DAVID (*irritably*). What's Sam selling now?

TECK. Bootleg munitions. He always has.

DAVID. You don't mind?

TECK. Mind? I have not thought about it.

FANNY. Well, you ought to think about it. Sam Chandler has always been a scoundrel. All the Chandlers are. They're cousins of mine. Mama used to say they never should have learned to walk on two feet. They would have been more comfortable on four.

TECK. Do you know the young Von Seitz, Herr Müller? He was your military attaché in Spain.

KURT. He was the German government attaché in Spain. I know his name, of course. He is a famous artillery expert. But the side on which I fought was not where he was stationed, Count de Brancovis.

ANISE (BABETTE *and* JOSHUA *begin to hum the song* KURT *is playing.* SARA *begins to hum*). It is time for the bath and the change of clothes. I will give you five more minutes—

FANNY. What is the song?

TECK. It was a German soldier's song. They sang it as they straggled back in '18. I remember hearing it in Berlin. Were you there then, Herr Müller?

KURT (*the playing and the humming continue*). I was not
in Berlin.

TECK. But you were in the war, of course?

KURT. Yes. I was in the war.

FANNY. You didn't think then you'd live to see another war.

KURT. Many of us were afraid we would.

FANNY. What are the words?

SARA. The Germans in Spain, in Kurt's Brigade, wrote new
words for the song.

KURT. This was what you heard in Berlin, in 1918. (*Begins
to sing.*)

> "Wir zieh'n Heim, wir zieh'n Heim,
> Mancher kommt nicht mit,
> Mancher ging verschütt,
> Aber Freunde sind wir stets."
> (*In English.*)
> "We come home. We come home.
> Some of us are gone, and some of us are lost, but
> we are friends:
> Our blood is on the earth together.
> Some day. Some day we shall meet again.
> Farewell."

(*Stops singing*) At a quarter before six on the morning
of November 7th, 1936, eighteen years later, five hundred Germans walked through the Madrid streets on
their way to defend the Manzanares River. We felt good
that morning. You know how it is to be good when it
is needed to be good? So we had need of new words to
say that. I translate with awkwardness, you understand.
(*Begins to sing.*)

> "And so we have met again.
> The blood did not have time to dry.
> We lived to stand and fight again.
> This time we fight for people.
> This time the bastards will keep their hands away.

Those who sell the blood of other men, this time,
They keep their hands away.
For us to stand.
For us to fight.
This time no farewell, no farewell."

(*Music dies out. There is silence for a minute*) We did
not win. (*Looks up, gently*) It would have been a different world if we had.

SARA. Papa said so years ago. Do you remember, Mama?
"For every man who lives without freedom, the rest of
us must face the guilt."

FANNY. Yes. "We are liable in the conscience-balance for
the tailor in Lodz, the black man in our South, the
peasant in—" (*Turns to* TECK. *Unpleasantly*) Your country, I think.

ANISE (*rises*). Come. Baths for everybody. (*To* BODO) Gather
the wires. You have wrecked my cure.

BODO. If you would allow me a few minutes more—

ANISE. Come along. I have been duped for long enough.
Come Joshua. Babette. Baths.

JOSHUA (*starts out after* ANISE. BABETTE *begins to gather
up her sewing*) My tub is a thing of glory. But I do not
like it so prepared for me and so announced by Miss
Anise. (*He exits.*)

BODO (*to* ANISE). You are angry about this. I do not blame
you with my heart or my head. I admit I have failed.
But Papa will repair it, Anise. Will you not, Papa? In a
few minutes—

TECK (*to* BODO). Your father is an expert electrician?

BODO. Oh yes, sir.

TECK. And as good with radio—

(BODO *begins to nod.*)

KURT (*sharply*). Count de Brancovis. Make your questions
to me, please. Not to my children.

(*The others look up, surprised.*)

TECK (*pleasantly*). Very well, Herr Müller.

ANISE (*as she exits with* BODO). Nobody can fix it. You have made a pudding of it.

BODO (*as he follows her*). Do not worry. In five minutes tonight, you will have a pad far better— (*As* BODO *reaches the door he bumps into* MARTHE *who is carrying large dress boxes*) Oh. Your pardon. Oh, hello. (*He disappears.*)

MARTHE (*gaily*). Hello. (*To* FANNY) I waited for them. I was afraid they wouldn't deliver this late in the day. (*To* SARA) Come on, Sara. I can't wait to see them.

SARA. What?

MARTHE. Dresses. From Fanny. A tan linen, and a dark green with wonderful buttons, a white net for Babbie, and a suit for you, and play dresses for Babbie, and a dinner dress in gray to wear for Babbie's birthday— gray should be good for you, Sara—all from Savitt's. We sneaked the measurements, Anise and I—

SARA (*she goes toward* FANNY). How nice of you, Mama. How very kind of you. And of you, Marthe, to take so much trouble— (*She leans down, kisses* FANNY) You're a sweet woman, Mama.

DAVID. That's the first time Mama's ever heard that word. (*He takes the boxes from* MARTHE, *puts them near the staircase.* MARTHE *smiles at him, touches his hand, as* TECK *watches them.*)

FANNY (*giggles*). I have a bottom sweetness, if you understand what I mean.

DAVID. I have been too close to the bottom to see it.

FANNY. That should be witty. I don't know why it isn't.

(BABETTE *goes over to stare at the boxes.*)

SARA. From Savitt's. Extravagant of you. They had such lovely clothes. I remember my coming-out dress—. (*Goes to* KURT) Do you remember the black suit with the braid, and the Milan hat? Not the *first* day we met, but the picnic day? (*He smiles up at her*) Well, they were from Savitt's. That was over twenty years ago—

I've known you a long time. Me, in an evening dress. Now you'll have to take me into Washington. I want to show off. Next week, and we'll dance, maybe— (*Sees that he is not looking at her*) What's the matter, darling? (*No answer. Slowly he turns to look at her*) What's the matter, Kurt? (*Takes his arms, very unhappily*) What have I done? It isn't that dresses have ever mattered to me, it's just that—

KURT. Of course, they have mattered to you. As they should. I do not think of the dresses. (*Draws her to him*) How many years have I loved that face?

SARA (*her face very happy*). So?

KURT. So. (*He leans down, kisses her, as if it were important.*)

SARA (*pleased, unembarrassed*). There are other people here.

MARTHE (*slowly*). And good for us to see.

TECK. Nostalgia?

MARTHE. No. Nostalgia is for something you have known. (FANNY *coughs.*)

BABETTE (*comes to* FANNY). Grandma, is it allowed to look at my dresses?

FANNY. Of course, child. Run along.

BABETTE (*picks up the boxes, goes toward the hall entrance, stops near* FANNY). I love dresses, I have a great fondness for materials and colors. Thank you, Grandma. (*She runs out of the room.*)

(JOSEPH *appears in the doorway.*)

(JOSEPH. There is a long-distance operator with a long-distance call for Mr. Müller. She wants to talk with him on the long-distance phone.

KURT. Oh— Excuse me, please—

(KURT *rises quickly.* SARA *turns sharply to look at him.* TECK *looks up.* KURT *goes quickly out.* TECK *watches him go.* SARA *stands staring after him.*)

MARTHE (*laughs*). I feel the same way as Babbie. Come on, Sara. Let's try them on.

(SARA *does not turn*.)

TECK. You also have a new dress?

MARTHE (*looks at him*). Yes. Fanny was kind to me, too.

TECK. You are a very generous woman, Madame Fanny. Did you also give her a sapphire bracelet from Barstow's?

FANNY. I beg your—

DAVID (*slowly*). No. I gave Marthe the bracelet. And I understand that it is not any business of yours.

(FANNY *rises*. SARA *turns*.)

FANNY. Really, David—

DAVID. Be still, Mama.

TECK (*after a second*). Did you tell him that, Marthe?

MARTHE. Yes.

TECK (*looks up at her*). I shall not forgive you for that. (*Looks at* DAVID) It is a statement which no man likes to hear from another man. You understand that? (*Playfully*) That is the type of thing about which we used to play at duels in Europe.

DAVID (*comes toward him*). We are not so musical comedy here. And you are not in Europe.

TECK. Even if I were, I would not suggest any such action. I would have reasons for not wishing it.

DAVID. It would be well for you not to suggest *any* action. And the reason for *that* is you might get hurt.

TECK (*slowly*). That would not be my reason. (*To* MARTHE) Your affair has gone far enough—

MARTHE (*sharply*). It is not an affair—

TECK. I do not care what it is. The time has come to leave here. Go upstairs and pack your things. (*She does not move.* DAVID *turns toward her*) Go on, Marthe.

MARTHE (*to* DAVID). I am not going with him. I told you that.

DAVID. I don't want you to go with him.

FANNY (*carefully*). Really, David, aren't you interfering in all this a good deal—

DAVID (*carefully*). Yes, Mama. I am.

TECK (*to* MARTHE). When you are speaking to me, please say what you have to say to me.

MARTHE (*comes to him*). You are trying to frighten me. But you are not going to frighten me any more. I will say it to you: I am not going with you. I am never going with you again.

TECK (*softly*). If you do not fully mean what you say, or if you might change your mind, you are talking unwisely, Marthe.

MARTHE. I know that.

TECK. Shall we talk about it alone?

MARTHE. You can't make me go, can you, Teck?

TECK. No, I can't make you.

MARTHE. Then there's no sense talking about it.

TECK. Are you in love with him?

MARTHE. Yes.

FANNY (*sharply*). Marthe! What is all this?

MARTHE (*sharply*). I'll tell *you* about it in a minute.

DAVID. You don't have to explain anything to anybody.

TECK (*ignores him*). Is he in love with you?

MARTHE. I don't think so. You won't believe it, because you can't believe anything that hasn't got tricks to it, but David hasn't much to do with this. I told you I would leave some day, and I remember where I said it—(*Slowly*)— and why I said it.

TECK. I also remember. But I did not believe you. I have not had much to offer you these last years. But if now we had some money and could go back—

MARTHE. No. I don't like you, Teck. I never have.

TECK. And I have always known it.

FANNY (*stiffly*). I think your lack of affections should be discussed with more privacy. Perhaps—

DAVID. Mama—

MARTHE. There is nothing to discuss. Strange. I've talked to myself about this scene for almost fifteen years. I knew a lot of things to say to you and I used to lie awake at night or walk along the street and say them. Now I don't want to. I guess you only want to talk that way, when you're not sure what you can do. When you're sure, then what's the sense of saying it? "This is why and this is why and this—" (*Very happily*) But when you know you can do it, you don't have to say anything; you can just go. And I'm going. There is nothing you can do. I would like you to believe that now.

TECK. Very well, Marthe. I think I made a mistake. I should not have brought you here. I believe you now.

MARTHE (*after a pause, she looks at* DAVID). I'll move into Washington, and—

DAVID. Yes. Later. But I'd like you to stay here for a while, with us, if you wouldn't mind.

SARA. It would be better for you, Marthe—

FANNY. It's very interesting that I am not being consulted about this. (*To* MARTHE) I have nothing against you, Marthe. I am sorry for you, but I don't think—

MARTHE. Thank you, Sara, David. But I'd rather move in now. (*Turns, comes toward* FANNY) But perhaps I have something against you. Do you remember my wedding?

FANNY. Yes.

MARTHE. Do you remember how pleased Mama was with herself? Brilliant Mama, handsome Mama—everybody thought so, didn't they? A seventeen-year-old daughter, marrying a pretty good title, about to secure herself in a world that Mama liked—she didn't ask me what I liked. And the one time I tried to tell her, she frightened me— (*Looks up*) Maybe I've always been frightened. All my life.

TECK. Of course.

MARTHE (*to* FANNY, *as if she had not heard* TECK). I remember Mama's face at the wedding—it was *her* wedding, really, not mine.

FANNY (*sharply*). You are very hard on your mother.

MARTHE. Nineteen hundred and twenty-five. No, I'm not hard on her. I only tell the truth. She wanted a life for me, I suppose. It just wasn't the life I wanted for myself. (*Sharply*) And that's what you have tried to do. With your children. In another way. Only Sara got away. And that made you angry—until so many years went by that you forgot.

FANNY. I don't usually mind people saying anything they think, but I find that—

MARTHE. I don't care what you mind or don't mind. I'm in love with your son—

FANNY (*very sharply*). That's unfortunate—

MARTHE. And I'm sick of watching you try to make him into his father. I don't think you even know you do it any more and I don't think he knows it any more, either. And that's what's most dangerous about it.

FANNY (*very angrily*). I don't know what you are talking about.

DAVID. I think you do. (*Smiles*) You shouldn't mind hearing the truth—and neither should I.

FANNY (*worried, sharply*). David! What does all this nonsense mean? I—

MARTHE (*to* FANNY). Look. That pretty world Mama got me into was a tough world, see? I'm used to trouble. So don't try to interfere with me, because I won't let you. (*She goes to* DAVID) Let's just have a good time. (*He leans down, takes both her hands, kisses them. Then slowly, she turns away, starts to exit. To* TECK) You will also be going today?

TECK. Yes.

MARTHE. Then let us make sure we go in different directions, and do not meet again. Good-bye, Teck.

TECK. Good-bye, Marthe. You will not believe me, but I tried my best, and I am now most sorry to lose you.

MARTHE. Yes. I believe you. (*She moves out. There is silence for a minute.*)

FANNY. Well, a great many things have been said in the last few minutes.

DAVID (*crosses to bell cord. To* TECK). I will get Joseph to pack for you.

TECK. Thank you. Do not bother. I will ring for him when I am ready. (KURT *comes in from the study door.* SARA *turns, stares at him, waits. He does not look at her*) It will not take me very long. (*He starts for the door, looking at* KURT.)

SARA. What is it, Kurt?

KURT. It is nothing of importance, darling— (*He looks quickly at* TECK, *who is moving very slowly.*)

SARA. Don't tell me it's nothing. I know the way you look when—

KURT (*sharply*). I said it was of no importance. I must get to California for a few weeks. That is all.

SARA. I—

TECK (*turns*). It is in the afternoon newspaper, Herr Müller. (*Points to paper on table*) I was waiting to find the proper moment to call it to your attention. (*He moves toward the table, as they all turn to watch him. He picks up the paper, turns it over, begins to read*) "Zurich, Switzerland: The Zurich papers today reprinted a despatch from the *Berliner Tageblatt* on the capture of Colonel Max Freidank. Freidank is said—(SARA *begins to move toward him*)—to be the chief of the Anti-Nazi Underground Movement. Colonel Freidank has long been an almost legendary figure. The son of the famous General Freidank, he was a World War officer and a distinguished physicist before the advent of Hitler." That is all.

SARA. Max—

KURT. Be still, Sara.

TECK. They told me of it at the Embassy last night. They also told me that with him they had taken a man who called himself Ebber, and a man who called himself Triste. They could not find a man called Gotter. (*He starts again toward the door*) I shall be a lonely man without Marthe. I am also a very poor one. I should like to have ten thousand dollars before I go.

DAVID (*carefully*) You will make no loans in this house.

TECK. I was not speaking of a loan.

FANNY (*carefully*). God made you not only a scoundrel but a fool. That is a dangerous combination.

DAVID (*suddenly leaps toward* TECK). Damn you, you—

KURT (*suddenly pounds on the top of the piano, as* DAVID *almost reaches* TECK). Leave him alone. (*Moves quickly to stop* DAVID) Leave him alone! *David! Leave him alone!*

DAVID (*angrily to* KURT). Keep out of it. (*Starts toward* TECK *again*) I'm beginning to see what Marthe meant. Blackmailing with your wife— You—

KURT (*very sharply*). He is not speaking of his wife. Or you. He means me. (*Looks at* TECK) Is that correct?

(SARA *moves toward* KURT. DAVID *draws back, bewildered.*)

TECK. Good. It was necessary for me to hear you say it. You understand that?

KURT. I understand it.

SARA. (*frightened, softly*). Kurt—

DAVID. What is all this about? What the hell are you talking about?

TECK (*sharply for the first time*). Be still. (*To* KURT) At your convenience. Your hands are shaking, Herr Müller.

KURT (*quietly*). My hands were broken: they are bad when I have fear.

TECK. I am sorry. I can understand that. It is not pleasant. (*Motions toward* FANNY *and* DAVID) Perhaps you would

like a little time to— I will go and pack, and be ready
to leave. We will all find that more comfortable, I think.
You should get yourself a smaller gun, Herr Müller.
That pistol you have been carrying is big and awkward.

KURT. You saw the pistol when you examined our bags?

TECK. You knew that?

KURT. Oh, yes. I have the careful eye, through many years
of needing it. And then you have not the careful eye.
The pistol was lying to the left of a paper package and
when you leave, it is to the right of the package.

SARA. Kurt! Do you mean that—

KURT (*sharply*). Please, darling, do not do that.

TECK. It is a German Army Luger?

KURT. Yes.

TECK. Keep it in your pocket, Herr Müller. You will have
no need to use it. And, in any case, I am not afraid of it.
You understand that?

KURT (*slowly*). I understand that you are not a man of
fears. That is strange to me, because I am a man who
has so many fears.

TECK (*laughs, as he exits*). Are you? That is most interesting. (*He exits.*)

DAVID (*softly*). What is this about, Kurt?

KURT. He knows who I am and what I do and what I
carry with me.

SARA (*carefully*). What about Max?

KURT. The telephone was from Mexico. Ilse received a
cable. Early on the morning of Monday, they caught
Ebber and Triste. An hour after they took Max in Berlin. (*She looks up at him, begins to shake her head. He
presses her arm*) Yes. It is hard.

FANNY (*softly*). You said he knew who you were and
what you carried with you. I don't understand.

KURT. I am going to tell you: I am an outlaw. I work with
many others in an illegal organization. I have so worked

for seven years. I am on what is called a desired list. But I did not know I was worth ten thousand dollars. My price has risen.

DAVID (*slowly*). And what do you carry with you?

KURT. Twenty-three thousand dollars. It has been gathered from the pennies and the nickels of the poor who do not like Fascism, and who believe in the work we do. I came here to bring Sara home and to get the money. I had hopes to rest here for a while, and then—

SARA (*slowly*). And I had hopes someone else would take it back and you would stay with us— (*Shakes her head, then*) Max is not dead?

KURT. No. The left side of his face is dead. (*Softly*) It was a good face.

SARA (*to* FANNY *and* DAVID, *as if she were going to cry*). It was a very good face. He and Kurt—in the old days— (*To* KURT) After so many years. If Max got caught, then nobody's got a chance. Nobody. (*She suddenly sits down.*)

DAVID (*points upstairs*). He wants to sell what he knows to you? Is that right?

KURT. Yes.

FANNY. Wasn't it careless of you to leave twenty-three thousand dollars lying around to be seen?

KURT. No, it was not careless of me. It is in a locked brief-case. I have thus carried money for many years. There seemed no safer place than Sara's home. It was careless of you to have in your house a man who opens baggage and blackmails.

DAVID (*sharply*). Yes. It was very careless.

FANNY. But you said you knew he'd seen it—

KURT. Yes. I knew it the first day we were here. What was I to do about it? He is not a man who steals. This is a safer method. I knew that it would come some other way. I have been waiting to see what the way would be. That is all I could do.

DAVID (*to* FANNY). What's the difference? It's been done (*To* KURT) If he wants to sell to you, he must have another buyer. Who?

KURT. The Embassy. Von Seitz, I think.

DAVID. You mean he has told Von Seitz about you and—

KURT. No. I do not think he has told him anything. As yet. It would be foolish of him. He has probably only asked most guarded questions.

DAVID. But you're here. You're in this country. They can't do anything to you. They wouldn't be crazy enough to try it. Is your passport all right?

KURT. Not quite.

FANNY. Why not? Why isn't it?

KURT (*wearily, as if he were bored*). Because people like me are not given visas with such ease. And I was in a hurry to bring my wife and my children to safety. (*Sharply*) Madame Fanny, you must come to understand it is no longer the world you once knew.

DAVID. It doesn't matter. You're a political refugee. We don't turn back people like you. People who are in danger. You will give me your passport and tomorrow morning I'll see Barens. We'll tell him the truth— (*Points to the door*) Tell de Brancovis to go to hell. There's not a damn thing he or anybody else can do.

SARA (*looks up at* KURT, *who is staring at her*). You don't understand, David.

DAVID. There's a great deal I don't understand. But there's nothing to worry about.

SARA. Not much to worry about as long as Kurt is in this house. But he's not going to—

KURT. The Count has made the guess that—

SARA. That you will go back to get Ebber and Triste and Max. Is that right, Kurt? Is that right?

KURT. Yes, darling, I will try. They were taken to Sonnenburg. Guards can be bribed— It has been done once before at Sonnenburg. We will try for it again. I must go back, Sara. I must start.

SARA. Of course, you must go back. I guess I was trying to think it wouldn't come. But— (*To* FANNY *and* DAVID) Kurt's got to go back. He's got to go home. He's got to buy them out. He'll do it, too. You'll see. (*She stops, breathes*) It's hard enough to get back. Very hard. But if they knew he was coming— They want Kurt bad. Almost as much as they wanted Max— And then there are hundreds of others, too— (*She gets up, comes to him. He holds her, puts his face in her hair. She stands holding him, trying to speak without crying. She puts her face down on his head*) Don't be scared, darling. You'll get back. You'll see. You've done it before— you'll do it again. Don't be scared. You'll get Max out all right. (*Gasps*) And then you'll do his work, won't you? That's good. That's fine. You'll do a good job, the way you've always done. (*She is crying very hard. To* FANNY) Kurt doesn't feel well. He was wounded and he gets tired— (*To* KURT) You don't feel well, do you? (*Slowly. She is crying too hard now to be heard clearly*) Don't be scared, darling. You'll get home. Don't worry, you'll get home. Yes, you will.

(*The curtain falls.*)

ACT THREE

SCENE: *The same. A half hour later.*

AT RISE: FANNY *is sitting in a chair.* KURT *is at the piano, his head resting on one hand. He is playing softly with the other hand.* SARA *is sitting very quietly on the couch.* DAVID *is pacing on the terrace.*

FANNY (*to* DAVID). David, would you stop that pacing, please? (DAVID *comes in*) And would you stop that one-hand piano playing? Either play, or get up.

(KURT *gets up, crosses to the couch, sits.* SARA *looks at him, gets up, crosses to the decanters, begins to make a drink.*)

SARA (*to* DAVID). A drink?

DAVID. What? Yes, please. (*To* KURT) Do you intend to buy your friends out of jail?

KURT. I intend to try.

FANNY. It's all very strange to me. I thought things were so well run that bribery and—

KURT (*smiles*). What a magnificent work Fascists have done in convincing the world that they are men from legends.

DAVID. They have done very well for themselves—unfortunately.

KURT. Yes. But not by themselves. Does it make us all uncomfortable to remember that they came in on the shoulders of the most powerful men in the world? Of course. And so we would prefer to believe they are men from the planets. They are not. Let me reassure you. They are smart, they are sick, and they are cruel. But given

309

men who know what they fight for— (*Shrugs*) I will
console you. A year ago last month, at three o'clock in
the morning, Freidank and I, with two elderly pistols,
raided the home of the Gestapo chief in Konstanz, got
what we wanted, and the following morning Friedank
was eating his breakfast three blocks away, and I was
over the Swiss border.

FANNY (*slowly*). You are brave men.

KURT. *I* do not tell you the story to prove we are remarkable, but to prove they are *not*.

(SARA *brings him a drink. Gives one to* DAVID.)

SARA (*softly, touching* KURT's *shoulder*). Kurt loves Max.

KURT. Always since I came here I have a dream: that he
will come into this room some day. How he would like
it here, eh, Sara? He loves good food and wine, and you
have books— (*Laughs happily*) He is fifty-nine years
of age. And when he was fifty-seven, he carried me on
his back, seven miles across the border. I had been
hurt— That takes a man, does it not?

FANNY (*to* KURT). You look like a sick man to me.

KURT. No. I'm only tired. I do not like to wait. It will go.
It is the waiting that is always most bad for me.

DAVID (*points upstairs*). Damn him! He's doing it deliberately.

KURT. It is then the corruption begins. Once in Spain I
waited for two days until the planes would exhaust
themselves. I think then why must our side fight always
with naked hands. The spirit and the hands. All is
against us but ourselves.

SARA. You will not think that when the time comes. It
will go.

KURT. Of a certainty.

FANNY. But does it have to go on being your hands?

KURT. For each man, his own hands. He has to sleep with
them.

DAVID (*uncomfortably, as if he did not like to say it*). That's right. I guess it's the way all of us should feel. But—but you have a family. Isn't there somebody else who hasn't a wife and children—

KURT. Each could have his own excuse. Some love for the first time, some have bullet holes, some have fear of the camps, some are sick, many are getting older. (*Shrugs*) Each could find a reason. And many find it. My children are not the only children in the world, even to me.

FANNY. That's noble of you, of course. But they are your children, nevertheless. And Sara, she—

SARA. Mama—

KURT (*after a slight pause*). One means always in English to insult with that word noble?

FANNY. Of course not, I—

KURT. It is not noble. It is the way I must live. Good or bad, it is what I am. (*Turns deliberately to look at* FANNY) And what I am is not what you wanted for your daughter, twenty years ago or now.

FANNY. You are misunderstanding me.

KURT (*smiles*). For our girl, too, we want a safe and happy life. And it is thus I try to make it for her. We each have our way. I do not convert you to mine.

DAVID. You are very certain of your way.

KURT (*smiles*). I seem so to you? Good.

(JOSEPH *appears in the hall doorway. He is carrying valises and overcoats.*)

JOSEPH. What'll I do with these, Miss Fanny?

FANNY. They're too large for eating, aren't they? What were you thinking of doing with them?

JOSEPH. I mean, it's Fred's day off.

DAVID. All right. You drive him into town.

JOSEPH. Then who's going to serve at dinner?

FANNY (*impatiently*). Belle can do it alone tonight.

JOSEPH. No she can't. Belle's upstairs packing with Miss

Marthe. My, there's quite a lot of departing, ain't there?

FANNY (*very impatiently*). All right, then cook can bring in dinner.

JOSEPH. I wouldn't ask her to do that, if I were you. She's mighty mad: the sink pipe is leaking again. You just better wait for your dinner till I get back from Washington.

FANNY (*shouting*). We are not cripples and we were eating dinner in this house before you arrived to show us how to use the knife and fork. (JOSEPH *laughs*) Go on. Put his things in the car. I'll ring for you when he's ready.

JOSEPH. You told me the next time you screamed to remind you to ask my pardon.

FANNY. You call that screaming?

JOSEPH. Yes'm.

FANNY. Very well. I ask your pardon. (*Waves him away*) Go on!

JOSEPH. Yes'm. (*Exits.*)

(TECK *appears in the door. He is carrying his hat and the brief-case we have seen in Act One.* SARA, *seeing the brief-case, looks startled, looks quickly at* KURT. KURT *watches* TECK *as he comes toward him.* TECK *throws his hat on a chair, comes to the table at which* KURT *is sitting, puts the brief-case on the table.* KURT *puts out his hand, puts it on the brief-case, leaves it there.*)

TECK (*smiles at the gesture*). Nothing has been touched, Herr Müller. I brought it from your room, for your convenience.

FANNY (*angrily*). Why didn't you steal it? Since you do not seem to—

TECK. That would have been very foolish of me, Madame Fanny.

KURT. Very.

TECK. I hope I have not kept you waiting too long. I

wanted to give you an opportunity to make any explanations—

DAVID (*angrily*). Does your price include listening to this tony conversation?

TECK (*turns to look at him*). My price will rise if I have to spend the next few minutes being interrupted by your temper. I will do my business with Herr Müller. And you will understand, I will take from you no interruptions, no exclamations, no lectures, no opinions of what I am or what I am doing.

KURT (*quietly*). You will not be interrupted.

TECK (*sits down at table with* KURT). I have been curious about you, Herr Müller. Even before you came here. Because Fanny and David either knew very little about you, which was strange, or wouldn't talk about you, which was just as strange. Have you ever had come to you one of those insistent half-memories of some person or some place?

KURT (*quietly, without looking up*). You had such a half-memory of me?

TECK. Not even a memory, but something. The curiosity of one European for another, perhaps.

KURT. A most sharp curiosity. You lost no time examining—(*Pats the case*)—this. You are an expert with locks?

TECK. No, indeed. Only when I wish to be.

FANNY (*angrily, to* TECK). I would like you out of this house as quickly as—

TECK (*turns to her*). Madame Fanny, I have just asked Mr. David not to do that. I must now ask you. (*Leans forward to* KURT) Herr Müller, I got one of the desired lists from Von Seitz, without, of course, revealing anything to him. As you probably know, they are quite easy to get. I simply told him that we refugees move in small circles and I might come across somebody on it. If, however, I have to listen to any more of this from any of you, I shall go immediately to him.

KURT (*to* DAVID *and* FANNY). Please allow the Count to do this in his own way. It will be best.

TECK (*takes a sheet of paper from his pocket*). There are sixty-three names on this list. I read them carefully, I narrow the possibilities and under "G" I find Gotter. (*Begins to read*) "Age, forty to forty-five. About six feet. One hundred seventy pounds. Birthplace unknown to us. Original occupation unknown to us, although he seems to know Munich and Dresden. Schooling unknown to us. Family unknown to us. No known political connections. No known trade-union connections. Many descriptions, few of them in agreement and none of them of great reliability. Equally unreliable, though often asked for, were Paris, Copenhagen, Brussels police descriptions. Only points on which there is agreement: married to a foreign woman, either American or English; three children; has used name of Gotter, Thomas Bodmer, Karl Francis. Thought to have left Germany in 1933, and to have joined Max Freidank shortly after. Worked closely with Freidank, perhaps directly under his orders. Known to have crossed border in 1934—February, May, June, October. Known to have again crossed border with Max Freidank in 1935—August, twice in October, November, January—"

KURT (*smiles*). The report is unreliable. It would have been impossible for God to have crossed the border that often.

TECK (*looks up, laughs. Then looks back at list*). "In 1934, outlaw radio station announcing itself as Radio European, begins to be heard. Station was located in Düsseldorf: the house of a restaurant waiter was searched, and nothing was found. Radio heard during most of 1934 and 1935. In an attempt to locate it, two probable

Communists killed in the tool-house of a farm near Bonn. In three of the broadcasts, Gotter known to have crossed border immediately before and after. Radio again became active in early part of 1936. Active attempt made to locate Freidank. Gotter believed to have then appeared in Spain with Madrid Government army, in one of the German brigades, and to have been a brigade commander under previously used name of Bodmer. Known to have stayed in France the first months of 1938. Again crossed German border some time during week when Hitler's Hamburg radio speech interrupted and went off the air." (*Looks up*) That was a daring deed, Herr Müller. It caused a great scandal. I remember. It amused me.

KURT. It was not done for that reason.

TECK. "Early in 1939, informer in Konstanz reported Gotter's entry, carrying money which had been exchanged in Paris and Brussels. Following day, home of Konstanz Gestapo chief raided for spy list by two men—" (KURT *turns to look at* FANNY *and* DAVID, *smiles*) My God, Herr Müller, that job took two good men.

SARA (*angrily*). Even you admire them.

TECK. Even I. Now I conclude a week ago that you are Gotter, Karl Francis—

KURT. Please. Do not describe me to myself again.

TECK. And that you will be traveling home—(*Points to brief-case*)—with this. But you seem in no hurry, and so I must wait. Last night when I hear that Freidank has been taken, I guess that you will now be leaving. Not for California. I will tell you free of charge, Herr Müller, that they have got no information from Freidank or the others.

KURT. Thank you. But I was sure they would not. I know all three most well. They will take what will be given them.

TECK (*looks down. Softly*). There is a deep sickness in the German character, Herr Müller. A pain-love, a death-love—

DAVID (*very angrily*). Oh, for God's sake, spare us *your* moral judgments.

FANNY (*very sharply*). Yes. They are sickening. Get on!

KURT. Fanny and David are Americans and they do not understand our world—as yet. (*Turns to* DAVID *and* FANNY) All Fascists are not of one mind, one stripe. There are those who give the orders, those who carry out the orders, those who watch the orders being carried out. Then there are those who are half in, half hoping to come in. They are made to do the dishes and clean the boots. Frequently they come in high places and wish now only to survive. They came late: some because they did not jump in time, some because they were stupid, some because they were shocked at the crudity of the *German* evil, and preferred their own evils, and some because they were fastidious men. For those last, we may well some day have pity. They are lost men, their spoils are small, their day is gone. (*To* TECK) Yes?

TECK (*slowly*). Yes. You have the understanding heart. It will get in your way some day.

KURT (*smiles*). I will watch it.

TECK. We are both men in trouble, Herr Müller. The world, ungratefully, seems to like your kind even less than it does mine. (*Leans forward*) Now. Let us do business. You will not get back if Von Seitz knows you are going.

KURT. You are wrong. Instead of crawling a hundred feet an hour in deep night, I will walk across the border with as little trouble as if I were a boy again on a summer walking trip. There are many men they would like to have. I would be allowed to walk directly to them— until they had all the names and all the addresses.

(*Laughs, points his finger at* TECK) *Roumanians* would pick me up ahead of time. *Germans* would not.

TECK (*smiles*). Still the national pride?

KURT. Why not? For that which is good.

FANNY (*comes over, very angrily, to* TECK). I have not often in my life felt what I feel now. Whatever you are, and however you became it, the picture of a man selling the lives of other men—

TECK. Is very ugly, Madame Fanny. I do not do it without some shame, and therefore I must sink my shame in large money. (*Puts his hand on the brief-case*) The money is here. For ten thousand, you go back to save your friends, nobody will know that you go, and I will give you my good wishes. (*Slowly, deliberately,* KURT *begins to shake his head.* TECK *waits, then carefully*) No?

KURT. This money is going home with me. It was not given to me to save my life, and I shall not so use it. It is to save the lives and further the work of more than I. It is important to me to carry on that work and to save the lives of three valuable men, and to do that with all speed. But— (*Sharply*) Count de Brancovis, the first morning we arrived in this house, my children wanted their breakfast with great haste. That is because the evening before we had been able only to buy milk and buns for them. If I would not touch this money for them, I would not touch it for you. (*Very sharply*) It goes back with me. The way it is. And if it does not get back, it is because I will not get back.

(*There is a long pause.* SARA *gets up, turns away.*)

TECK. Then I do not think you will get back. You are a brave one, Herr Müller, but you will not get back.

KURT (*as if he were very tired*). I will send to you a postal card and tell you about my bravery.

DAVID (*coming toward* KURT). Is it true that if this swine talks, you and the others will be—

SARA (*very softly*). Caught and killed. Of course. If they're lucky enough to get killed quickly. (*Quietly, points to the table*) You should have seen his hands in 1935.

FANNY (*violently, to* DAVID). We'll give him the money. For God's sake, let's give it to him and get him out of here.

DAVID (*to* SARA). Do you want Kurt to go back?

SARA. Yes. I do.

DAVID. All right. (*Goes to her, lifts her face*) You're a good girl.

KURT. That is true. Brave and good, my Sara. She is everything. She is handsome and gay and— (*Puts his hand over his eyes.* SARA *turns away.*)

DAVID (*after a second, comes to stand near* TECK). If we give you the money, what is to keep you from selling to Von Seitz?

TECK. I do not like your thinking I would do that. But—

DAVID (*tensely*). Look here. I'm sick of what you'd like or wouldn't like. And I'm sick of your talk. We'll get this over with now, without any more fancy talk from you, or as far as I am concerned, you can get out of here without my money and sell to any buyer you can find. I can't take much more of you at any cost.

TECK (*smiles*). It is your anger which delays us. I was about to say that I understood your fear that I would go to Von Seitz, and I would suggest that you give me a small amount of cash now and a check dated a month from now. In a month, Herr Müller should be nearing home, and he can let you know. And if you should not honor the check because Herr Müller is already in Germany, Von Seitz will pay a little something for a reliable description. I will take my chance on that. You will now say that I could do that in any case—and that is the chance you will take.

DAVID (*looks at* KURT, *who does not look up*). Is a month enough? For you to get back?

KURT (*shrugs*). I do not know.

DAVID (*to* TECK). Two months from today. How do you want the cash and how do you want the check?

TECK. *One month from today.* That I will not discuss. One month. Please decide now.

DAVID (*sharply*). All right. (*To* TECK) How do you want it?

TECK. Seventy-five hundred dollars in a check. Twenty-five hundred in cash.

DAVID. I haven't anywhere near that much cash in the house. Leave your address and I'll send it to you in the morning.

TECK (*laughs*). Address? I have no address, and I wish it now. Madame Fanny has cash in her sitting-room safe.

FANNY. Have you investigated that, too?

TECK (*laughs*). No. You once told me you always kept money in the house.

DAVID (*to* FANNY). How much have you got upstairs?

FANNY. I don't know. About fifteen or sixteen hundred.

TECK. Very well. That will do. Make the rest in the check.

DAVID. Get it, Mama, please. (*He starts toward the library door.* FANNY *starts for the hall exit.*)

FANNY (*turns, looks carefully at* TECK). Years ago, I heard somebody say that being Roumanian was not a nationality, but a profession. The years have brought no change.

KURT (*softly*). Being a Roumanian aristocrat is a profession.

(FANNY *exits. After her exit, there is silence.* KURT *does not look up,* SARA *does not move.*)

TECK (*awkwardly*). The new world has left the room. (*Looks up at them*) I feel less discomfort with you. We are Europeans, born to trouble and understanding it.

KURT. My wife is not a European.

TECK. Almost. (*Points upstairs*) They are young. The world has gone well for most of them. For us— (*Smiles*) The three of us—we are like peasants watching the big

frost. Work, trouble, ruin— (*Shrugs*) But no need to
call curses at the frost. There it is, it will be again, always—for us.

SARA (*gets up, moves to the window, looks out*). You
mean my husband and I do not have angry words for
you. What for? We know how many there are of you.
They don't, yet. My mother and brother feel shocked
that you are in their house. For us—we have seen you
in so many houses.

TECK. I do not say you *want* to understand me, Mrs. Müller. I say only that you do.

SARA. Yes. You are not difficult to understand.

KURT (*slowly gets up, stands stiffly. Then he moves toward
the decanter table*). A whiskey?

TECK. No, thank you. (*He turns his head to watch* KURT
move. He turns back.)

KURT. Sherry?

TECK (*nods*). Thank you, I will.

KURT (*as he pours*). You, too, wish to go back to Europe.

TECK. Yes.

KURT. But they do not much want you. Not since the Buda-
pest oil deal of '31.

TECK. You seem as well informed about me as I am about
you.

KURT. That must have been a conference of high comedy,
that one. Everybody trying to guess whether Kessler
was working for Fritz Thyssen, and what Thyssen *really*
wanted—and whether this "National Socialism" was a
smart blind of Thyssen's, and where was Wolff—I
should like to have seen you and your friends. It is too
bad: you guessed an inch off, eh?

TECK. More than an inch.

KURT. And Kessler has a memory? (*Almost playfully*) I do
not think Von Seitz would pay you money for a description of a man who has a month to travel. But I think
he would pay you in a visa and a cable to Kessler. I

think you want a visa almost as much as you want money. Therefore, I conclude you will try for the money here, and the visa from Von Seitz. (*He comes toward the table carrying the sherry glass*) I cannot get anywhere near Germany in a month and you know it. (*He is about to place the glass on the table*) I have been bored with this talk of paying you money. If they are willing to try you on this fantasy, I am not. Whatever made you think I would take such a chance? Or *any* chance? You are a gambler. But you should not gamble with your life. (TECK *has turned to stare at him, made a half motion as if to rise. As he does so, and on the words,* "*gamble with your life*," KURT *drops the glass, hits* TECK *in the face. Struggling,* TECK *makes a violent effort to rise.* KURT *throws himself on* TECK, *knocking him to the floor. As* TECK *falls to the floor,* KURT *hits him on the side of the head. At the fourth blow,* TECK *does not move.* KURT *rises, takes the gun from his pocket, begins to lift* TECK *from the floor. As he does so,* JOSHUA *appears in the hall entrance. He is washed and ready for dinner. As he reaches the door, he stops, sees the scene, stands quietly as if he were waiting for orders.* KURT *begins to balance* TECK, *to balance himself. To* JOSHUA) Hilf mir. (JOSHUA *comes quickly to* KURT) Mach die Tür auf! (JOSHUA *runs toward the doors, opens them, stands waiting*) Bleib da! Mach die Tür zu! (KURT *begins to move out through the terrace. When he is outside the doors,* JOSHUA *closes them quickly, stands looking at his mother.*)

SARA. There's trouble.

JOSHUA. Do not worry. I will go up now. I will pack. In ten minutes all will be ready. I will say nothing. I will get the children ready— (*He starts quickly for the hall, turns for a second to look toward the terrace doors. Then almost with a sob*) This was a nice house.

SARA (*softly*). We're not going this time, darling. There's
no need to pack.

JOSHUA (*stares at her, puzzled*). But Papa—

SARA. Go upstairs, Joshua. Take Babbie and Bodo in your
room, and close the door. Stay there until I call you.
(*He looks at her,* SARA *sits down*) There's nothing to be
frightened of, darling. Papa is all right. (*Then very
softly*) Papa is going home.

JOSHUA. To Germany?

SARA. Yes.

JOSHUA. Oh. Alone?

SARA. Alone. (*Very softly*) Don't say anything to the children. He will tell them himself.

JOSHUA. I won't.

SARA (*as he hesitates*). I'm all right. Go upstairs now. (*He
moves slowly out, she watches him, he disappears. For
a minute she sits quietly. Then she gets up, moves to
the terrace doors, stands with her hands pressed against
them. Then she crosses, picks up the overturned chair,
places it by the table, picks up the glass, puts it on the
table. As if without knowing what she is doing, she
wipes the table with her handkerchief.*)

(FANNY *comes in from hall. After a second,* DAVID *comes
in from library. Stops, looks around room.*)

DAVID. Where is he? Upstairs?

SARA. No. They went outside.

FANNY. Outside? They went outside. What are they doing,
picking a bouquet together?

SARA (*without turning*). They just went outside.

DAVID (*looks at her*). What's the matter, Sara?

(SARA *shakes her head. Goes to the desk, opens the telephone book, looks at a number, begins to dial the
telephone.*)

FANNY. Eleven hundred, eleven hundred and fifty, twelve,
twelve-fifty—

DAVID. For God's sake, stop counting that money.

FANNY. All right. I'm nervous. And I don't like to think of giving him too much.

SARA. It's very nice of you and Mama. All that money— (*Into the telephone*) Hello. What time is your next plane? Oh. To— South. To El Paso, or—Brownsville. Yes.

DAVID (*to* FANNY). Is Joseph ready?

FANNY. I don't know. I told him I'd call him.

SARA. To Brownsville? Yes. Yes. That's all right. At what time? Yes. No. The ticket will be picked up at the airport. (DAVID *begins to cross to the bell cord. She looks up*) No. David. Don't call Joseph. *David! Please!* (*He draws back, stares at her. Looking at him, she goes on with the conversation*) Ritter. R-I-T-T-E-R. From Chicago. Yes. Yes. (*She hangs up, walks away.*)

DAVID. Sara! What's happening? What is all this? (*She does not answer*) Where is Kurt? What— (*He starts for the terrace door.*)

SARA. David. *Don't go out.*

FANNY (*rises*). Sara! What's happening—

SARA. For seven years now, day in, day out, men have crossed the German border. They are always in danger. They always may be going in to die. Did you ever see the face of a man who never knows if this day will be the last day? (*Softly*) Don't go out on the terrace, David. Leave Kurt alone.

FANNY (*softly*). Sara! What is—

SARA (*quietly*). For them, it may be torture, and it may be death. Some day, when it's all over, maybe there'll be a few of them left to celebrate. There aren't many of Kurt's age left. He couldn't take a chance on them. They wouldn't have liked it. (*Suddenly, violently*) He'd have had a bad time trying to explain to them that because of this house and this nice town and my mother and my brother, he took chances with their work and with their lives. (*Quietly*) Sit down, Mama. I think it's all over now. (*To* DAVID) There's nothing you can do about it. It's the way it had to be.

DAVID. Sara—

FANNY. Do you mean what I think you— (*She sits down.*)

SARA (*she turns, looks out toward the doors. After a pause*). He's going away tonight and he's never coming back any more. (*In a sing-song*) Never, never, never. (*She looks down at her hands, as if she were very interested in them*) I don't like to be alone at night. I guess everybody in the world's got a time they don't like. Me, it's right before I go to sleep. And now it's going to be for always. All the rest of my life. (*She looks up as* KURT *comes in from the terrace*) I've told them. There is an eight-thirty plane going as far south as Brownsville. I've made you a reservation. In the name of Ritter.

KURT (*stands looking at her*). Liebe Sara! (*Then he goes to the table at which* FANNY *is sitting. To* FANNY) It is hard for you, eh? (*He pats her hand*) I am sorry.

FANNY (*without knowing why, she takes her hand away*). Hard? I don't know. I— I don't— I don't know what I want to say.

KURT (*looks at the hand she has touched, then turns to look at* DAVID). Before I come in, I stand and think. I say, I will make Fanny and David understand. I say, how can I? Does one understand a killing? No. To hell with it, I say. I do what must be done. I have long sickened of words when I see the men who live by them. What do you wish to make them understand, I ask myself. Wait. Stand here. Just stand here. What are you thinking? Say it to them just as it comes to you. And this is what came to me. When you kill in a war, it is not so lonely; and I remember a cousin I have not seen for many years; and a melody comes back and I begin to make it with my fingers; a staircase in a house in Bonn years ago; an old dog who used to live in our town; Sara in a hundred places— Shame on us. Thousands of years and we cannot yet make a world. Like a child I am. I have stopped a man's life. (*Points to the place on the couch where he had been sitting opposite* TECK) I sit here. I listen to him. You will not believe— but I pray that I will not have to touch him. Then I know I will have to. I know that if I do not, it is only that I pamper myself, and risk the lives of others. I want you from the room. I know what I must do. (*Loudly*) All right. Do I now pretend sorrow? Do I now pretend it is not I who act thus? No. I do it. I have done it. I will do it again. And I will keep my hope that we may make a world in which all men can die in bed. I have a great hate for the violent. They are the sick of the world. (*Softly*) Maybe I am sick now, too.

SARA. You aren't sick. Stop that. It's late. You must go soon.

KURT (*he puts out his hands, she touches them*). I am going to say good-bye now to my children. Then I am going to take your car— (*Motions with his head*) I will take him with me. After that, it is up to you. Two ways: You can let me go and keep silent. I believe I can hide him and the car. At the end of two days, if they have not been found, you will tell as much of the truth as is safe for you to say. Tell them the last time you saw us we were on our way to Washington. You did not worry at the absence, we might have rested there. Two crazy foreigners fight, one gets killed, you know nothing of the reason. I will have left the gun, there will be no doubt who did the killing. If you will give me those two days, I think I will be far enough away from here. If the car is found before then—(*Shrugs*) I will still try to move with speed. And all that will make you, for yourselves, part of a murder. For the world, I do not think you will be in bad trouble. (*He pauses*) There is another way. You can call your police. You can tell them the truth. I will not get home. (*To* SARA) I wish to see the children now. (*She goes out into the hall and up the stairs. There is silence.*)

FANNY. What are you thinking, David?

DAVID. I don't know. What are you thinking?

FANNY. Me? Oh, I was thinking about my Joshua. I was thinking that a few months before he died, we were sitting out there. (*Points to terrace*) He said, "Fanny, the Renaissance American is dying, the Renaissance man is dying." I said what do you mean, although I knew what he meant, I always knew. "A Renaissance man," he said, "is a man who wants to know. He wants to know how fast a bird will fly, how thick is the crust of the earth, what made Iago evil, how to plow a field. He knows there is no dignity to a mountain, if there is no dignity to man. You can't put that in a man, but when it's *really* there, and he will fight for it, put your trust in him."

DAVID (*gets up, smiles, looks at* FANNY). You're a smart woman sometimes. (SARA *enters with* JOSHUA. *To* KURT) Don't worry about things here. My soul doesn't have to be so nice and clean. I'll take care of it. You'll have your two days. And good luck to you.

FANNY. You go with my blessing, too. I like you. (BODO *enters.*)

SARA. See? I come from good stock. (KURT *looks at* DAVID. *Then he begins to smile. Nods to* DAVID. *Turns, smiles at* FANNY.)

FANNY. Do you like me?

KURT. I like you, Madame, very much.

FANNY. Would you be able to cash that check?

KURT (*laughs*). Oh, no.

FANNY. Then take the cash. I, too, would like to contribute to your work.

KURT (*slowly*). All right. Thank you. (*He takes the money from the table, puts it in his pocket.*)

BODO (*to* KURT). You like Grandma? I thought you would, with time. I like her, too. Sometimes she dilates with screaming, but— Dilates is correct? (BABETTE *enters.* JOSHUA *stands away from the others, looking at his father.* KURT *turns to look at him.*)

JOSHUA. Alles in Ordnung?

KURT. Alles in Ordnung.

BODO. What? What does that mean, all is well? (*There is an awkward silence.*)

BABETTE (*as if she sensed it*). We are all clean for dinner. But nobody else is clean. And I have on Grandma's dress to me—

FANNY (*very nervously*). Of course. And you look very pretty. You're a pretty little girl, Babbie.

BODO (*looks around the room*). What is the matter? Everybody is acting like such a ninny. I got that word from Grandma.

KURT. Come here. (*They look at him. Then slowly* BABETTE *comes toward him, followed by* BODO. JOSHUA *comes more slowly, to stand at the side of* KURT's *chair*) We have said many good-byes to each other, eh? We must now say another. (*As they stare at him, he smiles, slowly, as if it were difficult*) This time, I leave you with good people to whom I believe you also will be good. (*Half playfully*) Would you allow me to give away my share in you, until I come back?

BABETTE (*slowly*). If you would like it.

KURT. Good. To your mother, her share. My share, to Fanny and David. It is all I have to give. (*Laughs*) There. I have made a will, eh? Now. We will not joke. I have something to say to you. It is important for me to say it.

JOSHUA (*softly*). You are talking to us as if we were children.

KURT (*turns to look at him*). Am I, Joshua? I wish you were children. I wish I could say love your mother, do

not eat too many sweets, clean your teeth— (*Draws*
BODO *to him*) I cannot say these things. You are not
children. I took it all away from you.

BABETTE. We have had a most enjoyable life, Papa.

KURT (*smiles*). You are a gallant little liar. And I thank you
for it. I have done something bad today—

FANNY (*shocked, sharply*). Kurt—

SARA. Don't, Mama. (BODO *and* BABETTE *have looked at*
FANNY *and* SARA, *puzzled. Then they have turned again
to look at* KURT.)

KURT. It is not to frighten you. In a few days, your mother
and David will tell you.

BODO. You could not do a bad thing.

BABETTE (*proudly*). You could not.

KURT (*shakes his head*). Now let us get straight together.
The four of us. Do you remember when we read
"Les Misérables"? Do you remember that we talked
about it afterward and Bodo got candy on Mama's bed?

BODO. I remember.

KURT. Well. He stole bread. The world is out of shape we
said, when there are hungry men. And until it gets in
shape, men will steal and lie and—(*A little more slowly*)
—kill. But for whatever reason it is done, and whoever
does it—you understand me—it is all bad. I want you
to remember that. Whoever does it, it is bad. (*Then
very gaily*) But you will live to see the day when it
will not have to be. All over the world, in every place
and every town, there are men who are going to make
sure it will not have to be. They want what I want: a
childhood for every child. For my children, and I for
theirs. (*He picks* BODO *up, rises*) Think of that. It will
make you happy. In every town and every village and
every mud hut in the world, there is always a man who
loves children and who will fight to make a good world
for them. And now good-bye. Wait for me. I shall try to
come back for you. (*He moves toward the hall, fol-*

lowed by BABETTE, *and more slowly, by* JOSHUA) Or you shall come to me. At Hamburg, the boat will come in. It will be a fine, safe land— I will be waiting on the dock. And there will be the three of you and Mama and Fanny and David. And I will have ordered an extra big dinner and we will show them what our Germany can be like— (*He has put* BODO *down. He leans down, presses his face in* BABETTE'S *hair. Tenderly, as her mother has done earlier, she touches his hair.*)

JOSHUA. Of course. That is the way it will be. Of course. But—but if you should find yourself delayed— (*Very slowly*) Then I will come to you. Mama.

SARA (*she has turned away*). I heard you, Joshua.

KURT (*he kisses* BABETTE). Gute Nacht, Liebling!

BABETTE. Gute Nacht, Papa. Mach's gut!

KURT (*leans to kiss* BODO). Good night, baby.

BODO. Good night, Papa. Mach's gut! (BABETTE *runs up the steps. Slowly* BODO *follows her.*)

KURT (*kisses* JOSHUA). Good night, son.

JOSHUA. Good night, Papa. Mach's gut! (*He begins to climb the steps.* KURT *stands watching them, smiling. When they disappear, he turns to* DAVID.)

KURT. Good-bye, and thank you.

DAVID. Good-bye, and good luck.

KURT (*he moves to* FANNY). Good-bye. I have good children, eh?

FANNY. Yes, you have. (KURT *kisses her hand.*)

KURT (*slowly, he turns toward* SARA). Men who wish to live have the best chance to live. I wish to live. I wish to live with you. (*She comes toward him.*)

SARA. For twenty years. It is as much for me today— (*Takes his arms*) Just once, and for all my life. (*He pulls her toward him*) Come back for me, darling. If you can. (*Takes brief case from table and gives it to him.*)

KURT (*simply*). I will try. (*He turns*) Good-bye, to you all. (*He exits. After a second, there is the sound of a car starting. They sit listening to it. Gradually the noise begins to go off into the distance. A second later,* JOSHUA *appears.*)

JOSHUA. Mama— (*She looks up. He is very tense*) Bodo cries. Babette looks very queer. I think you should come.

SARA (*gets up, slowly*). I'm coming.

JOSHUA (*to* FANNY *and* DAVID. *Still very tense*). Bodo talks so fancy, we forget sometimes he is a baby. (*He waits for* SARA *to come up to him. When she reaches him, she takes his hand, goes up the steps, disappears.* FANNY *and* DAVID *watch them.*)

FANNY (*after a minute*). Well, here we are. We're shaken out of the magnolias, eh?

DAVID. Yes. So we are.

FANNY. Tomorrow will be a hard day. But we'll have Babbie's birthday dinner. And we'll have music afterward. You can be the audience. I think you'd better go up to Marthe now. Be as careful as you can. She'd better stay here for a while. I daresay I can stand it.

DAVID (*turns, smiles*). Even your graciousness is ungracious, Mama.

FANNY. I do my best. Well, I think I shall go and talk to Anise. I like Anise best when I don't feel well. (*She begins to move off.*)

DAVID. Mama. (*She turns*) We are going to be in for trouble. You understand that?

FANNY. I understand it very well. We will manage. You and I. I'm not put together with flour paste. And neither are you—I am happy to learn.

DAVID. Good night, Mama. (*As she moves out, the curtain falls.*)

The Best of the World's Best Books
COMPLETE LIST OF TITLES IN
THE MODERN LIBRARY
For convenience in ordering use number at right of title

MODERN LIBRARY GIANTS

A series of full-sized library editions of books that formerly were available only in cumbersome and expensive sets.
THE MODERN LIBRARY GIANTS REPRESENT A SELECTION OF THE WORLD'S GREATEST BOOKS

These volumes contain from 600 to 1,400 pages each
